Ripe

RIPE
New Design in Australia

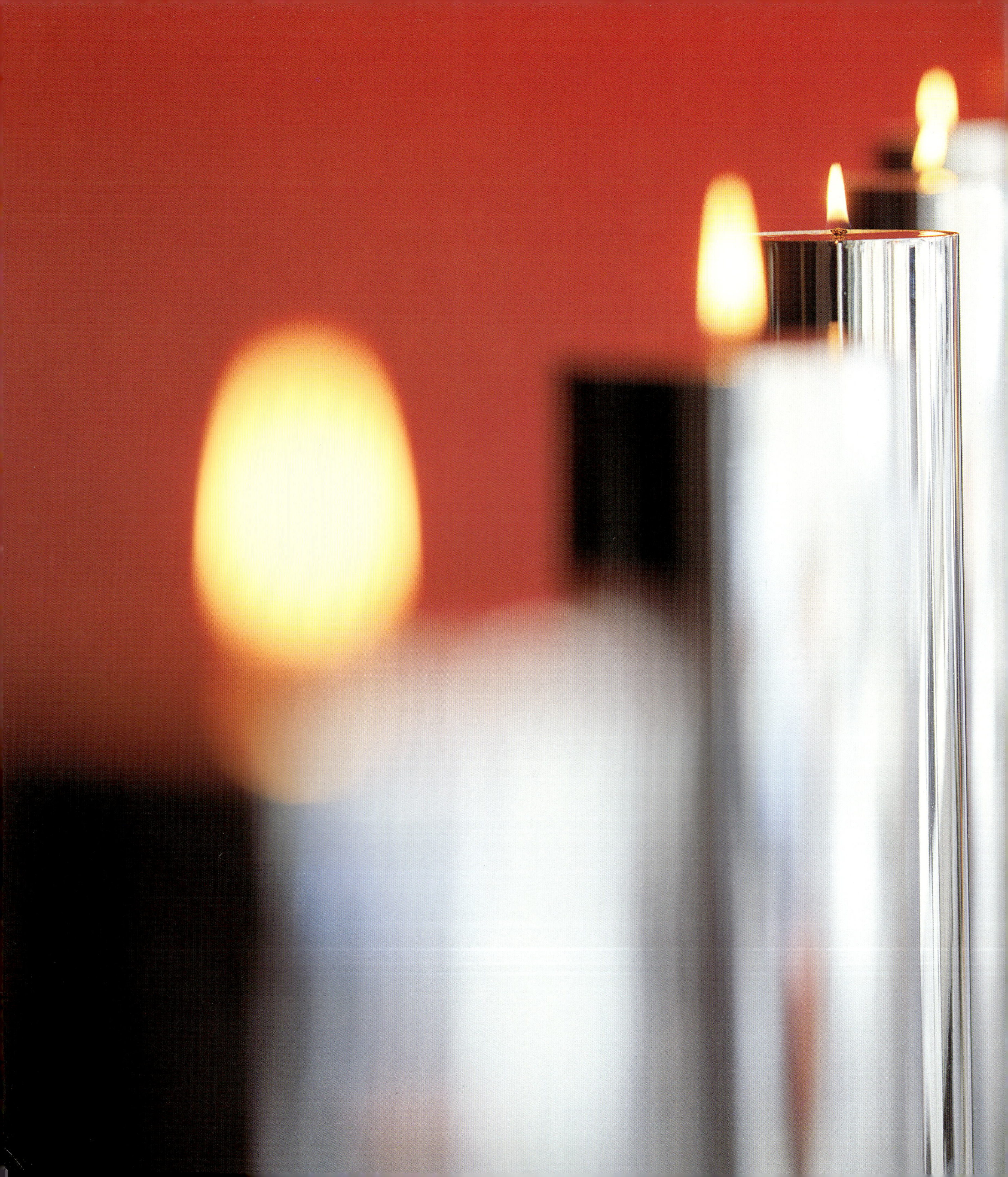

RIPE
New Design in Australia

CRAFTSMAN HOUSE
G+B ARTS INTERNATIONAL

Distributed in Australia by Craftsman House,
Tower A, 112 Talavera Road,
North Ryde, Sydney, NSW 2113
in association with G+B Arts International:
www.gbhap.com
Australia, Canada, France, Germany, India,
Japan, Luxembourg, Malaysia, The Netherlands,
Russia, Singapore, Switzerland

Copyright © 2000 Cornwell Design Pty Ltd
All rights reserved

This book is copyright. Apart from any fair dealing for
the purpose of private research, criticism or reviews,
as permitted under the Copyright Act, no part may be
reproduced by any process without written permission.

ISBN 90 5703 422 0

Design by Steven Cornwell, Domenic Minieri

Printed by Kyodo Printing Co., Singapore

Contents

Introduction — 7 — Steven Cornwell

Architecture — 8 — Introduction
10 — Tina Engelen / Ian Moore
18 — David Balestra-Pimpini / Serge Biguzas
26 — Sean Godsell
34 — Shelley Penn
40 — Steven Whiting
48 — Kerstin Thompson
56 — Christopher Connell
64 — Iain Halliday

Graphic Design — 72 — Introduction
74 — Steven Cornwell / Jane Sinclair
84 — David Band / Fiona Mahon
92 — Visnja Brdar
100 — Andrew Hoyne
108 — Atia Cader / Philippa Penndelberry / Andrew Majzner
116 — David Ansett / Dean Butler
124 — Hanna Cutts
130 — Andrew Ashton / Rick Nelmes / Graeme Smith
138 — Ashley Durrans / Dean Hastie

Industrial Design — 146 — Introduction
148 — Simon Christopher / Celina Clarke
156 — Marc Pascal
162 — Hugo Davidson
170 — Malte Wagenfeld
178 — Mark Armstrong
186 — Peter Cooper / Stephen Neil

Interior Design — 194 — Introduction
196 — Nik Karalis
206 — Andrew Parr
214 — Jackie Johnston
220 — Paul Hecker
228 — Kerry Phelan
236 — Jeffery Copolov
242 — Hamish Guthrie / Kate Hart / Olivia Jackson / Rowan Lodge / Jane Mackay / Geraldine Maher

List of Works — 250

Why are we producing this book? What is this obsession with age? Why do we need it? Who is going to buy it? Do we have enough young design talent to fill a book? What design disciplines are we going to publish? Young designers aren't interested. Good luck getting the text. Do you have any idea how difficult it is to get information out of young people? Why now? Etc. Etc. Why not! As a young designer I have often felt that during the many functions and events I have attended the greatest reward and source of valuable information has come from discussing issues with designers close to my age. Not specifically because I get the right answers, or because I feel that they are more in tune, but more so because I get a different answer. A little separatist? Perhaps. I found that the energy and passion which young designers embody allowed me to talk freely about design issues. To ask questions about its future and most importantly provide me with options, not black and white answers. The more I travelled around the country the more I've realised how great an impact the Generation X designer is having on our design landscape. New ideas, new approaches, new culture. Why *Ripe*? The definition of the word 'ripe' is mature and ready. Ready to be recognised, ready to take on major projects, ready to contribute with committed focus. The designers in this book have much in common. All aspire to reach a level of unsurpassed quality, all have established themselves as some of the future leaders within their given discipline and all of them provide us with inspirational work. The difficulties in remaining impartial and choosing the talent has been an ordeal. Some designers, to my amazement, weren't interested. But others responded with the kind of enthusiasm that has made this book a pleasure to work on. As you read this book and marvel at the work you get an overwhelming sense of comfort. Comfort in the expression, comfort in the diversity, comfort in the fact that our design future is well looked after. **Steven Cornwell**

Architecture

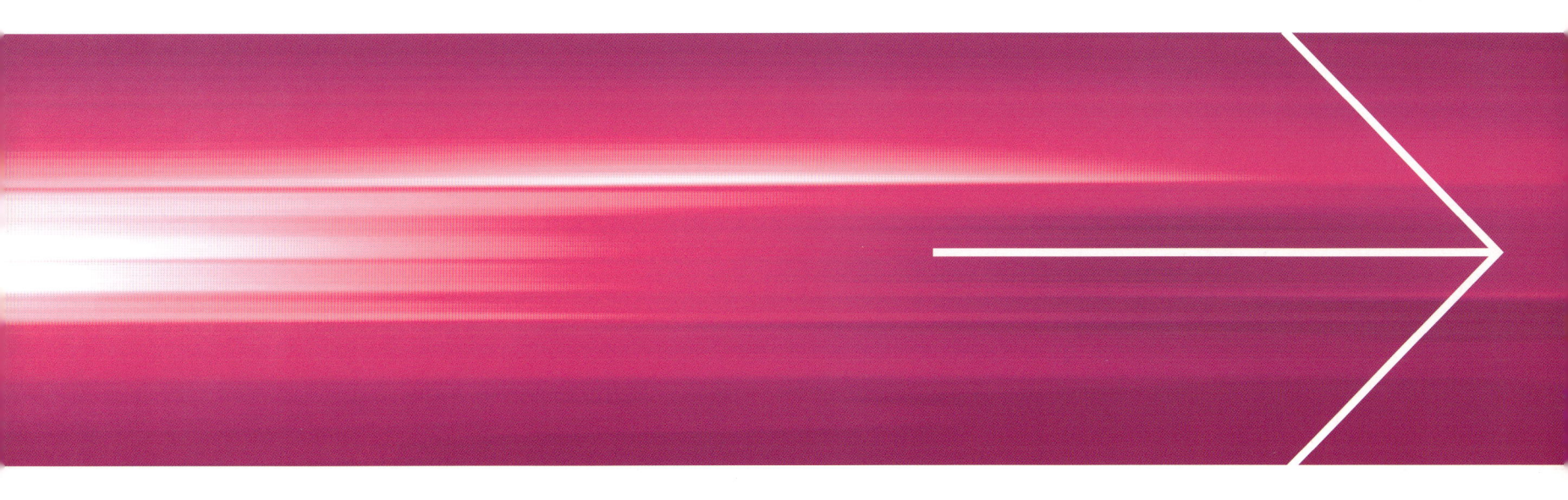

Tina Engelen
Ian Moore
Engelen Moore

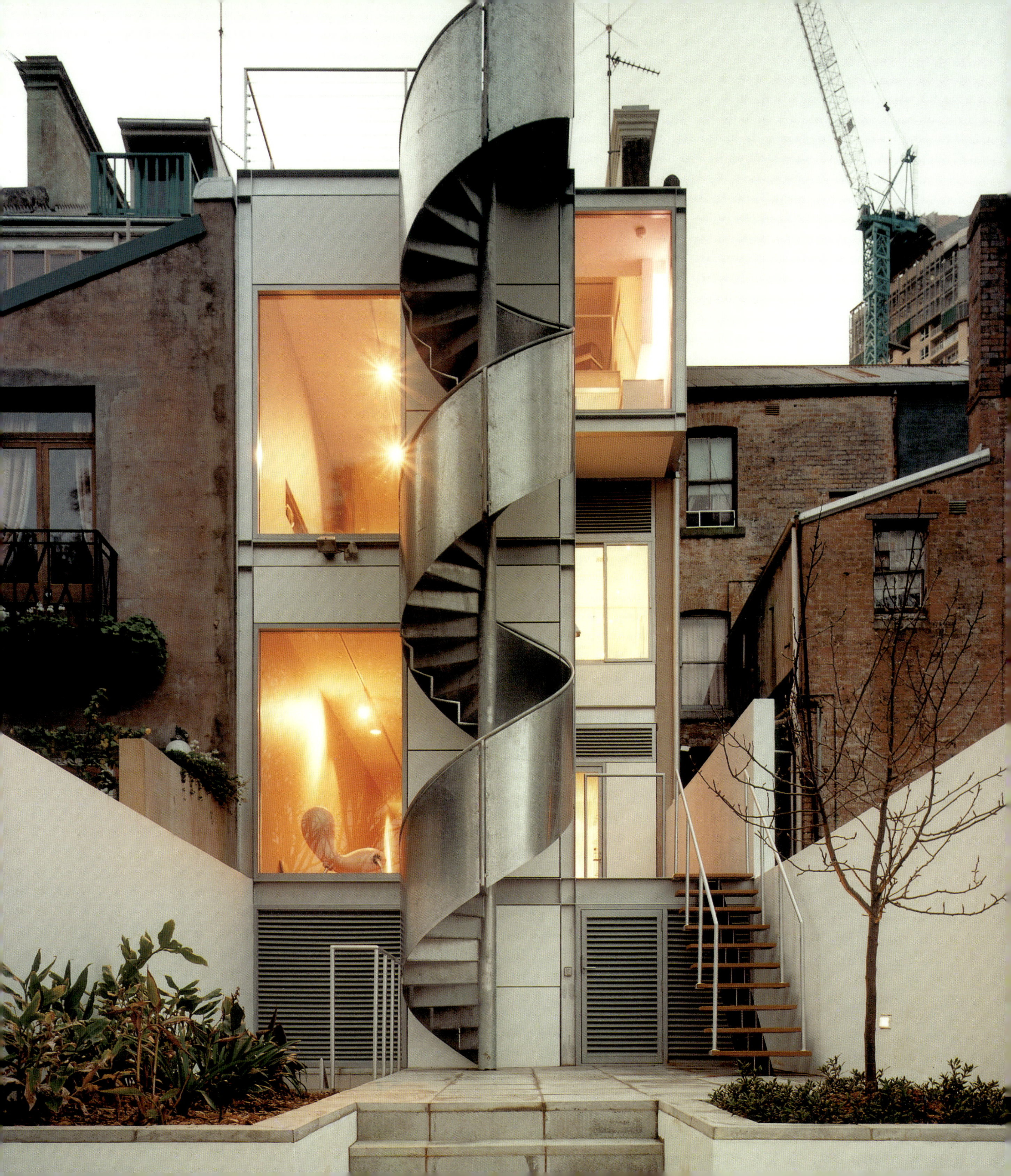

Inspired by the Weissenhofseidlung, the California case study house program and Mies van der Rohe's Farnsworth House, the architects of Engelen Moore seek to build on the fine tradition of the modern house. Houses of the twenty-first century will be responsive to place and climate, flexible in use, providing a neutral background for the usually hectic life of their occupants. Being modern in this context implies a confidence in the future, an understanding of what has gone before. Engelen Moore shares an optimism with the authors of all modern houses produced this century. The work is not new. It is a development and reworking of well-known architectural principles and prototypes. From this base, adjustments are made to suit the individual circumstances, climate, new technology and changing lifestyles. The principle remains the same. Limited budgets lend themselves to a few well-chosen ideas. Space is always the driving force. The primary goal is to create the largest possible space with the least possible amount of materials. Proportions and physical dimensions are also manipulated. Space can be borrowed from an external courtyard, or from the garden. Engelen Moore's planning reflects spatial concerns and a desire to discard the superfluous. Provide only that which is absolutely necessary. Simplicity and rigour. The construction techniques and material are similarly driven. The larger each element, the fewer in number required to enclose the space. Frames and panels as opposed to bricks and mortar. An assertion of principles often intended but rarely accomplished.

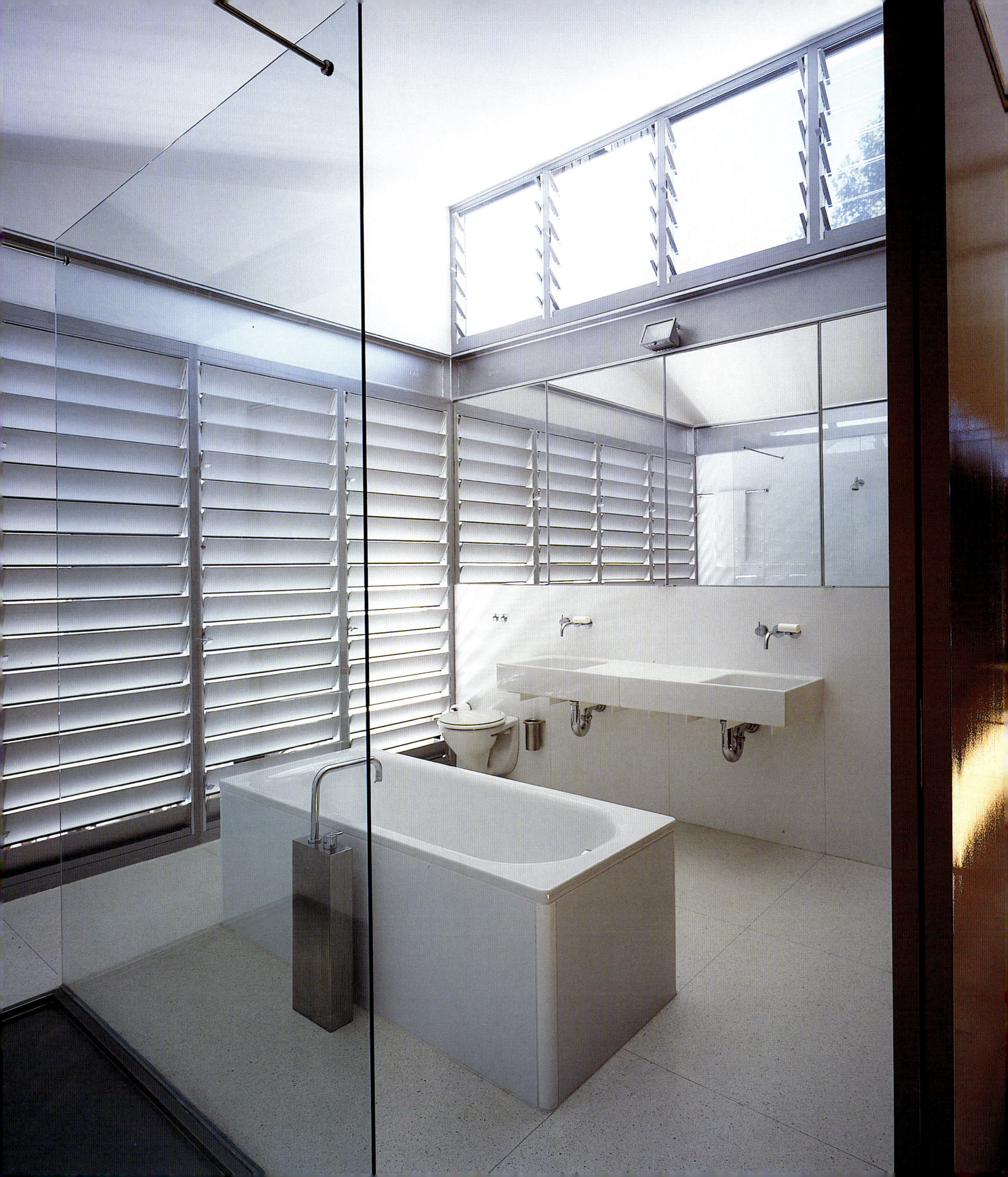

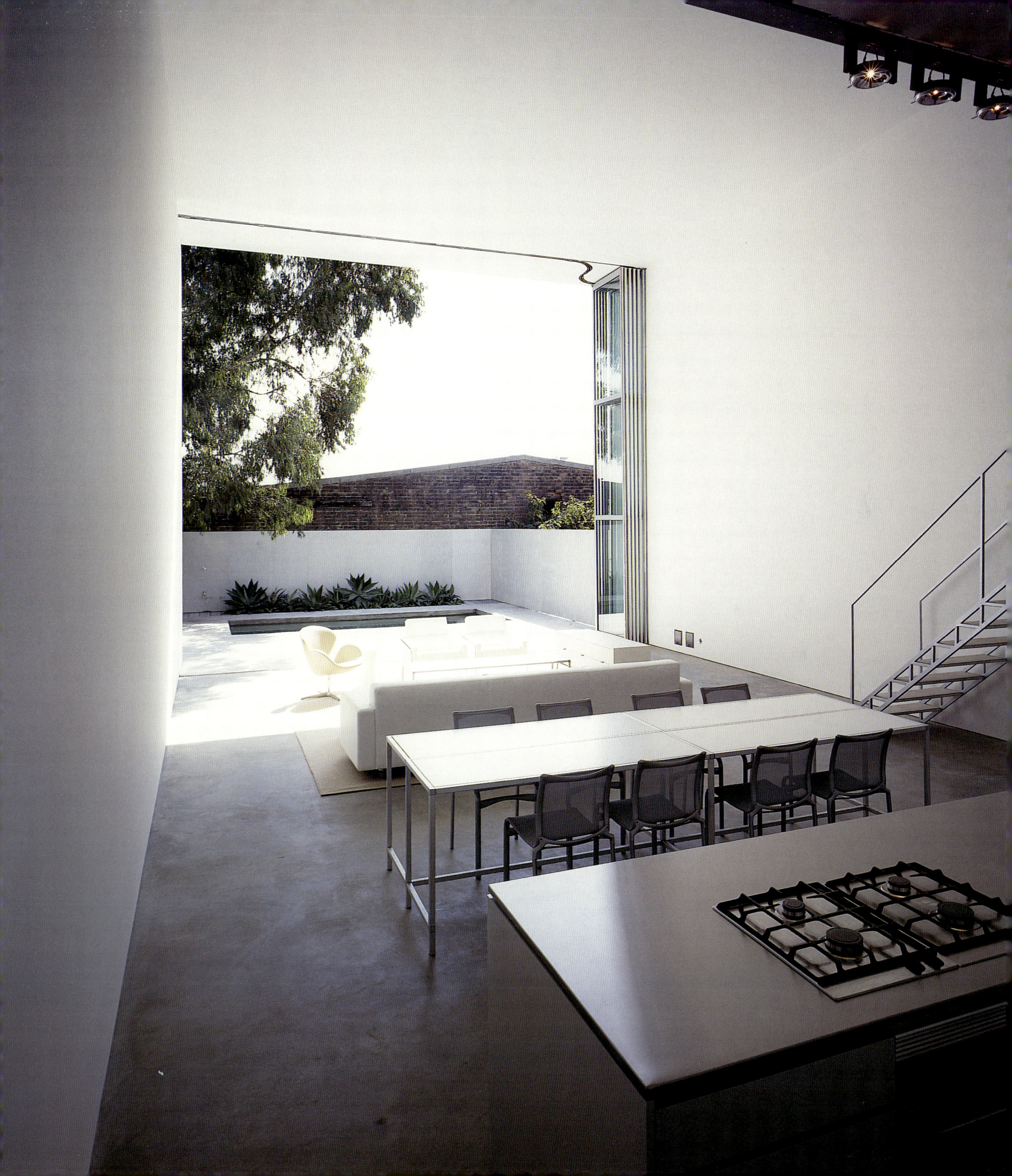

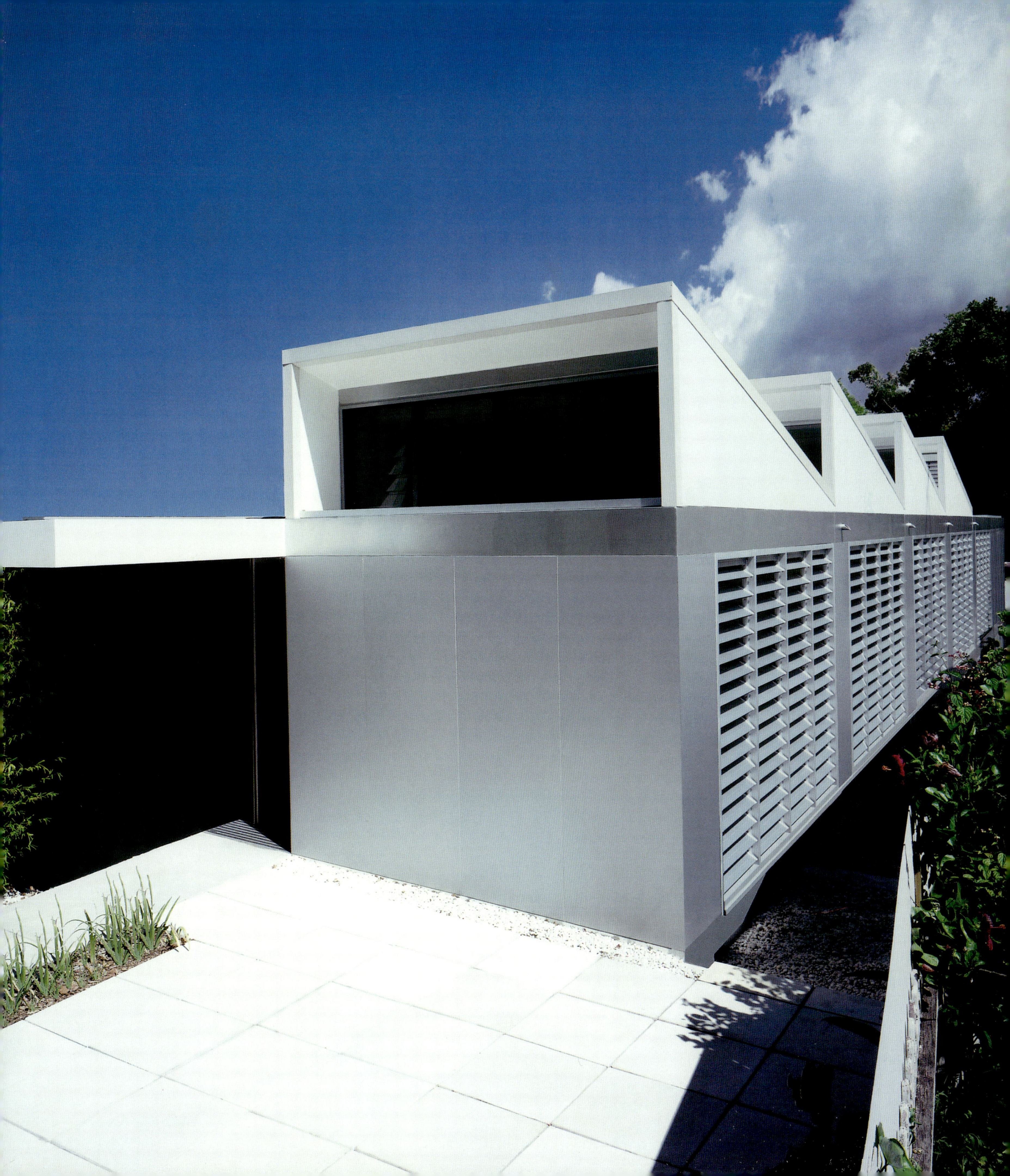

David Balestra-Pimpini
Serge Biguzas
BBP Architects

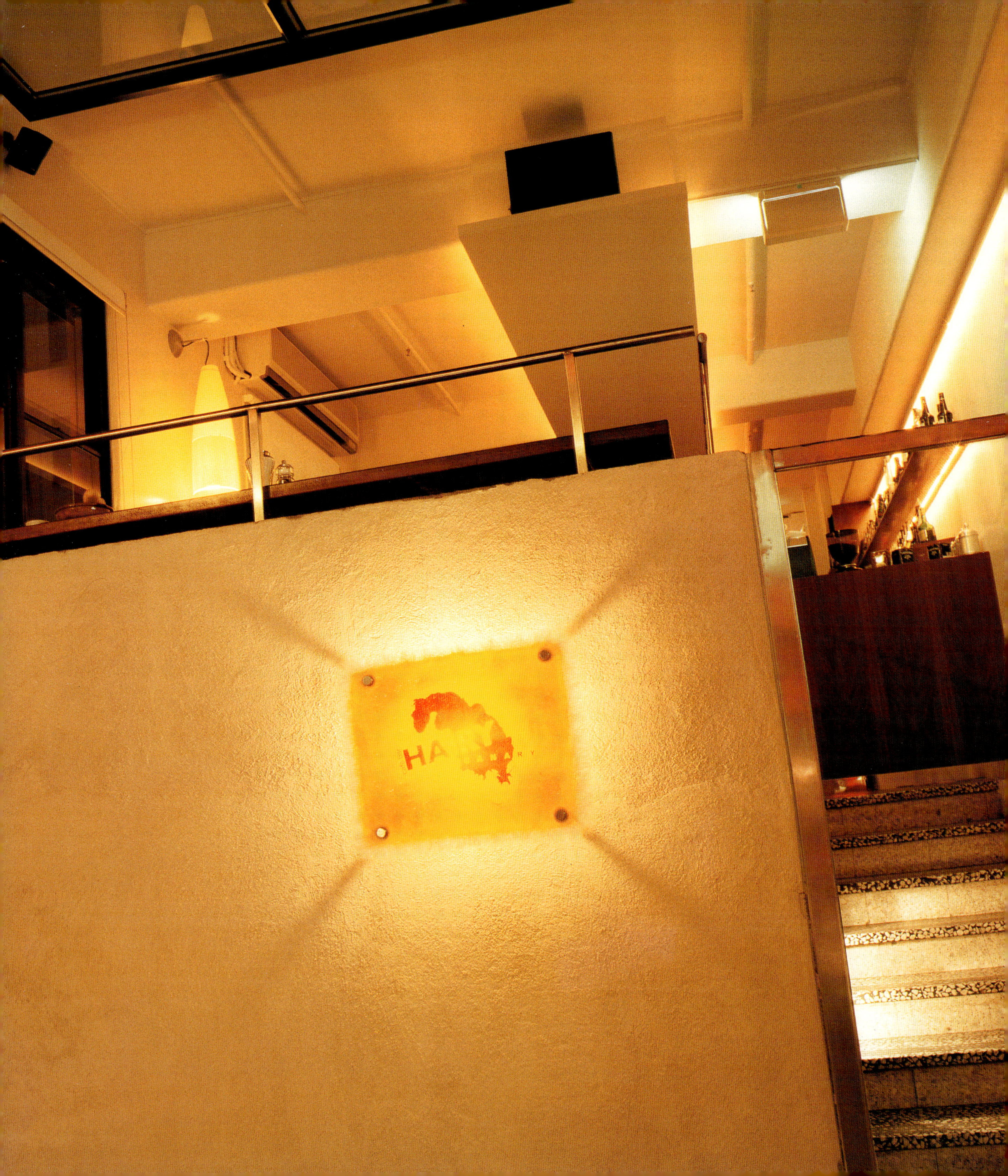

As subscribers to the modernist theories, Serge Biguzas and David Balestra-Pimpini of BBP Architects look to an international style of architectural expression. Rem Koolhaas. Jean Nouvel. Renzo Piano. Serge and David believe in the notion that less is more. Their strongest interest lies in the manipulation of the planes of a cube as a method of generating space and form. Legibility is achieved by creating tensions. Cantilevering and articulated spaces maintain order. The contrast of solid voids and openings give their buildings transparency. The BBP team does not ignore the obvious. Buildings should be functional. People need to use them. Urban planning and interior design have equal standing in their overall design philosophy. They believe they have a role to play in social change. In environmental change, too. They are concerned with improving the built environment. It's a balance between creativity and a practical understanding of materials and structure. BBP has no intention of replicating the past. Rather, its architects work to enhance through the exploration and orchestration of a new language within an existing urban context. These partners feel that the education of architecture remains integral to the practice of architecture. Community discourse and debate. The energy and rigour of students. The design process is not a linear experience. An idea is had. Tested. Tried. Reconsidered. Reworked. Re-evaluated. Eventually a conclusion is drawn for that project, but the design process continues. It's a journey of discovery that does not conclude. For Serge and David, the articulation and expression of space remains paramount in their design position and attitude. Fundamental criteria are clear. Attention to detail. The creative use of materials. A consistent expression of intent. These lead to innovation and significant architectural achievement.

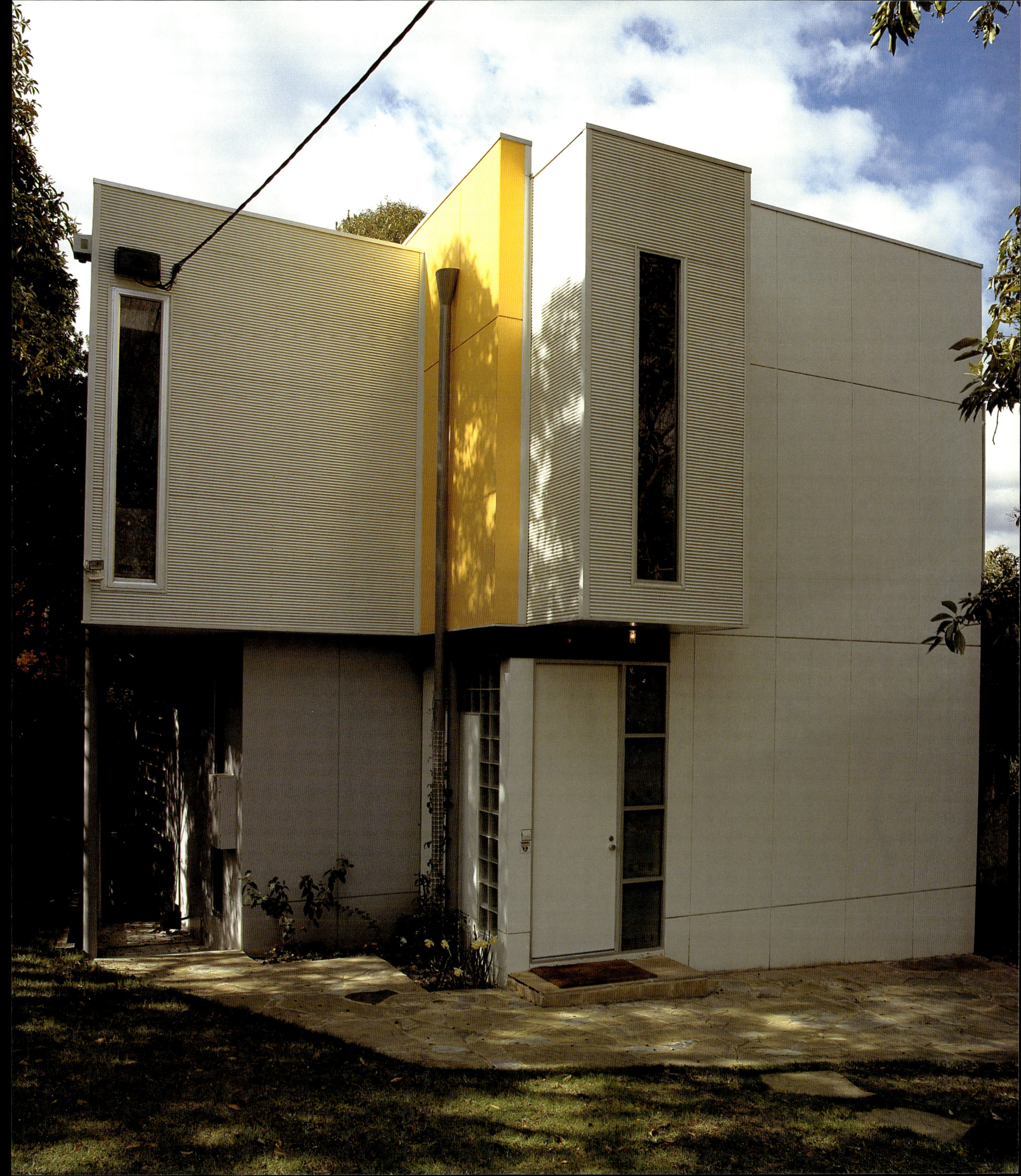

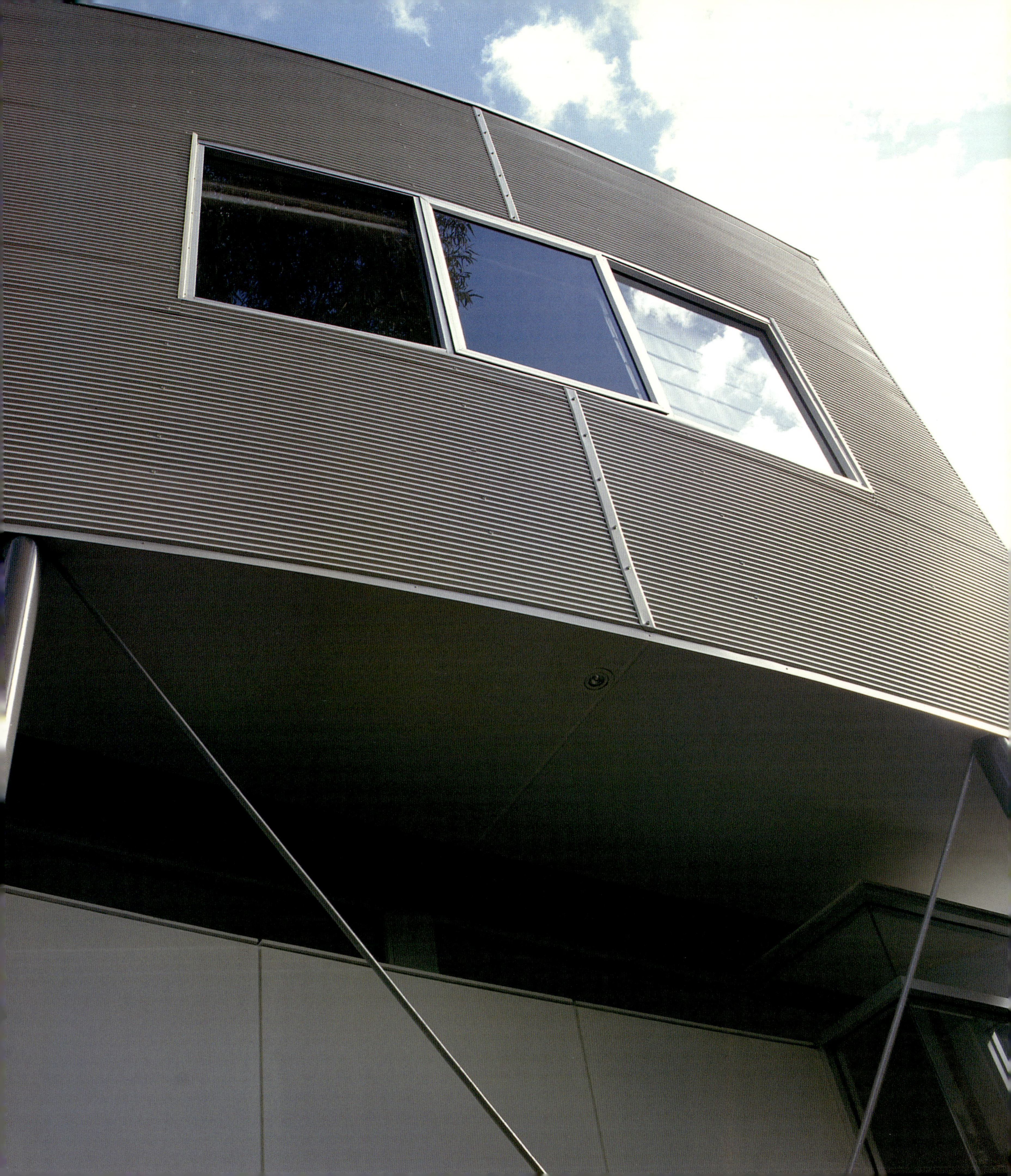

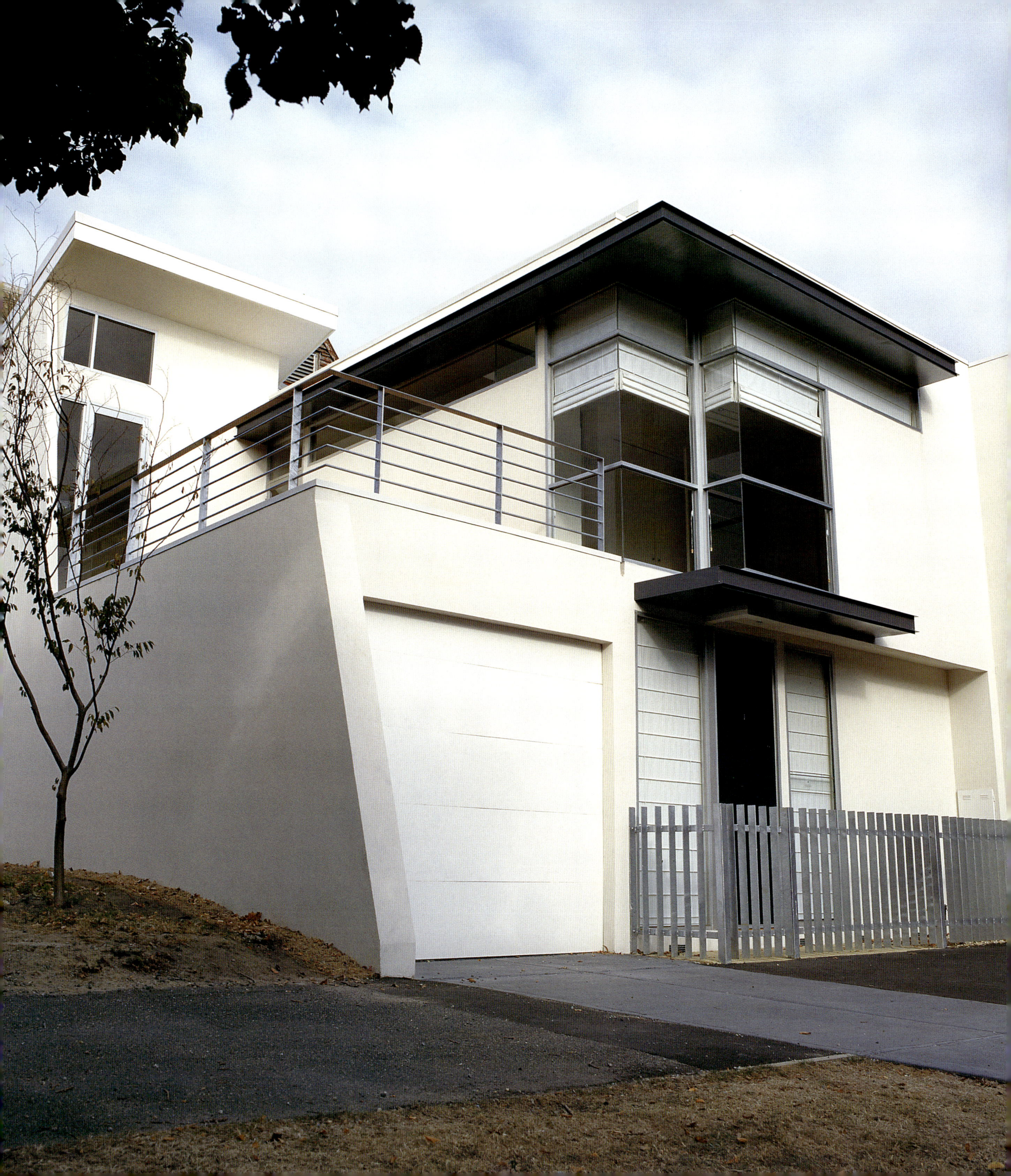

Sean Godsell
Architect Sean Godsell

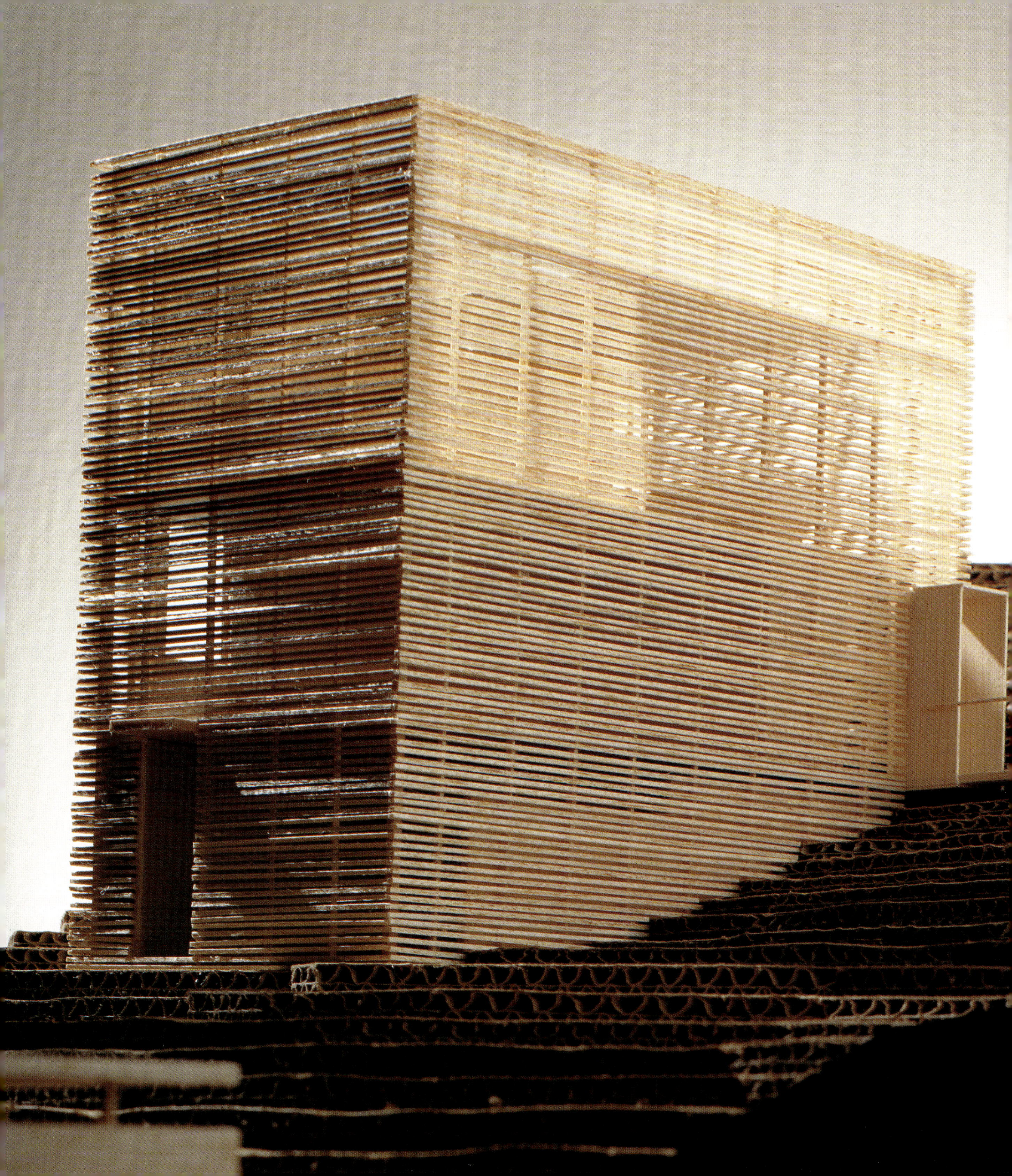

Born 1960. Grew up in Beaumaris, Melbourne. A beautiful Frank Lloyd Wright–inspired house. Architecture was instilled in Sean Godsell at an early age. His father ran a practice from home. A wonderful detailer, lateral thinker and pragmatist. He made site visits a regular occurrence for young Sean. Architectural terminology was the daily dialogue. The accumulated influence led to a degree at Melbourne University. Travel immediately followed. Japan first, Europe later. Finally, three years in London. A postgraduate self-education. Sean saw great buildings. He drew them, photographed them, understood them. Aalto, Le Corbusier, Mies, Palladio, Michelangelo, Terragni, Shinohara, Ando, Foster were all influential. Sir Denys Lasdun, who was passionate and committed to architecture, in his seventies, a significant man. After working in the practices of others, in 1993 Sean stepped out on his own. Beginning with small residential projects, a diverse client base was gradually built. There is definite methodology in the conceptual and schematic stages of a project. A lesson learnt in Lasdun's office and observed in Norman Foster's work. Several concepts are developed during the early stages of a project, each then allowed to exist autonomously, develop lives of their own. One ultimately emerges as a clear winner. This 'bucket of water' technique, as de Bono describes it, ensures that all possibilities are considered before a final decision is reached. Nietzsche would then describe the rejected designs as positive. They have, by their very existence, contributed to the final result. The Godsell House in Kew is a pivotal work for Sean, as it summarises all the work that precedes it. At the same time, it provides a starting point for the next phase. The plan is significant. It speculates on the future design of the Australian house. It signifies the emerging influence of Asian culture on contemporary Australian design. Interconnected rooms. Dividing sliding doors. This eastern planning gesture is countered by the introduction of a table seven metres long. The kitchen table, for generations the centre of Australian family life, has been extended to become a universal work surface, dining area, meeting point – the high altar. In Sean's design, this hybrid of east and west acknowledges the economic cultural and geographic reality of Australia in the twenty-first century.

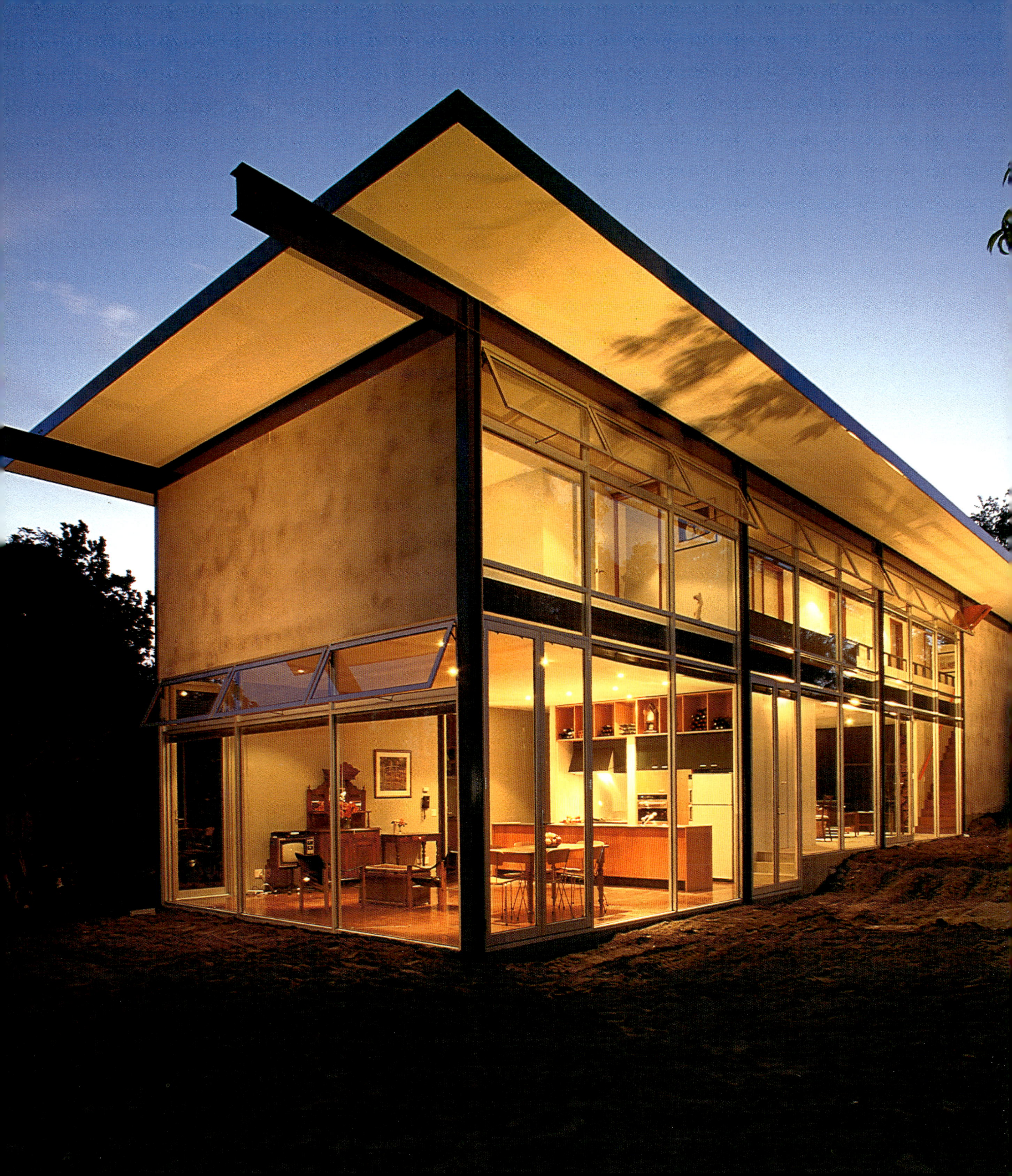

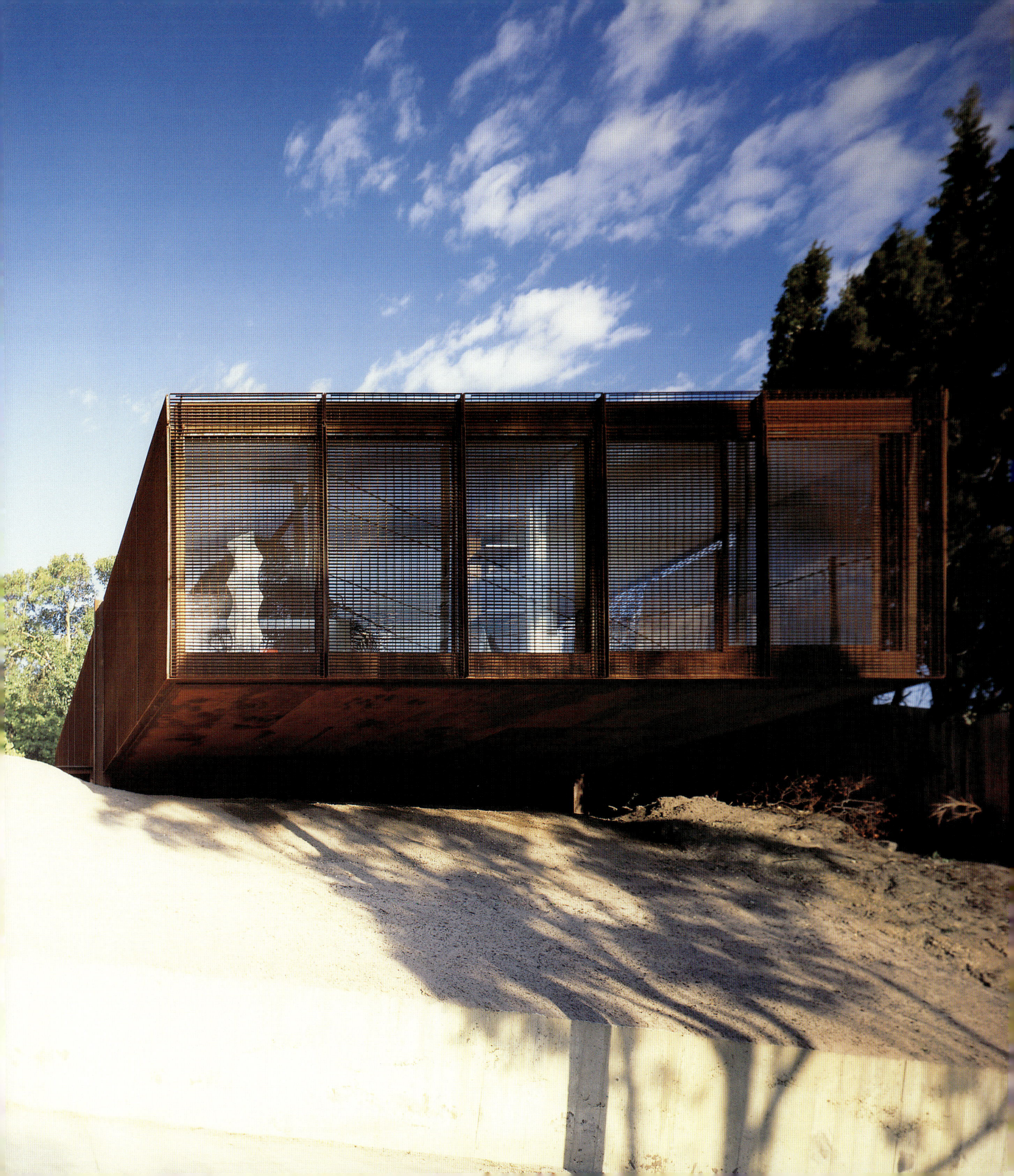

Shelley Penn
Shelley Penn Architect

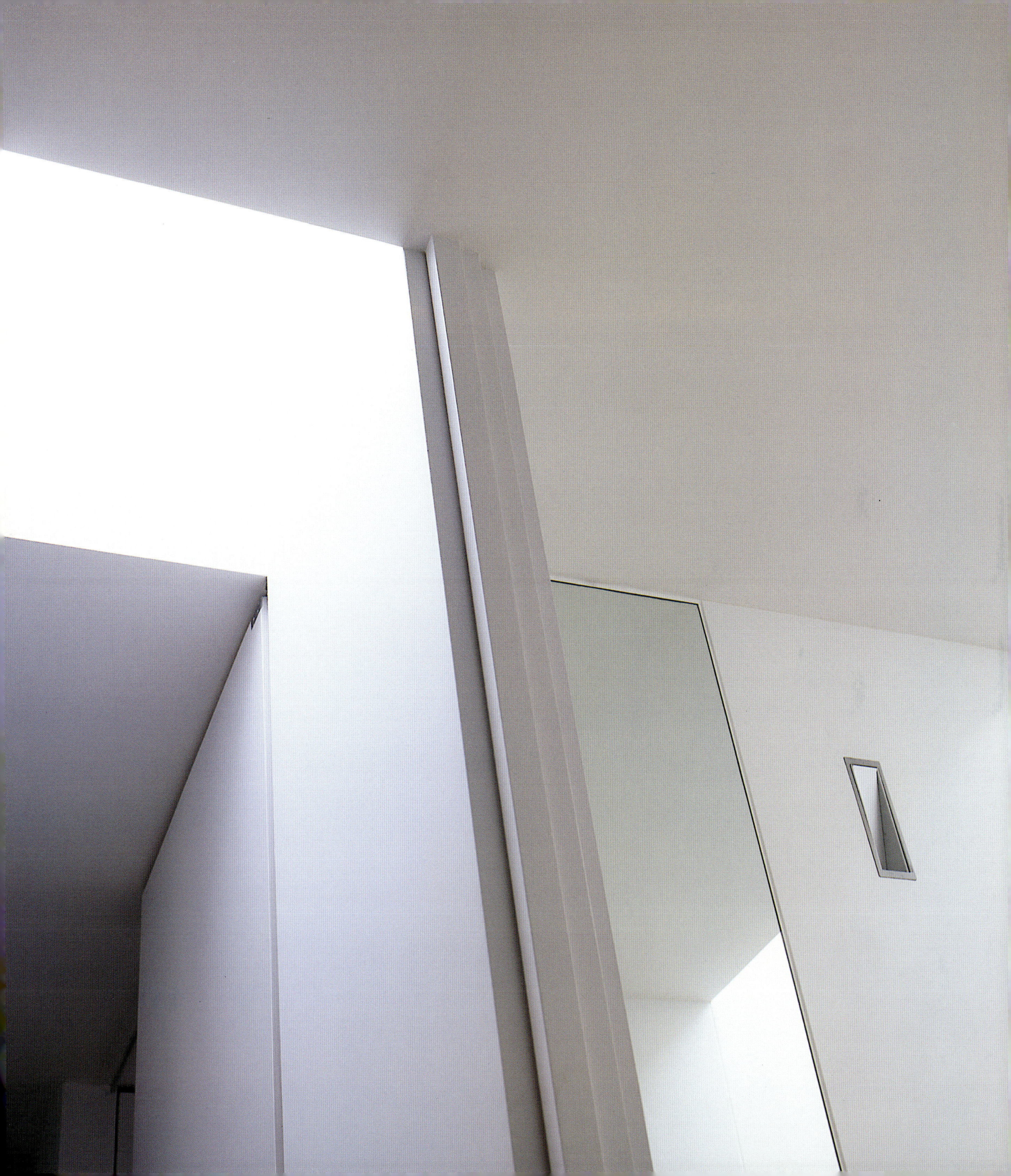

It began in Japan. A university study tour in 1985. An encounter with traditional and contemporary Japanese architecture. A sense of architecture's capacity to enrich and transform the human experience. It was the beginning of Shelley Penn's intense exploration into the emotive power of design. On her return to Australia, Penn began work as a student architect in the office of Robinson Chen. The job evolved into a highly influential relationship that spanned seven years. The architectural process adopted, the buildings produced and the single-minded passion with which the partners approached their work instilled in Penn a deep faith in the value and meaning of architecture. She came to an intimate understanding of the complexities of production. Rich travelling experiences in Asia and Europe heightened her confidence in the opportunities Australia afforded a young architect. An adolescent design culture offering a fertile environment. Penn believes the resonance of a building lies in those parts which are not there. For Penn, each line in the building is imperative in the creation of a space. She aims to limit the distinction between interior and exterior volumes and is less interested in the object than in the way space is made or altered by that object. Penn's work is characterised by spatial fluidity. It is a consistent concern that's evident in her articulation of volume and form through the manipulation of natural light. Her use of colour is restrained. Her palette of materials is limited. A mature subtlety results. In the design of structure and the detailing of surface and junction, Penn's desire is to de-limit space. She focuses on movement and passage through a building. She has learnt that the essence of space is often richer for being revealed slowly.

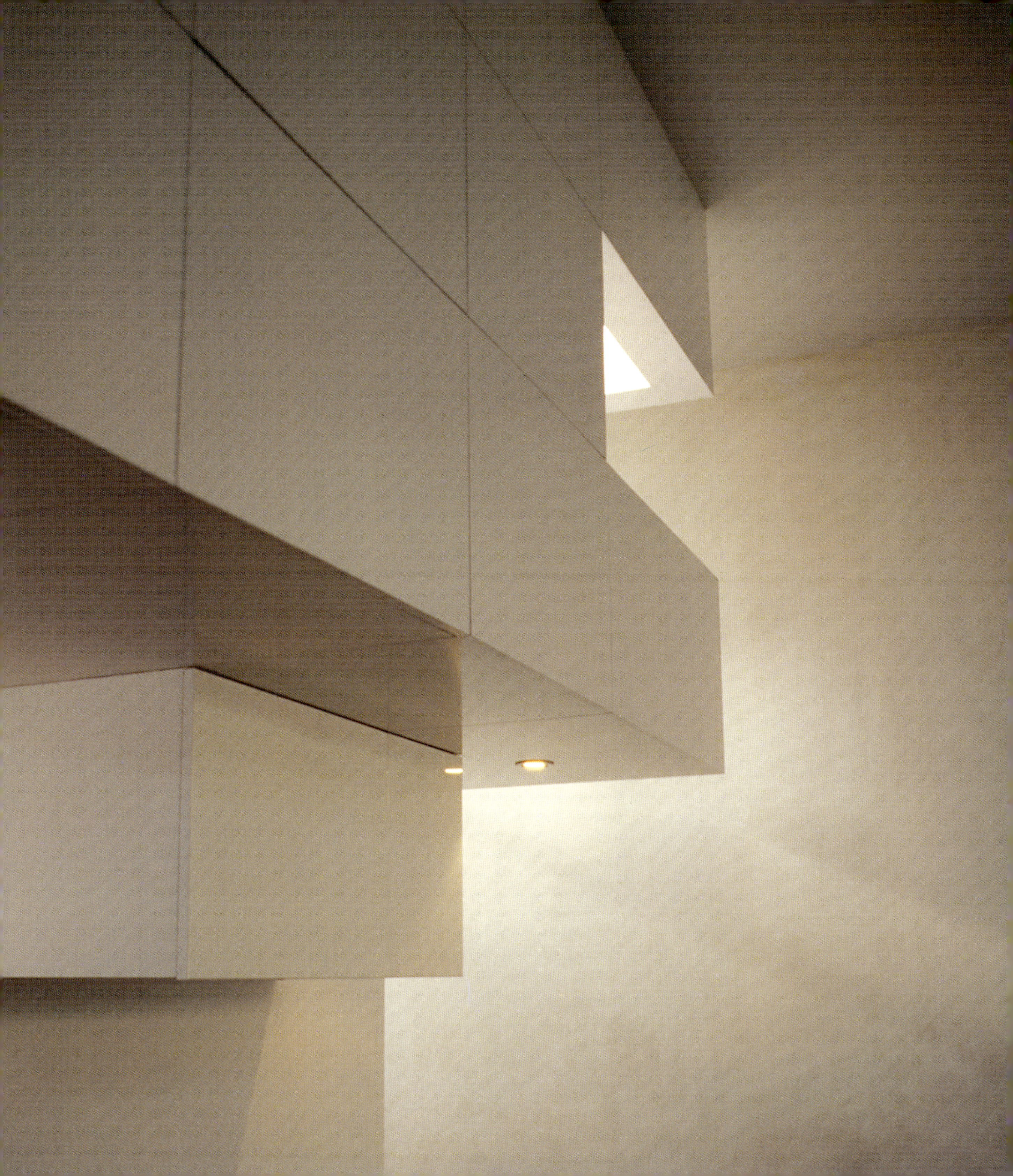

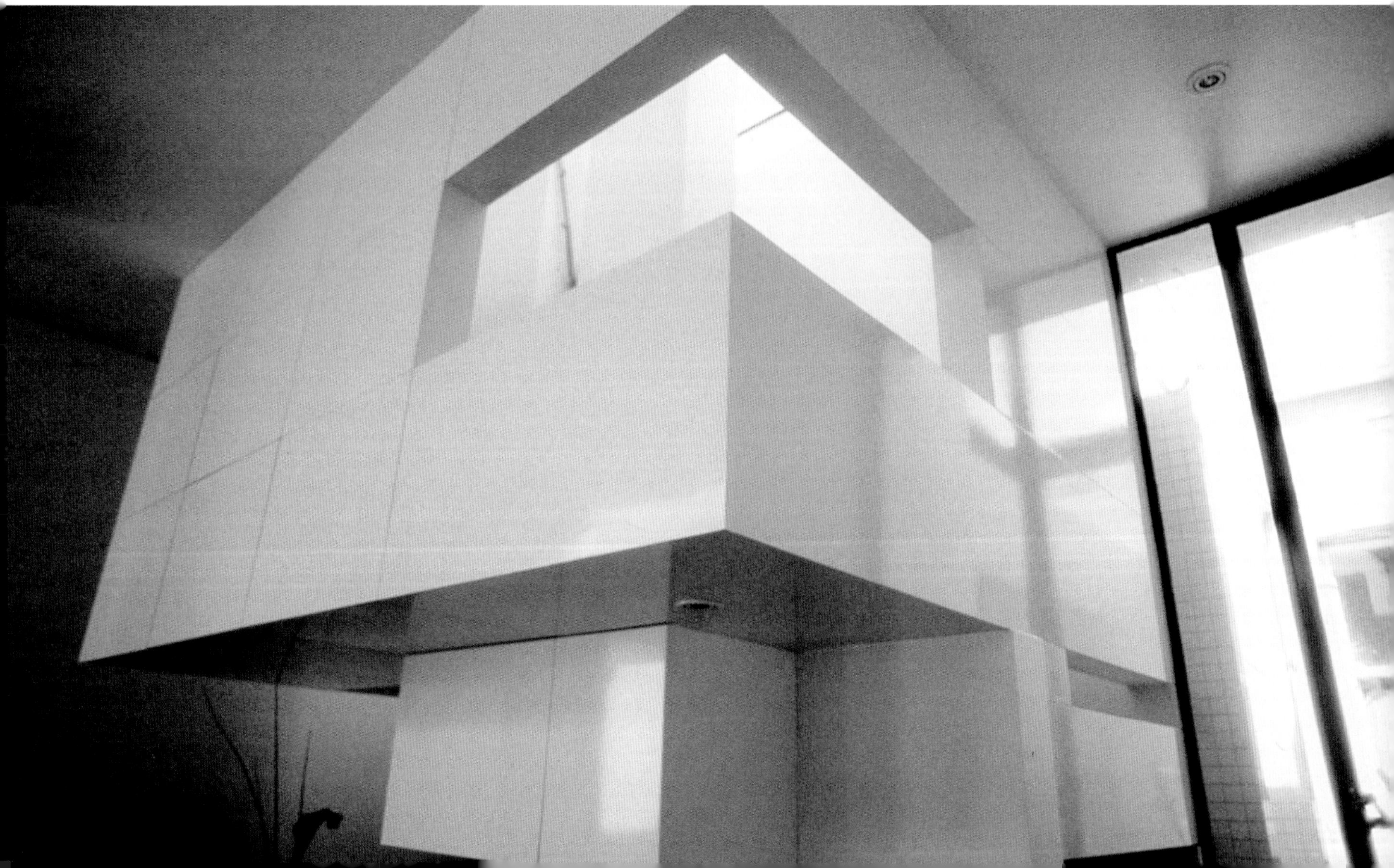

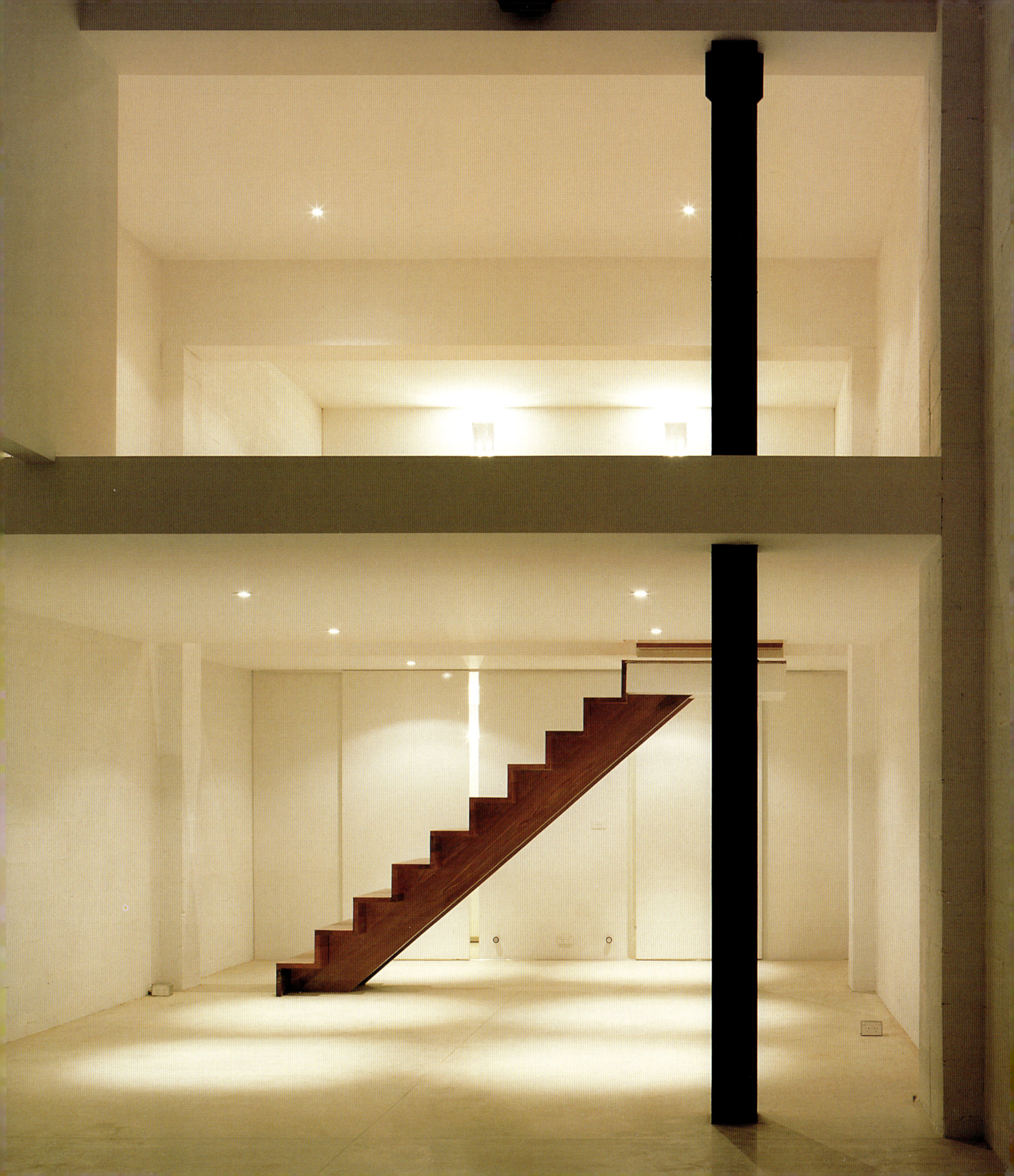

Steven Whiting believes design is a natural process. Finding different ways of looking at previously established modes. Innovation. Improvising. In his mind, architecture is not the primary asset to be bought, sold and borrowed against. The brief should be about creating suitable, personal architecture. The solution lies in the appreciation of form and interior. Steven imagines that the interior is a personal interactive museum, curated by its new owner who will fill the space with many aspects of his or her personality. Artwork and furniture serve to complement the interior space of a building. They give colour and texture. Light is important. Activity within the space is encouraged to be the statement. The architecture should always remain secondary to the activities it facilitates. This is no excuse for complacency. Nothing about the building should be reduced to the mundane. Take nothing for granted. Detail all the parts and the rest will follow. This process results in a compositional architecture of primary forms. It is as much about what Steven chooses to leave out of the composition as it is about what he chooses to include. His design principles are rooted in Japanese-inspired modernism. Dignified simplicity. Texture. Fine materials. Simple forms. In retail design work, Steven approaches every project from an architectural standing. Fittings and fixtures become structural elements. Operational meshes with aesthetic. The values of service and quality must be inherent in all levels of the design. Gimmicks and themes should be avoided. In recent years, Steven Whiting's style has begun to emerge. His work is evolving a 'look'. It's individual. It's consistent. It's his own.

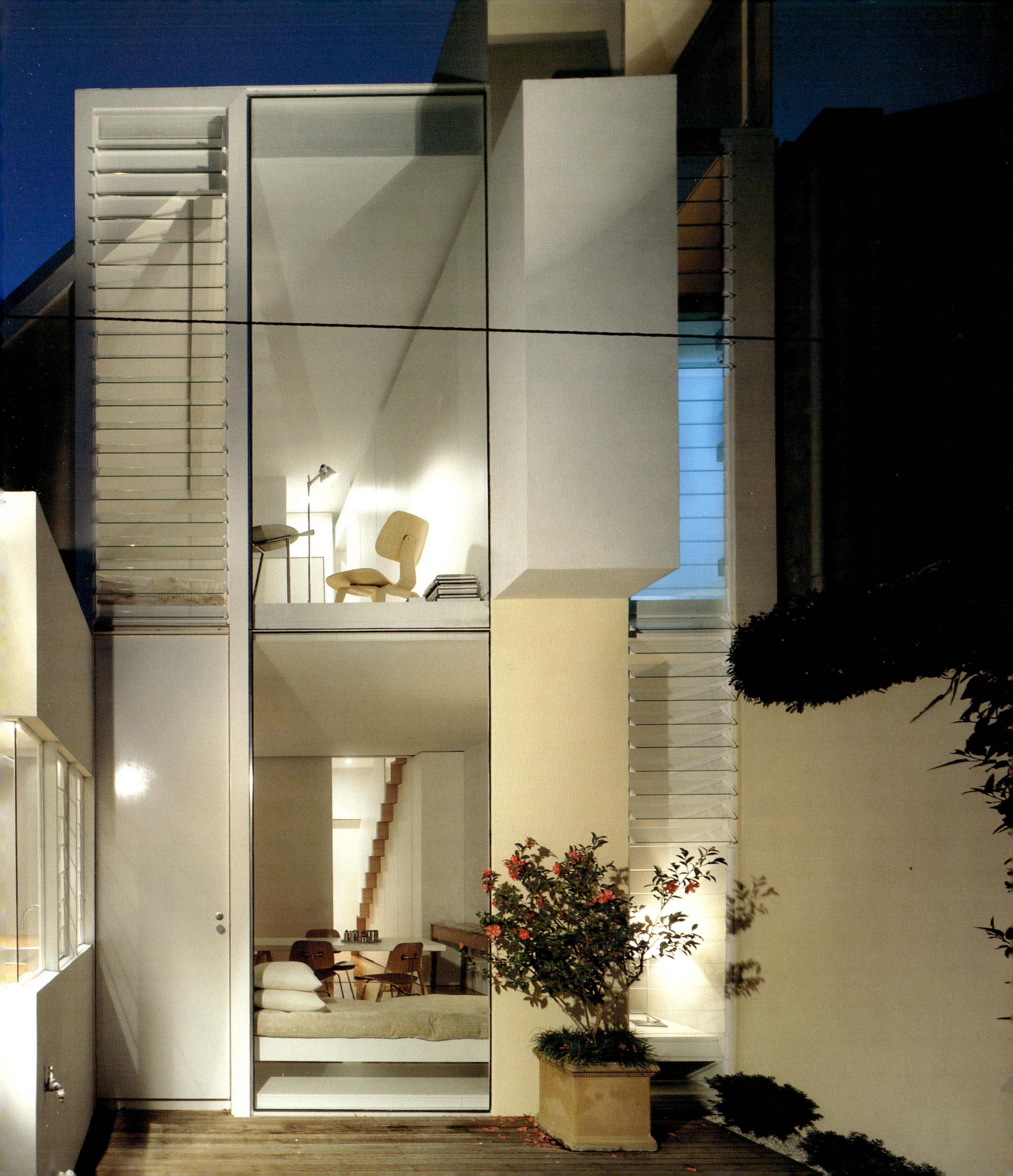

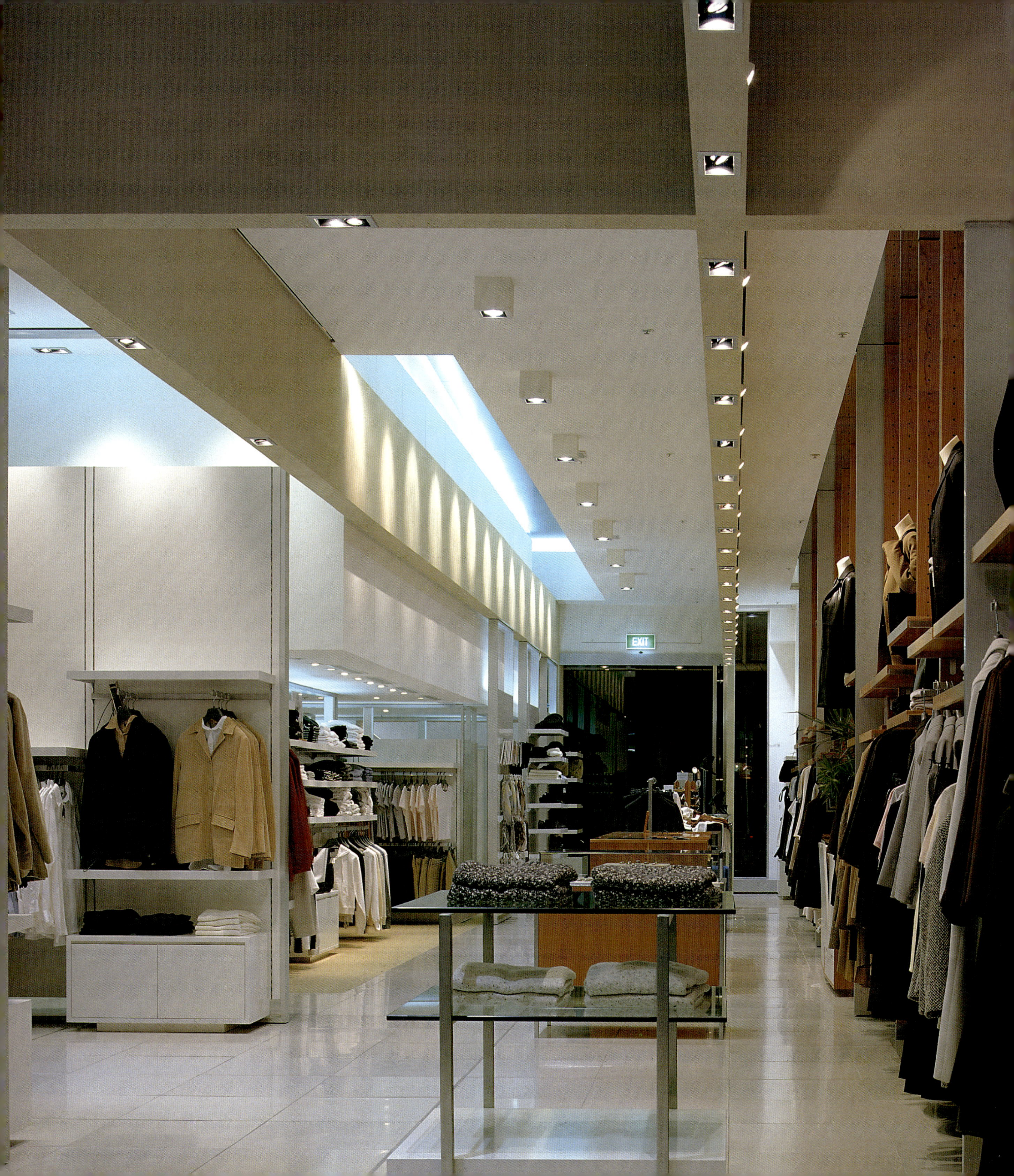
EXIT

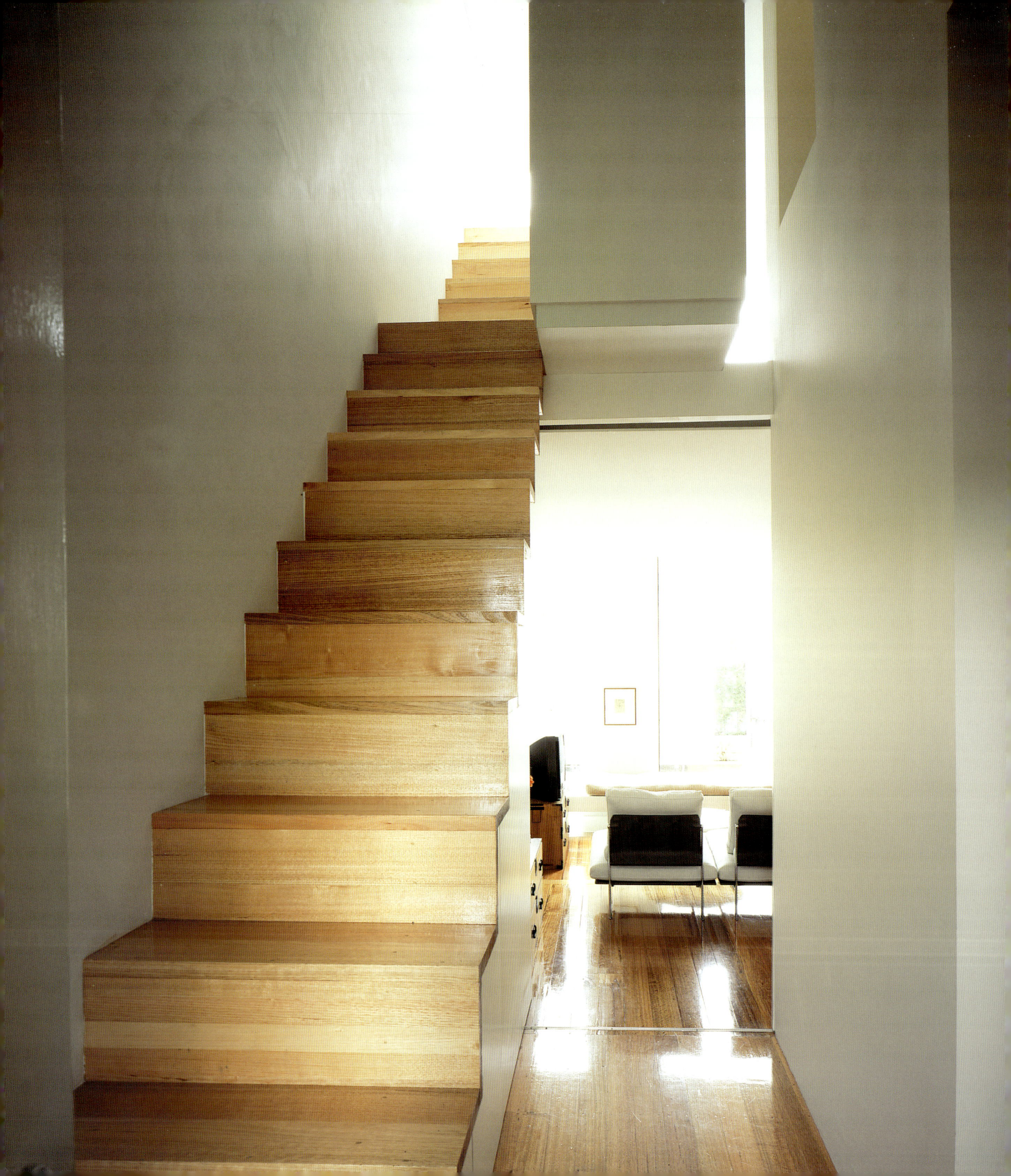

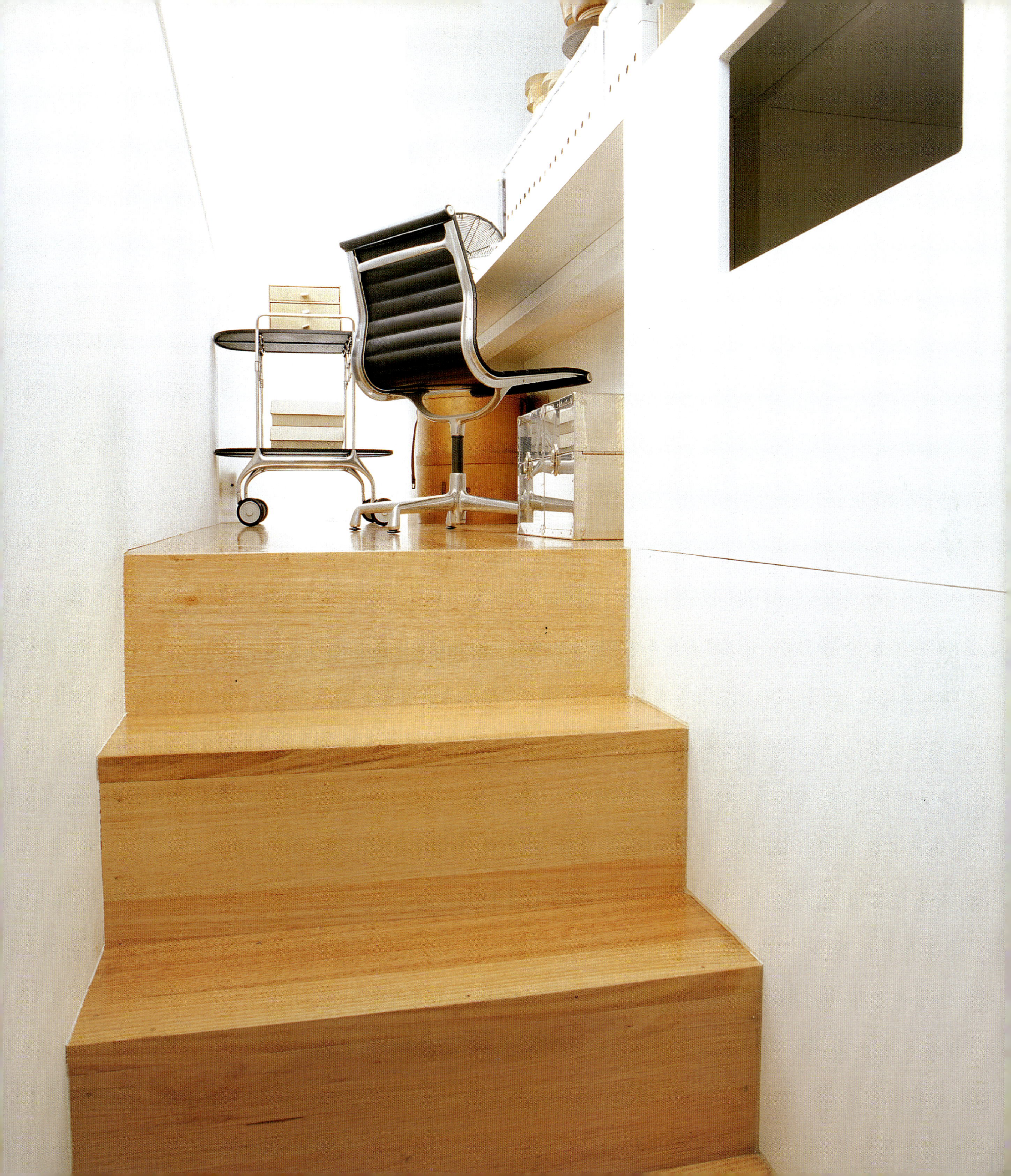

Kerstin Thompson
Kerstin Thompson Architects

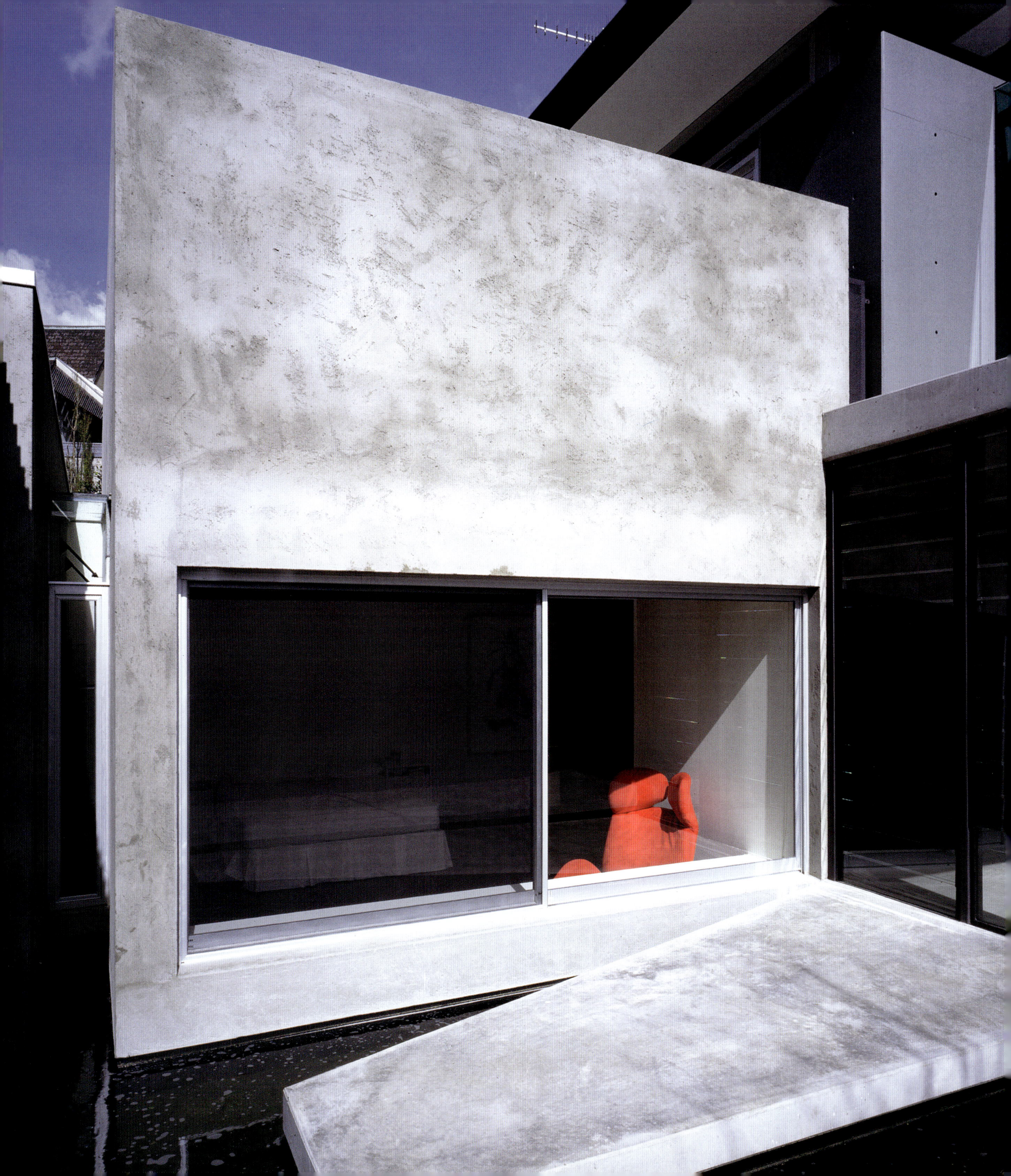

Contemporary culture raises a key predicament. The inheritance of a global discipline in architecture – rich and restrictive – is juxtaposed against particular influences of location, skills and personal stories. It suggests a choice between an international perspective and a regional one. Nonsense. Each depends on the other. It is in this playground that Kerstin Thompson spends her time. Climbing through it. Exploring it. Resolving the issues as she sees them. Kerstin's work challenges the notion of geographic space. It generates conversation. It speaks a particular language. It has its own ideogram, slang, inflections, vocabulary and dialect. Rather than conceptualising architecture as being about individual buildings, she is interested in exploring how architecture interacts with and relates to what is around it. The built environment. Relationships between elements. Building and street. Figure and ground. Inside and out. Public and private. Nature and culture. Postmodernity creates the possibility for hybrid utterances. The creativity of Creole. The uses to which architecture can be put are unpredictable, fluid, improvisational. Kerstin wonders about the modalities with which she represents architecture. Is it possible to provide a chance experience of a view through a stud frame on site with the formal training received in sections and perspectives? For her, buildings are in fact an index of the limited possibilities for negotiation between abstract schemes and determinants of place. Between people and institutions. Buildings are a record of petty quarrels, odd obsessions and personal relationships. Kerstin's vision of architecture is removed from issues of purity and image. She looks more towards an architecture that's alive to the potential created by materials, site characteristics and the ideas which underpin the project.

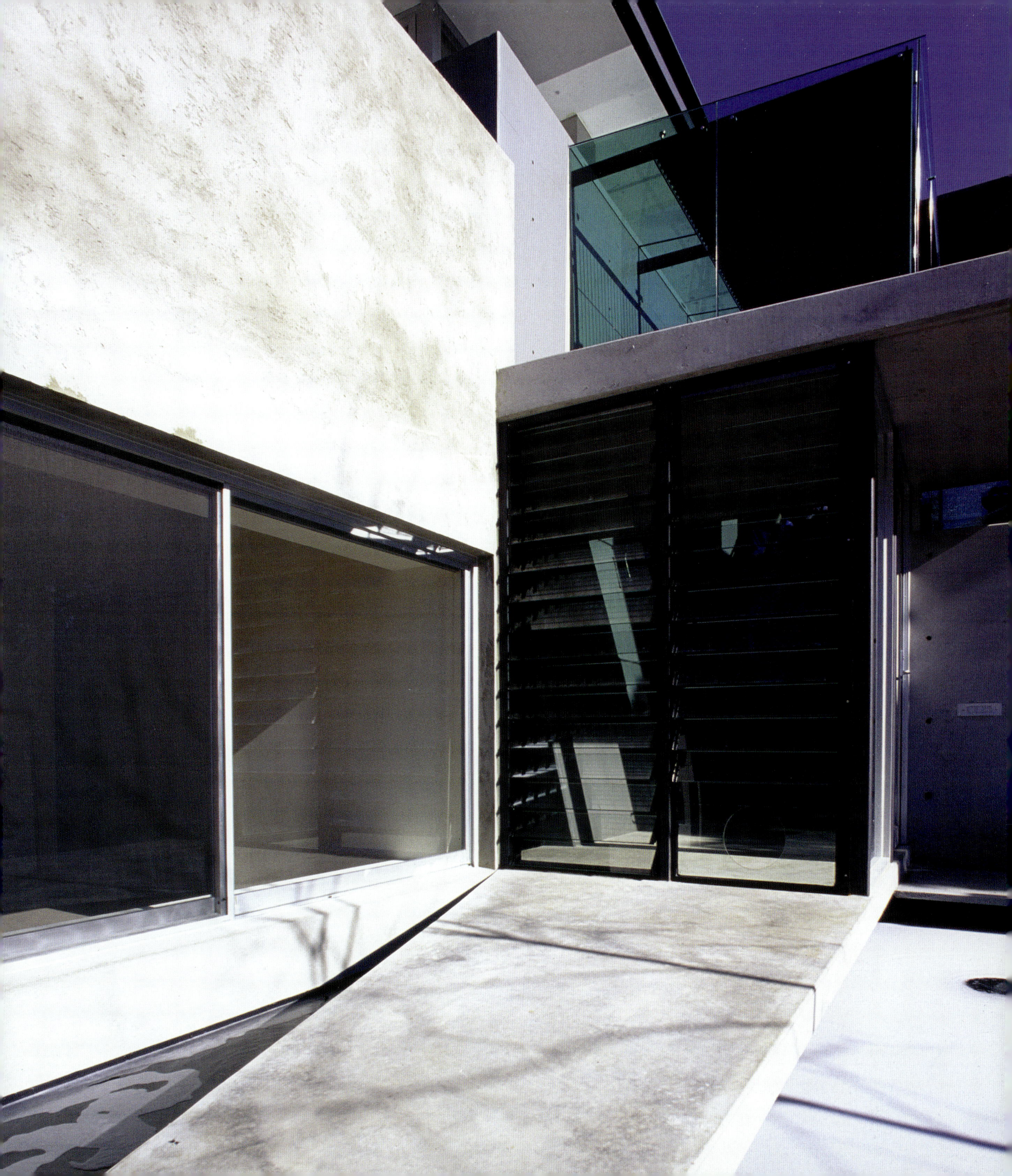

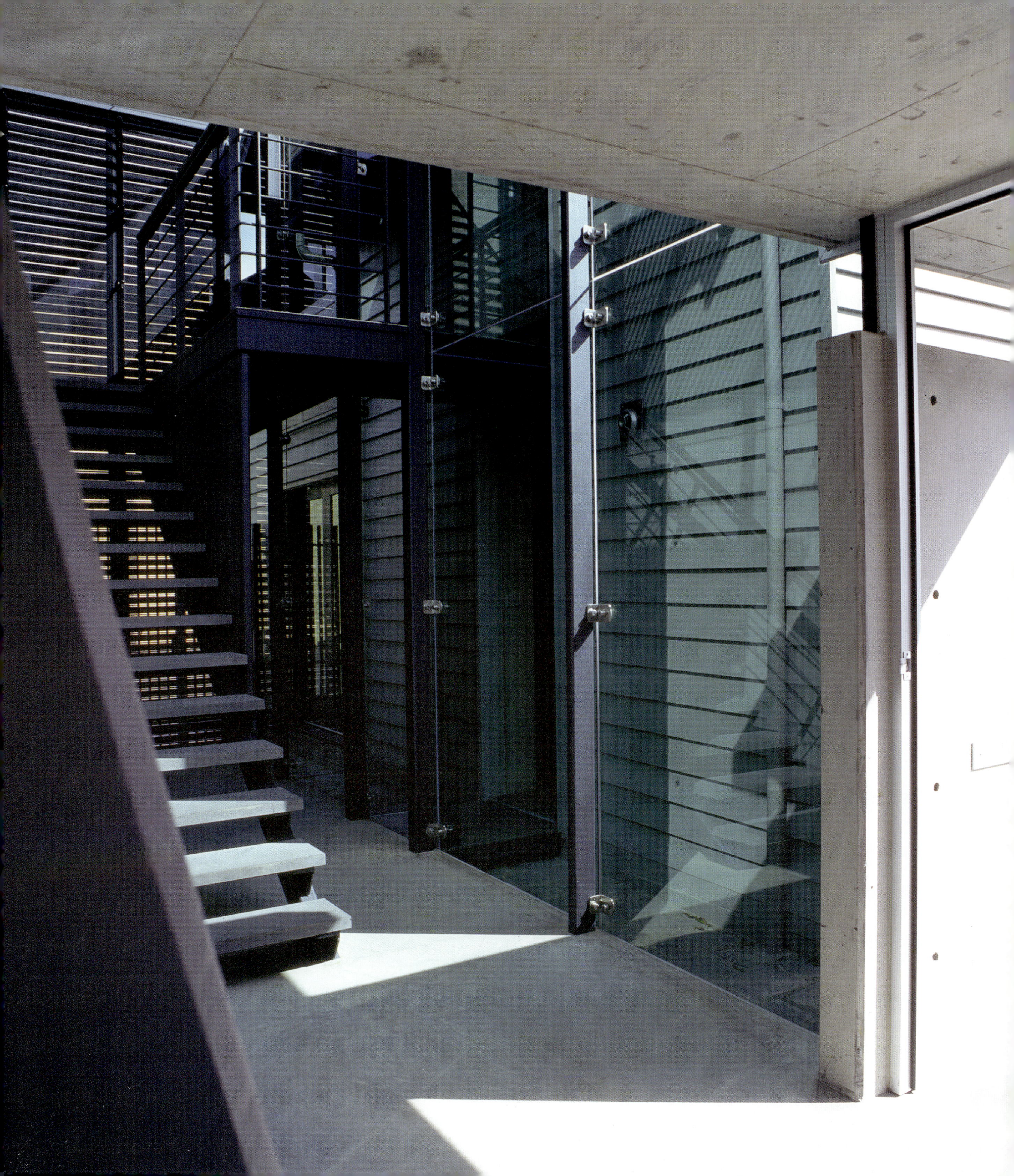

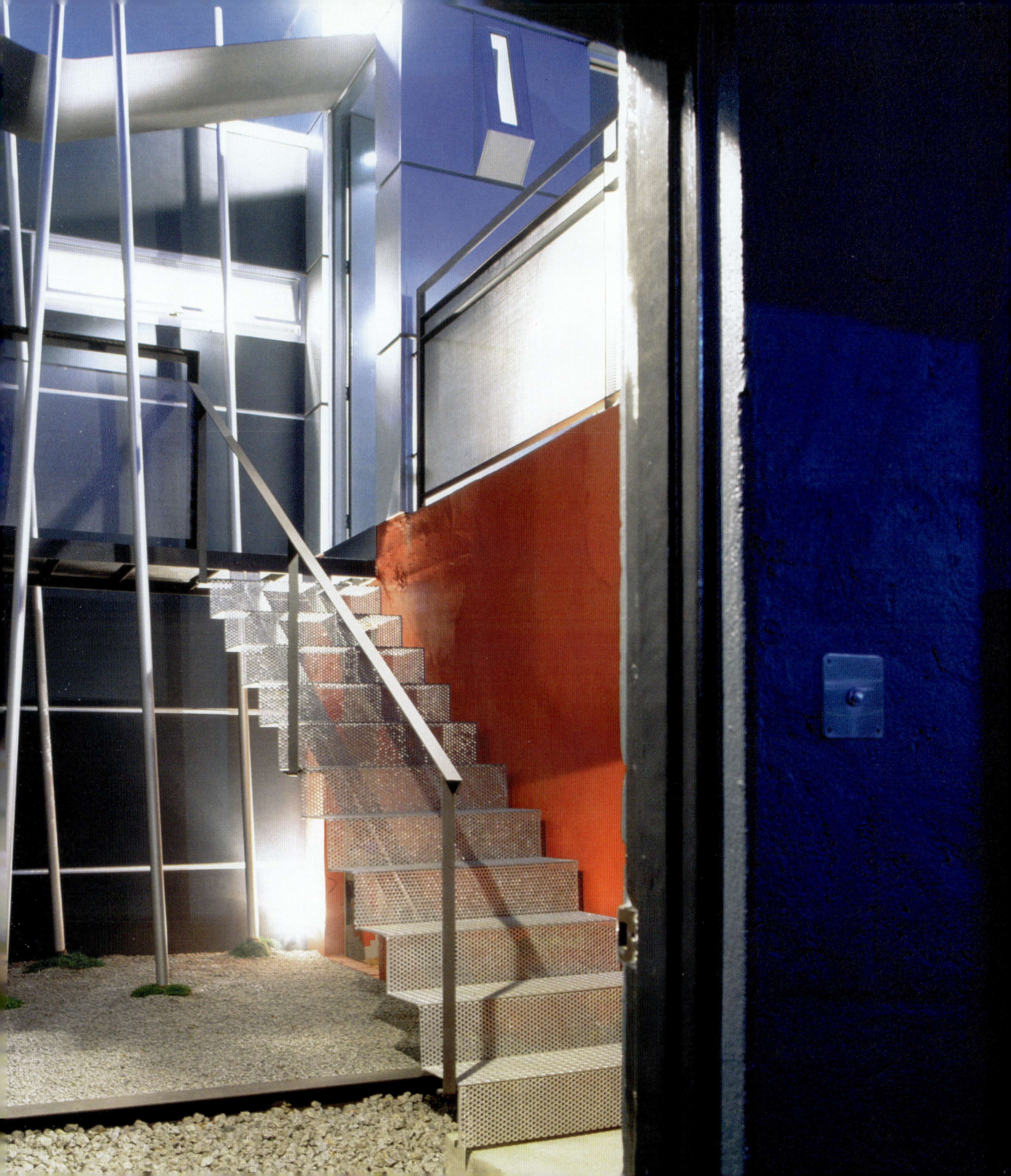

Christopher Connell
Christopher Connell Design

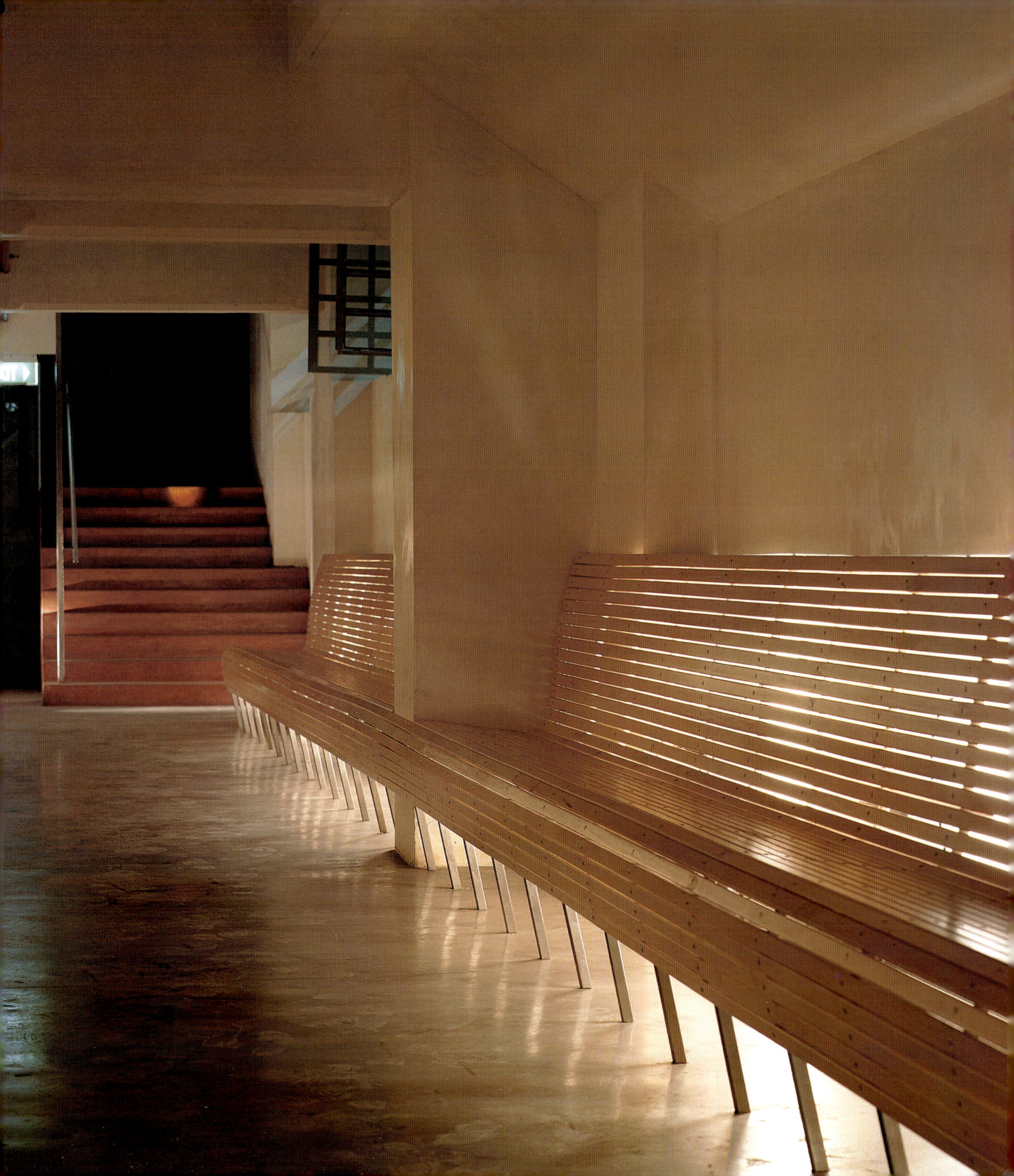

Design and travel. They are accomplices. Partners. A way of life for Christopher Connell. The simple pleasure of a salad and wine in Mikonos. Long hot summers and stolen weekends in the surf at Lorne. The international style and rapture of Milan. Shops. Restaurants. Scenery. Travel has always inspired Christopher. He draws in the qualities that surround him and immerses himself in the creative expressions that beg for his attention. The simple buildings and clear blue water of Greece. The beautiful tailoring of Prada. The sleek production of expensive motor cars. The quirky air of furniture by Sottsass. In Christopher's world, design is an experimental process – ever-changing, refining, eliminating and purifying its expression to establish a style. A learning process. Throughout his career, Connell's style has developed and evolved, encompassing furniture and interiors that reflect the qualities of life he enjoys. Simplistic form. Space. In Dinosaur Designs, we see a clean white space. Understated. It does not overwhelm. It concentrates on what's important – the treasures. The illumination comes from within. It works. Christopher enjoys the variety of cultures and diverse landscapes of Australia. Removed yet accessible to global ideas. An international style. It inspires him. The future of design in Australia? For Christopher Connell, it lies in the support of the patrons. They must encourage. Opportunity must arise for the young to create. In his own words, 'Give young designers carte blanche – a vibrant place to create, where design is foremost and ideas paramount.'

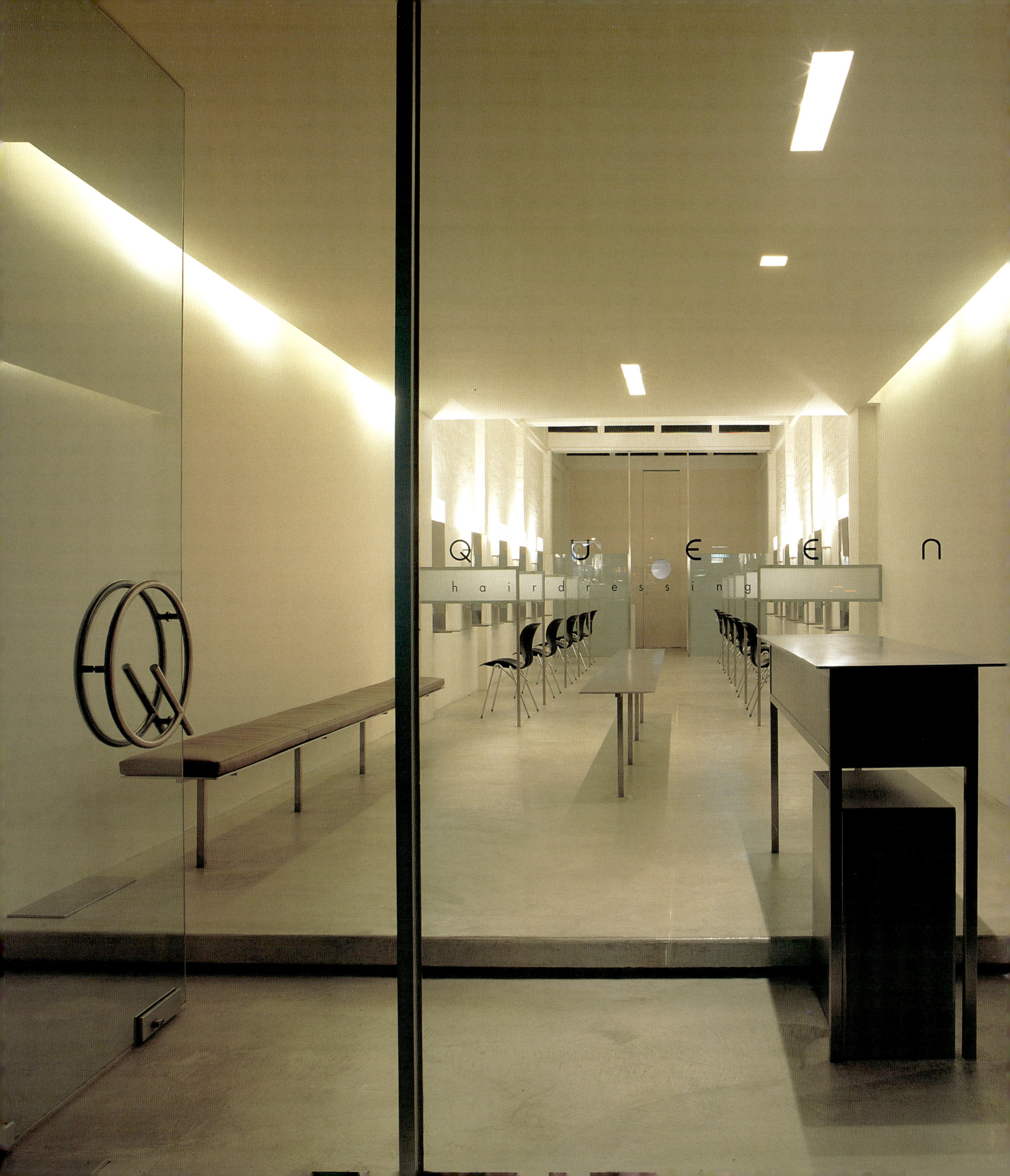
Q U E E N
hairdressing

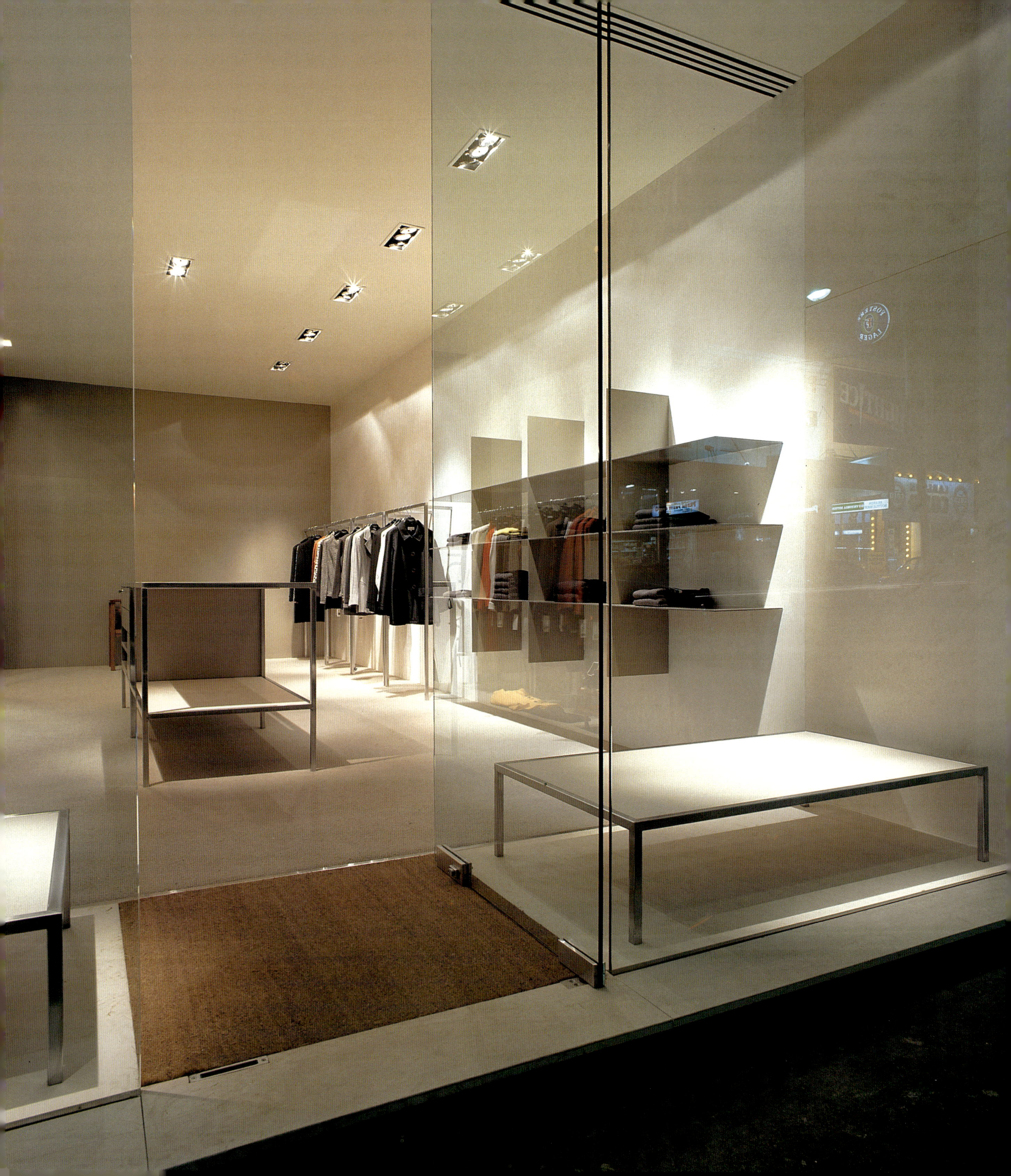

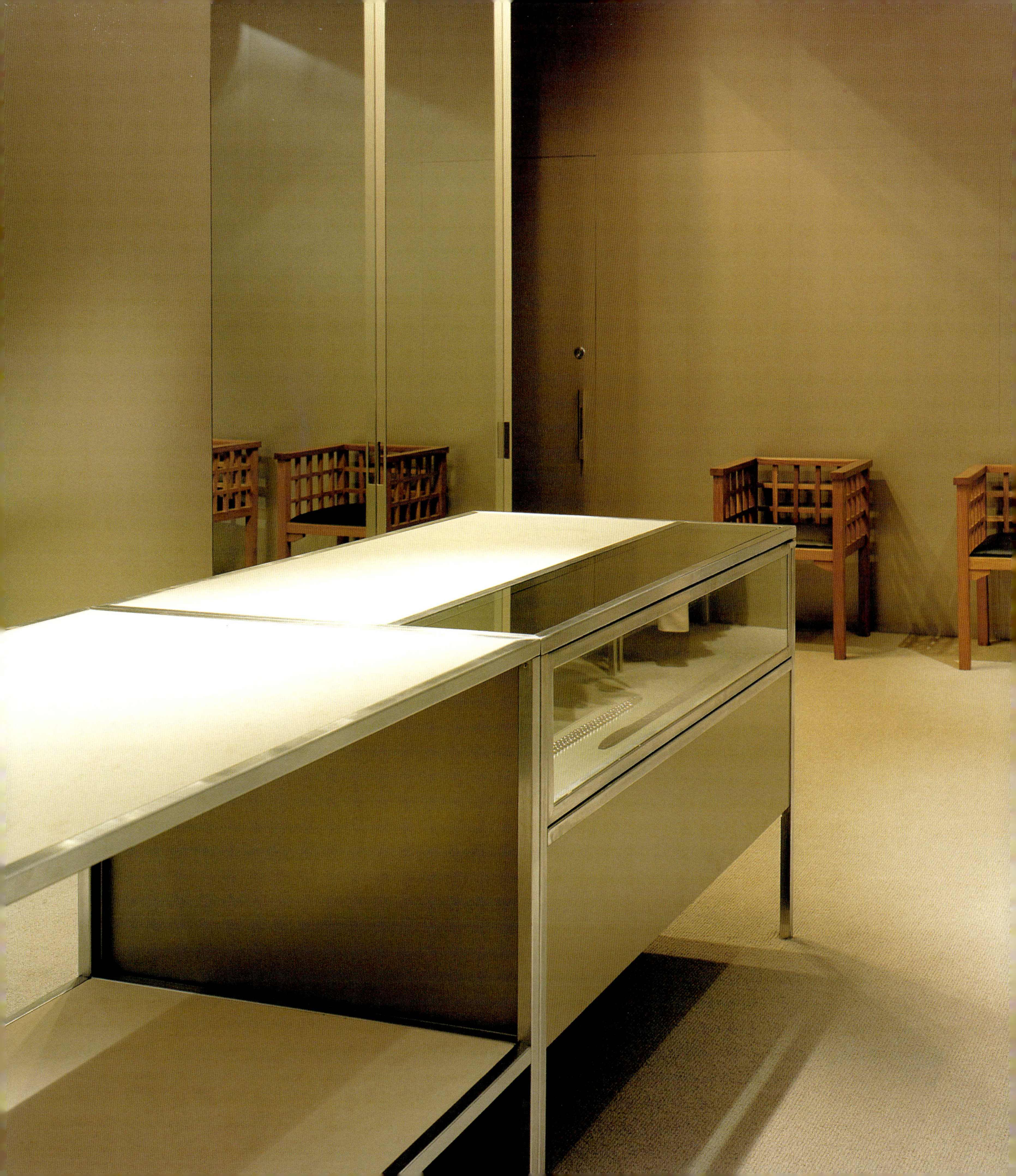

Iain Halliday
Burley Katon Halliday

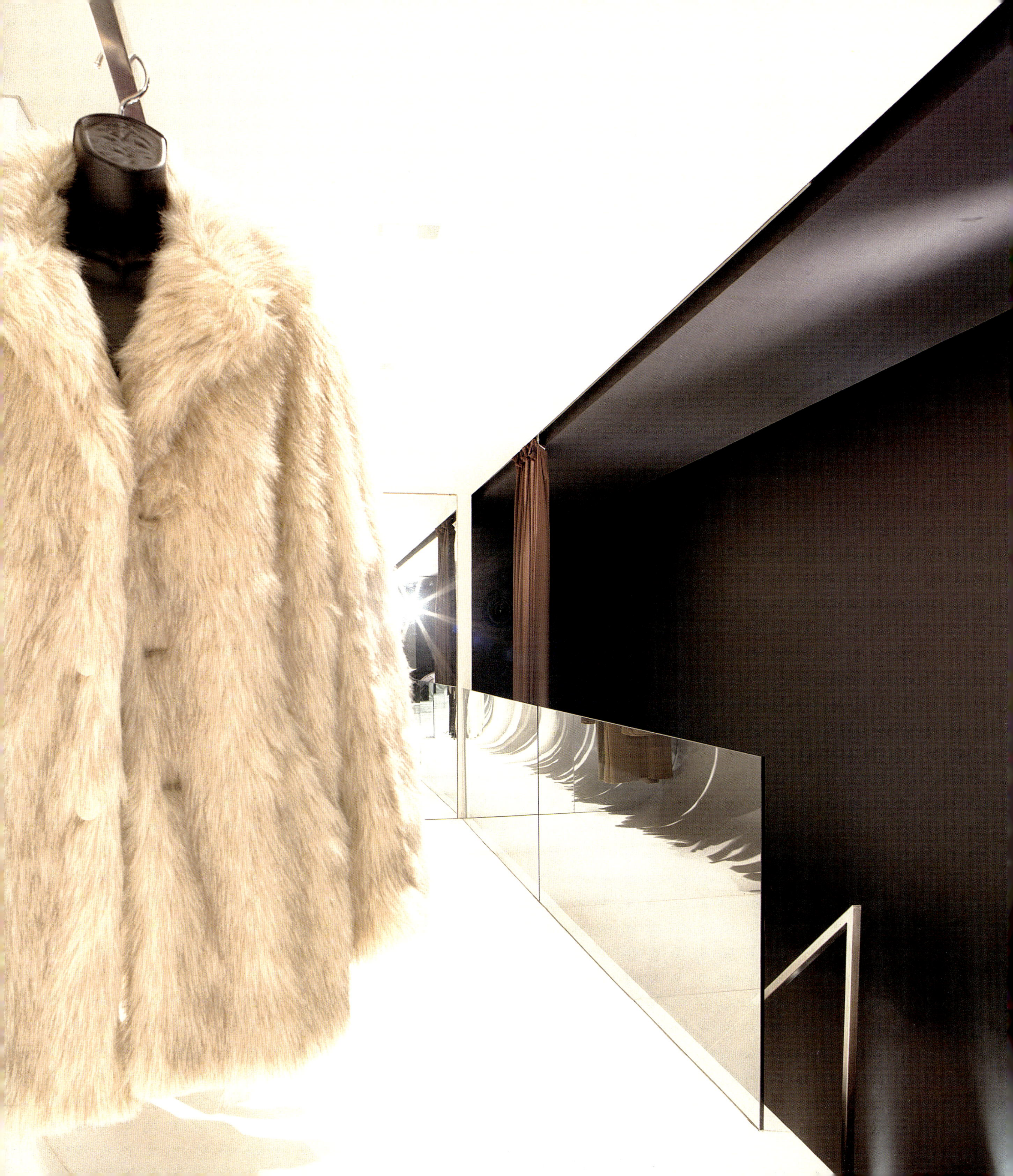

A cool guy dressed in urban black. No clear reflection of a very Australian upbringing on Sydney's northern beaches. His everyday is now spent in the inner city. An environment in Paddington created by the partners in Burley Katon Halliday. A team with a passion for contemporary luxury. Design engaging contrast. A graduate of interior design. A student of architecture. A teacher of students. A presenter to the design community. Iain Halliday is a ready supporter of the industry. After a stint with Mash Freedman and Associates, then Neil Burley and Partners, Iain was made a director and partner of Burley Katon Halliday in 1984. His work is recognised. His signature respected. In 1989, Iain was selected as one of '30 under 30' designers for a New York exhibition. His design works for a variety of media. Museums. Retail environments. Restaurants. Domestic and hotels. His work is glamorous. Joyful. His confidence understated. His precision defined. Iain expresses a pragmatic attention to detail. He gently directs his clients to an understanding of his design. Operating with foresight. Determined. Exhibiting the strength that comes with planning. Iain Halliday sells lifestyles. He makes people live better. Feel richer.

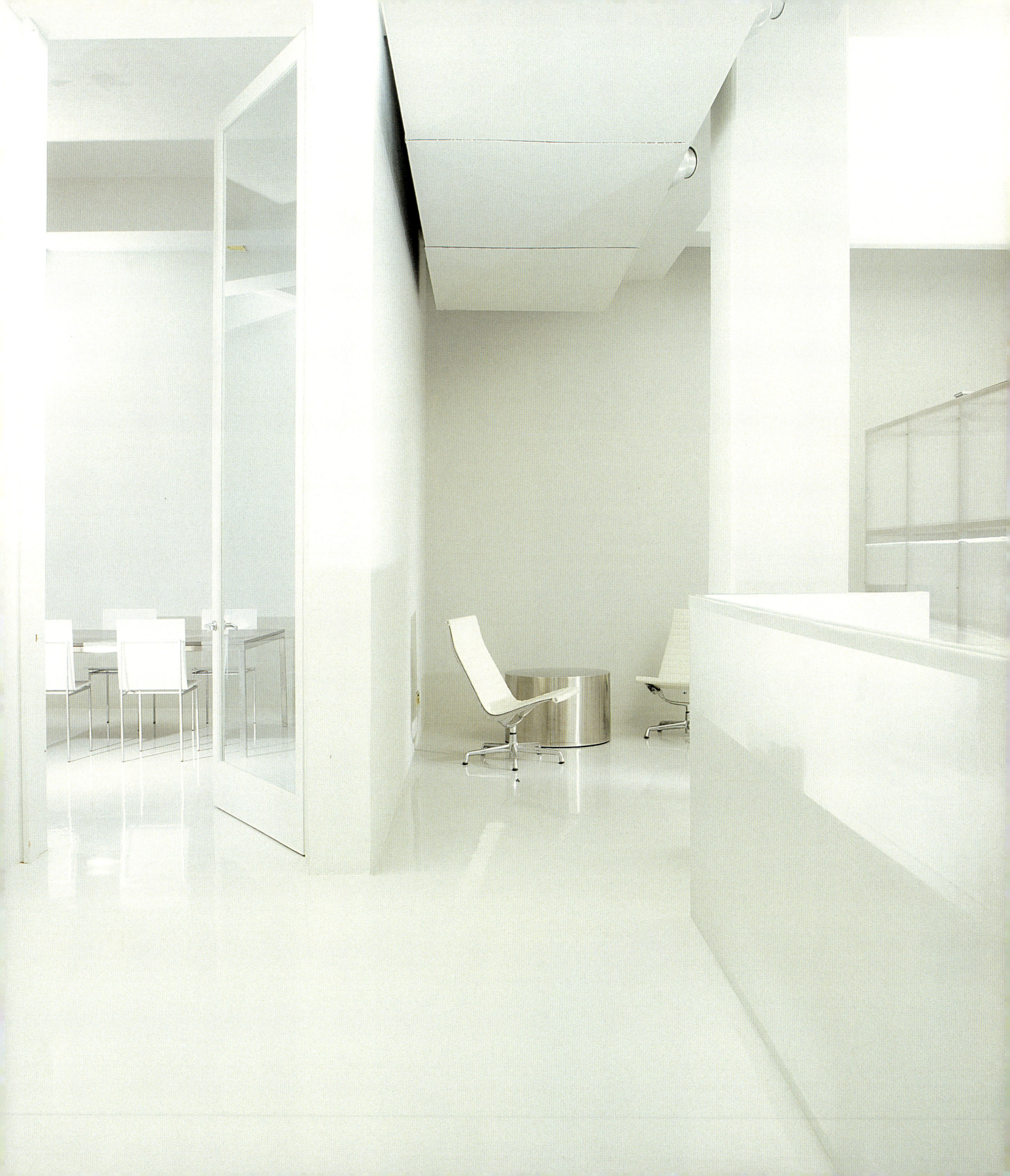

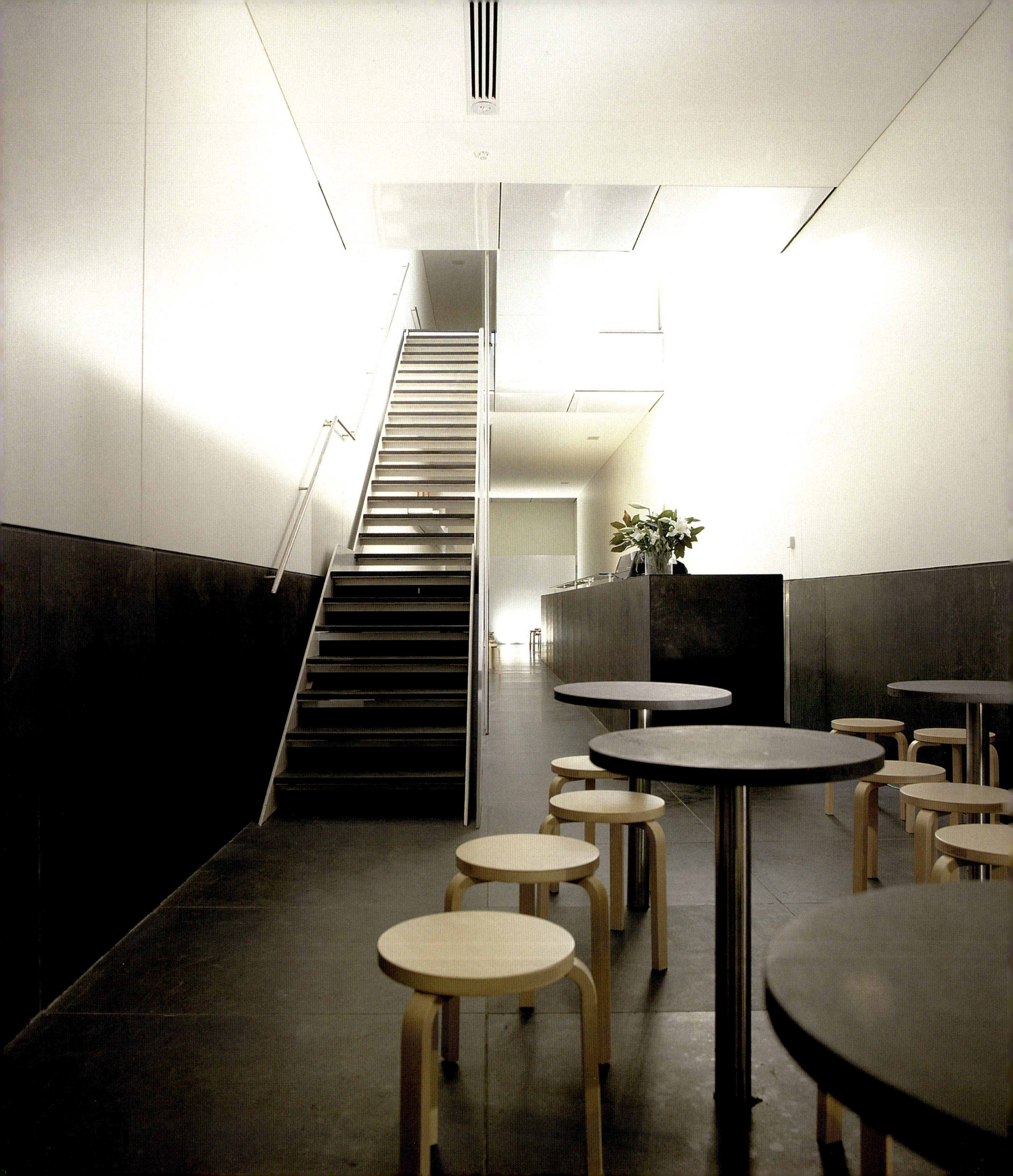

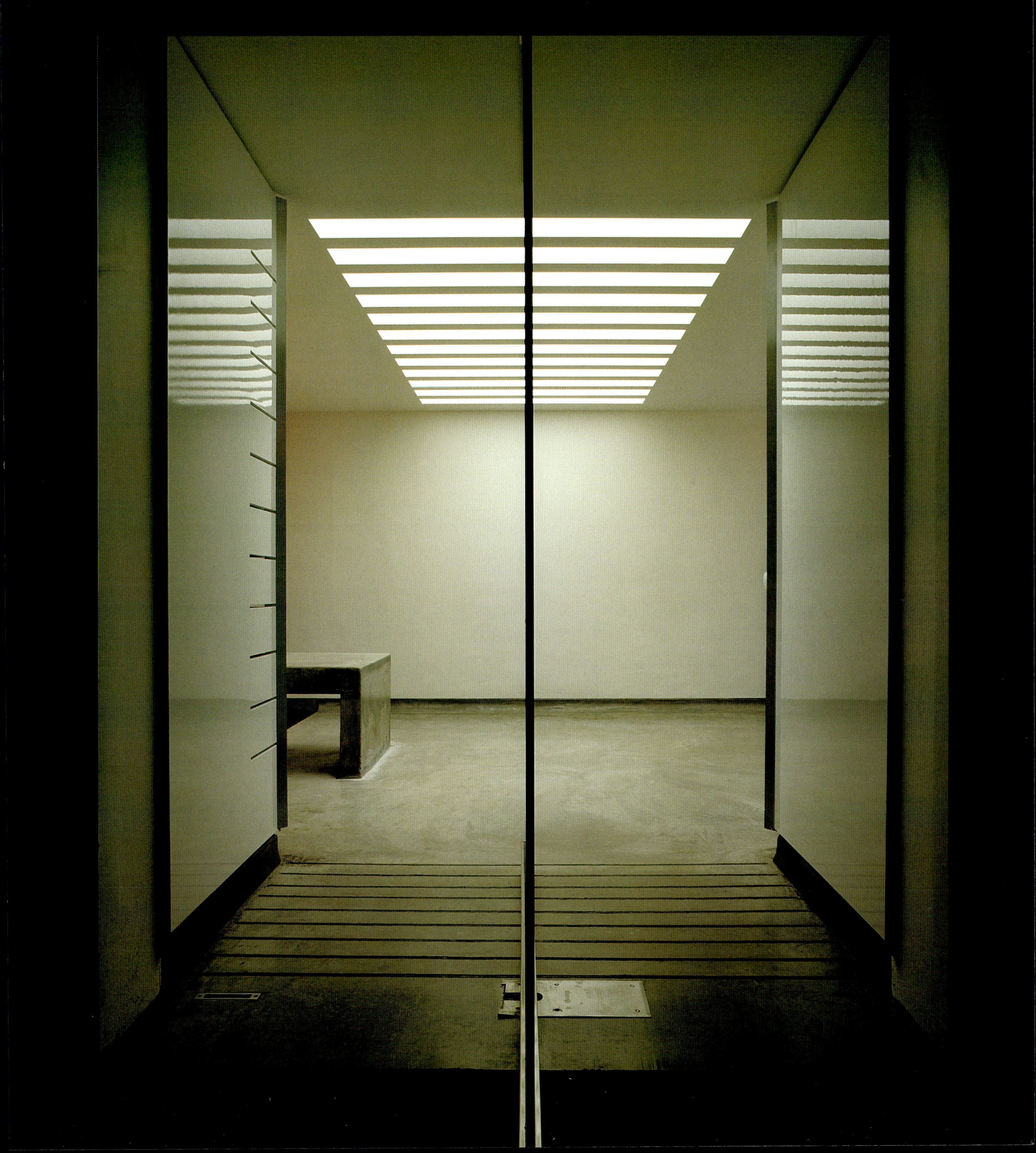

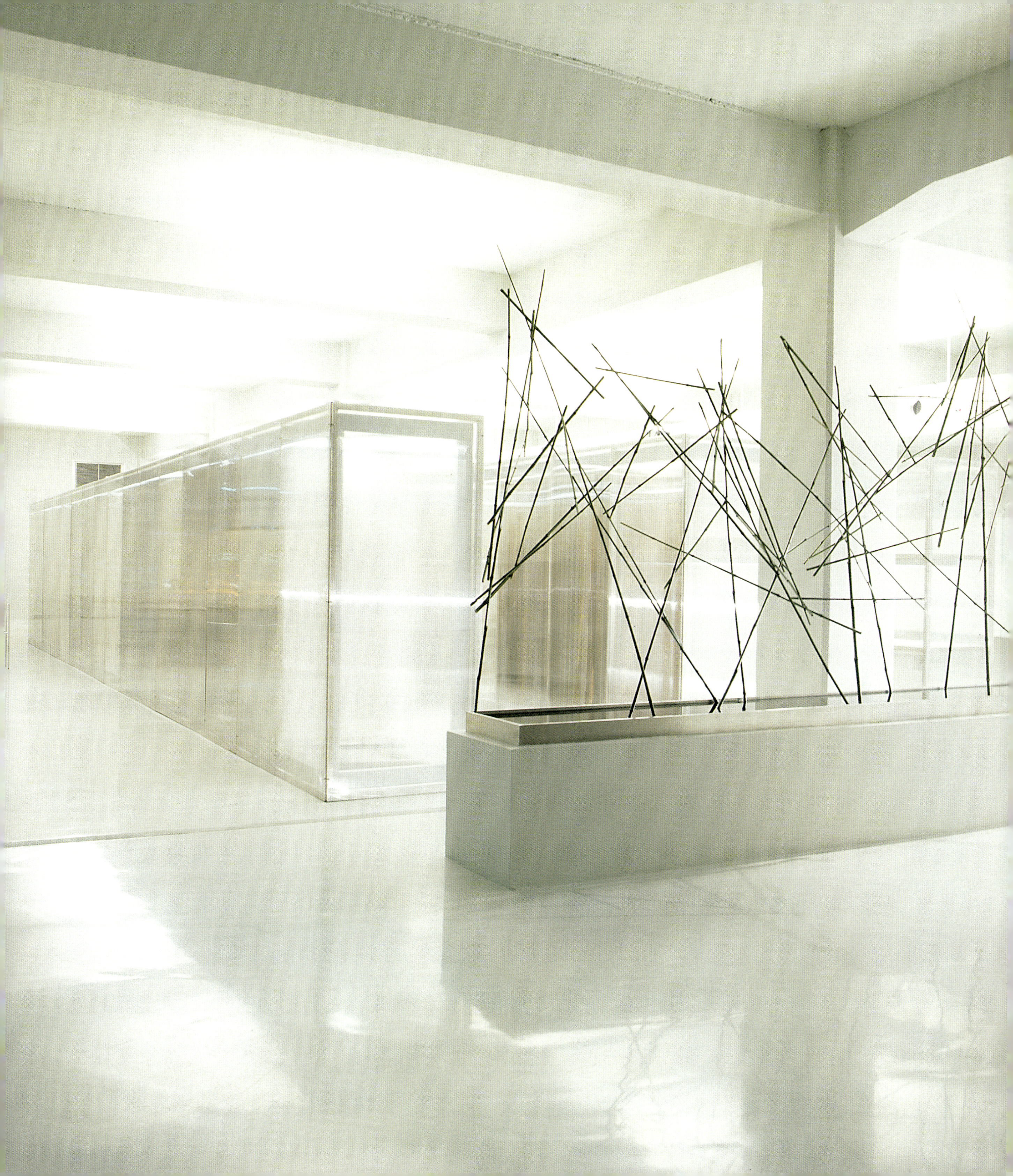

Graphic Design

Steven Cornwell
Jane Sinclair
Cornwell Design

2

Paper over time:
a story of paper
EDWARDS DUNLOP AND CO

Cornwell Design's way of working is infectious among clients and studio alike. Together, Steven Cornwell and Jane Sinclair create wonderful design that works, that communicates, that reaches into hearts and minds. To produce consistently outstanding work also takes an approach which is insightful, visionary and intelligent, yet rooted firmly in careful process. When creative talent meets its match in planning and systems, the outcome will always land a powerful punch. They follow processes specially developed by astute project management principles. But most of all, they know how to take a brief which is at the very core of visual communication strategy. Every step is careful, every outcome incisive.

Solving, Searching, Supporting and Surprising

Floor 2

2 Floor

Floor 2
customer relations decision making industrial relations
tality management gaming operations resort development crowd control computer spreadsheets management computing hospitality accounting keyboarding leadership customer relations decision making industrial relations quality assurance
ccounting
floor 2

e.g.etal

DESIGN
design481

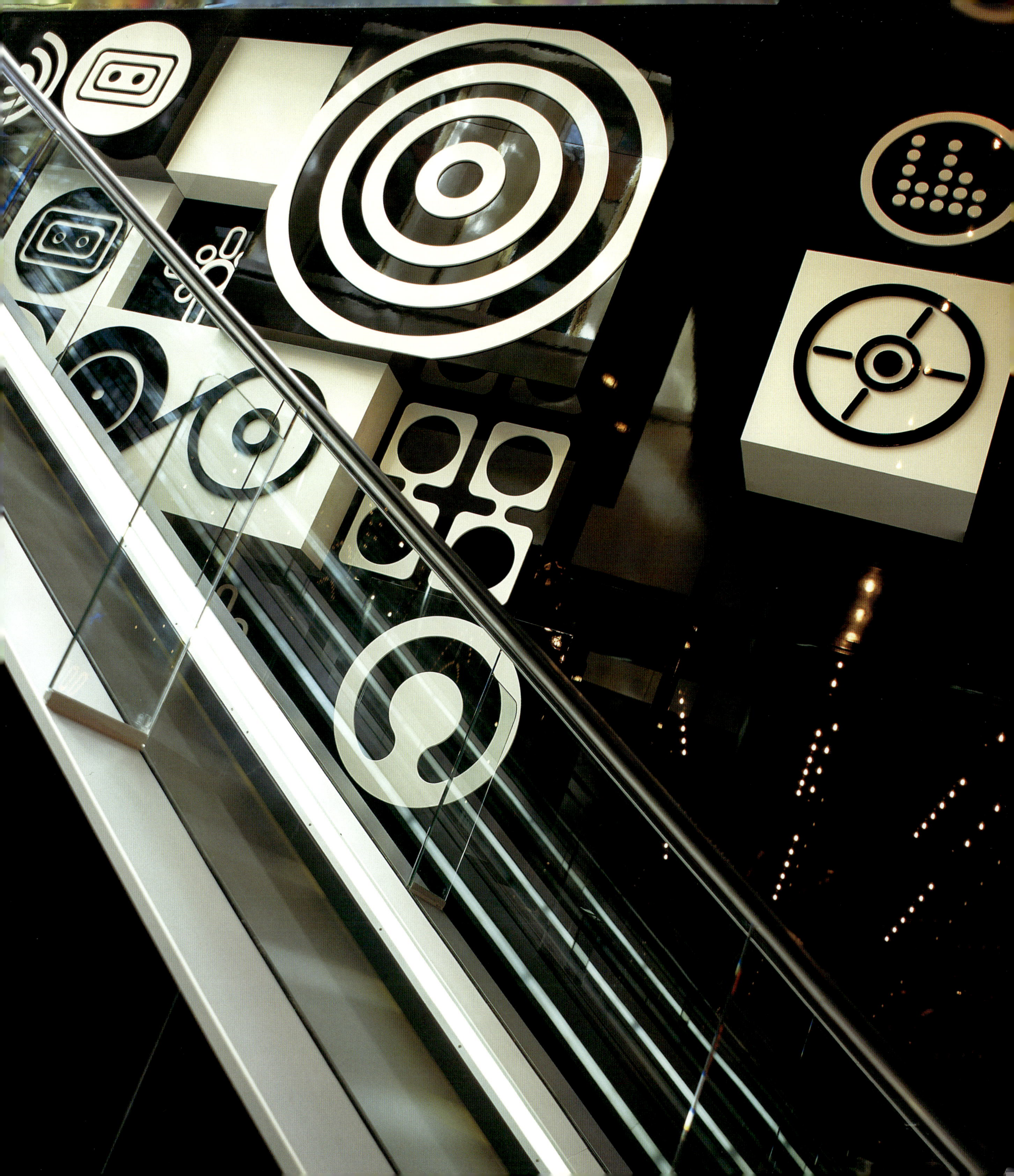

David Band
Fiona Mahon
Mahon&Band

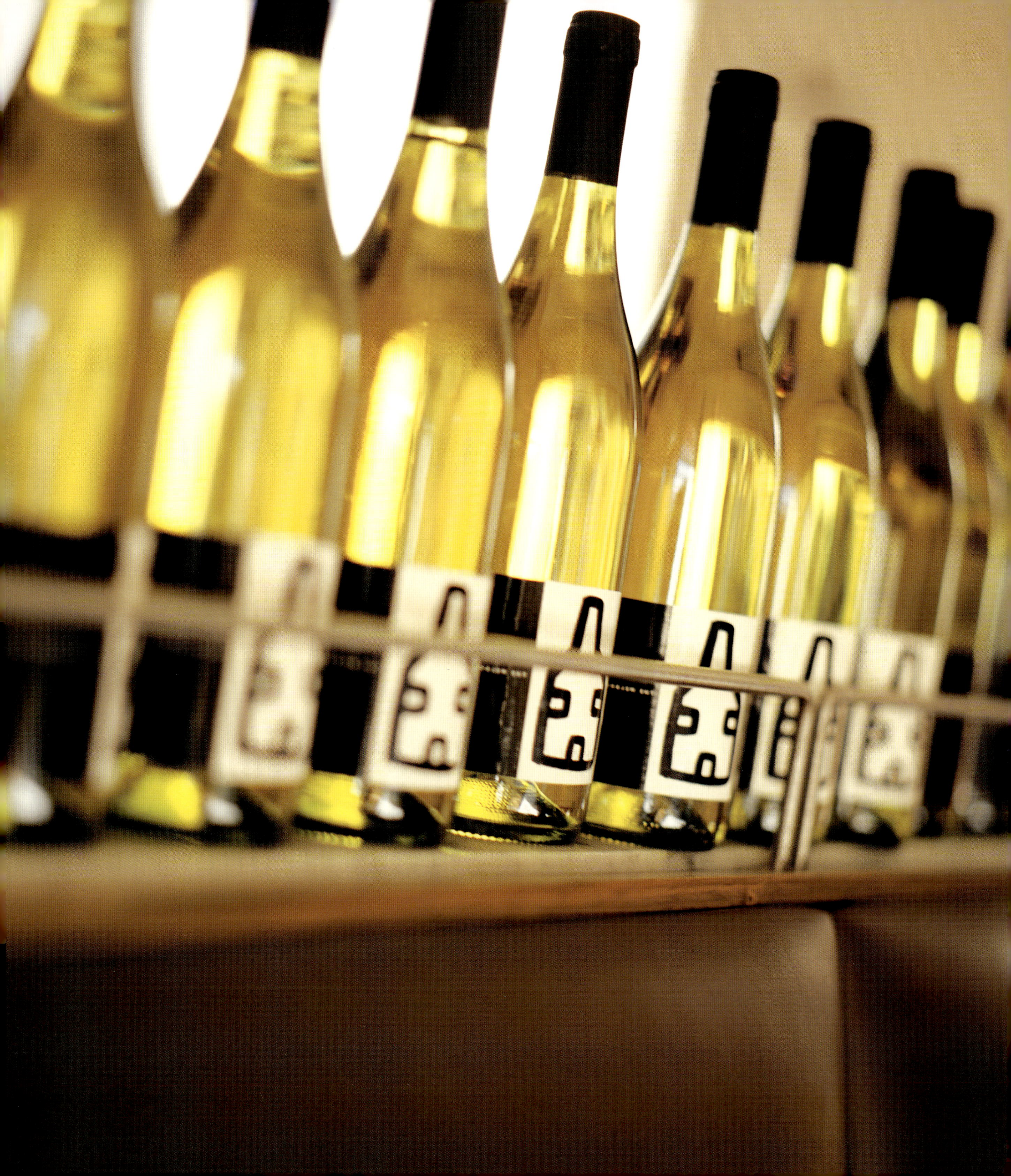

Mahon&Band is what you get when Glasgow-born artist David Band and Melbourne-born graphic designer Fiona Mahon decide there's work to be done. Together. The partnership arose out of the realms of book publishing when the pair discovered a common creative spirit that begged collaboration. Immediately. In the early days, their foray into image-making as a duo was representative of two divergent artistic backgrounds – David honing an intuitive and painterly approach to form, shape and colour in Britain's fine-arts schools, Fiona crafting commercial needs with technology. But, soon, the conceptual interests of the artist began to respond to the commercial exigencies of a fast-growing client base, and the promotional concerns of the graphic designer started to accommodate the gut feeling of the artist. A powerful economy of image began to emerge. Beguilingly seductive images. Intent is communicated in an instant. Take the identity designed for Pomme restaurant in Melbourne. The diner refers to a menu emblazoned with the image of a single apple. There is no type. Why bother telling the diner what they already know? In its deceptive simplicity, the minimalist photo of an apple shot in a very opulent way tells us everything we need to know about this dining venue. Upmarket. Unpretentious. Adventurous. More would be superfluous. This reductionist approach buys the image longevity. It is universally identifiable. Memorable. With Café a Taglio, Mahon&Band took the iconic Leaning Tower of Pisa and put it on a postcard. No words. A clear message to take-away customers. The pizza is made to traditional Italian specifications. At the Melbourne Wine Room, a strong illustrative reference to Band's art school roots is apparent. Here, the figurative sketch style is entirely appropriate. It knows its audience – young arty types who appreciate good food and drink in unassuming surrounds. In a world so oversubscribed with dense imagery and type, Mahon&Band relies on the premise that if you reduce the message to a simple, strong visual, you will make a simple, memorable impression.

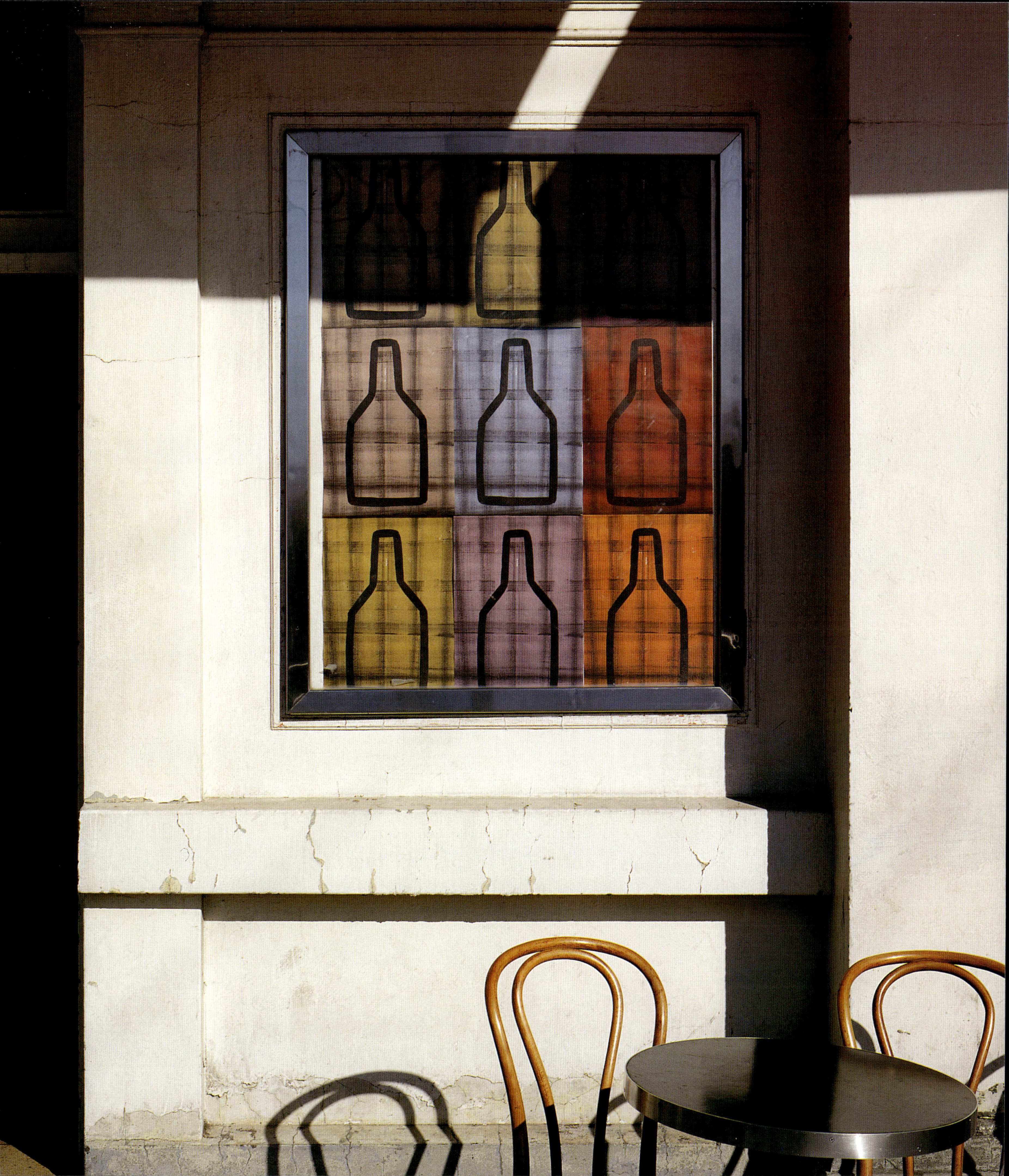

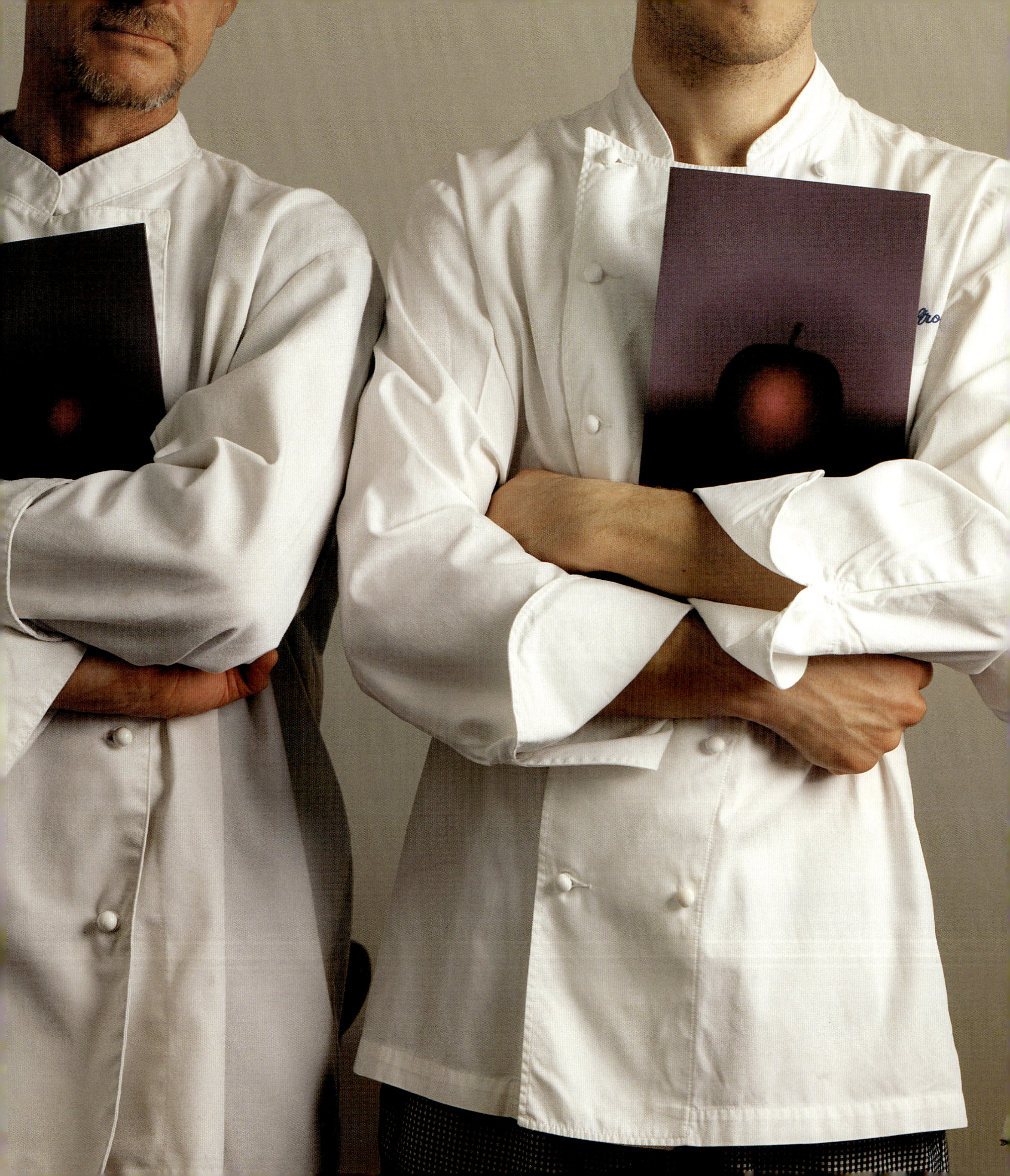

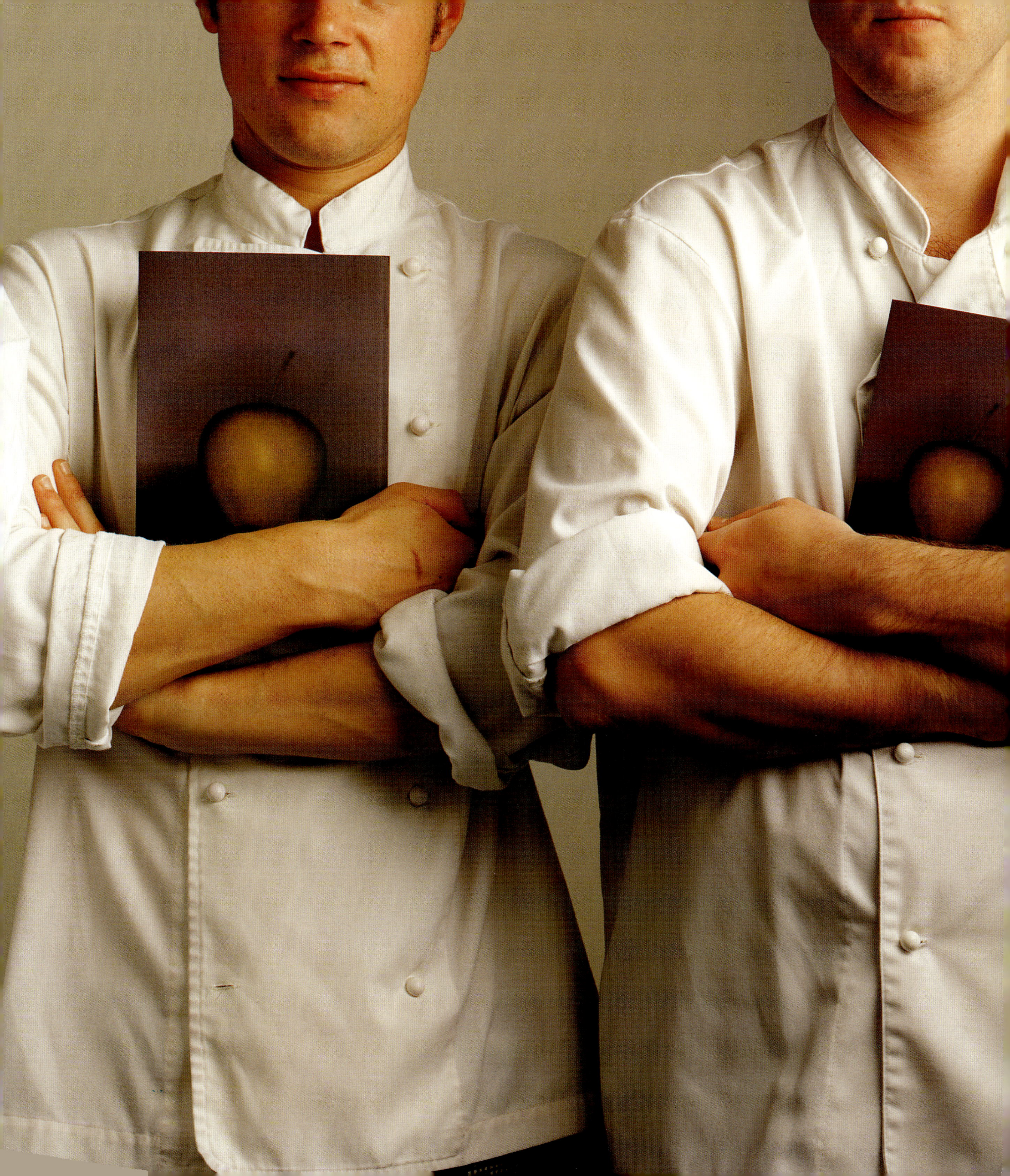

a soup of mixed
baked vegetables $6.50

PIATTO ALLA ROMANA $10.50
two whole artichokes &
"friselle" with tomato

BRUSCHETTA AGLIO & OLIO $1.50

cote a taglio heating instructions:
we recommend you pre-heat
your grill on high heat and warm
your pizza for 2-3 minutes.

157 mirror street st kilda 3182 telephone 9534 1344

Visnja Brdar
Brdar Design

Old Food by Jill Dupleix

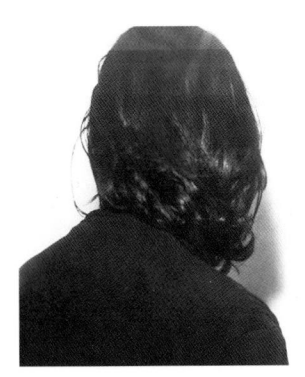

Born a Virgo in Australia, 1969. Speaks Croatian first. English second. Mother and Father paint walls. Their favourite paint is white. Father wears white shirts every day. Without fail. White shirts inspire. Visnja does four years at Swinburne University. Has many job offers. Chooses freedom. Starts her own business and designs for some chic Melburnians. Goes to Europe aged 22. First night in Amsterdam, the red-light district. Glossy red inspires. Then to Dubrovnik where the white stone city is white. Very sublime white white. The Croatian War continues. In the mornings, bombs drop nearby as she puts on Chanel moisturiser. Immersion in blue on the islands of Croatia – Rab, Krk, Brac, Vis, Hvar. Good-looking words. Not many vowels. Brdar. In Milan, meets Memphis maestro Sottsass. In Paris, the Newson book is a labour of love. In Rome, spends long days in the *Colors Magazine* office. Kalman says not to stop until the right picture is found. Doesn't stop until the right picture is found. Walks past the Pantheon every day. Stops in front of it every day. Graphics can be monumental like the Pantheon. Graphics should taste as good as pea risotto. Chases the robber who steals her purse. Doesn't stop. Catches him. In London, lives with seventy-year-old Sayma, who wears a different Hermès scarf every day. In New York and speechless. In Melbourne, designs a very minimal cookbook and wins a $20,000 design award.

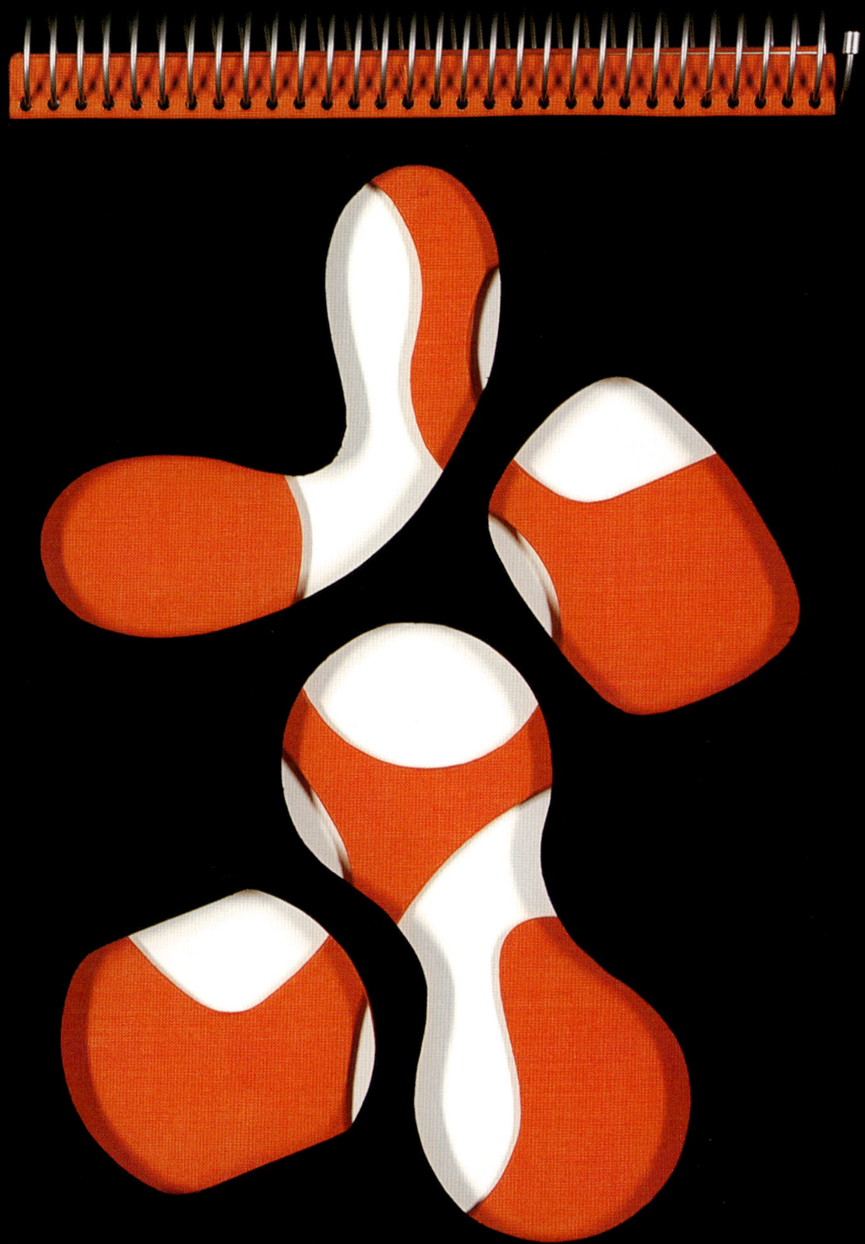

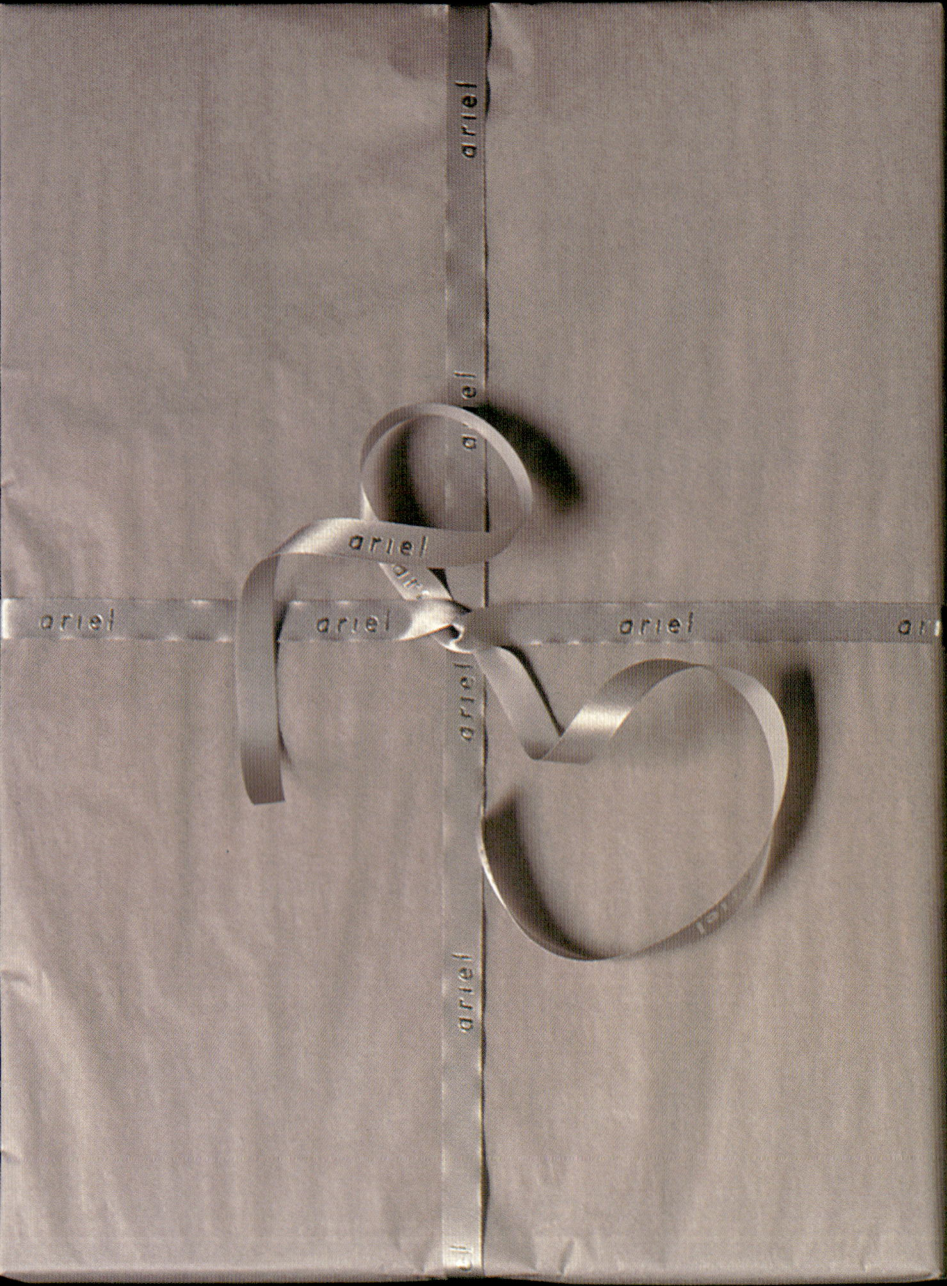
ariel

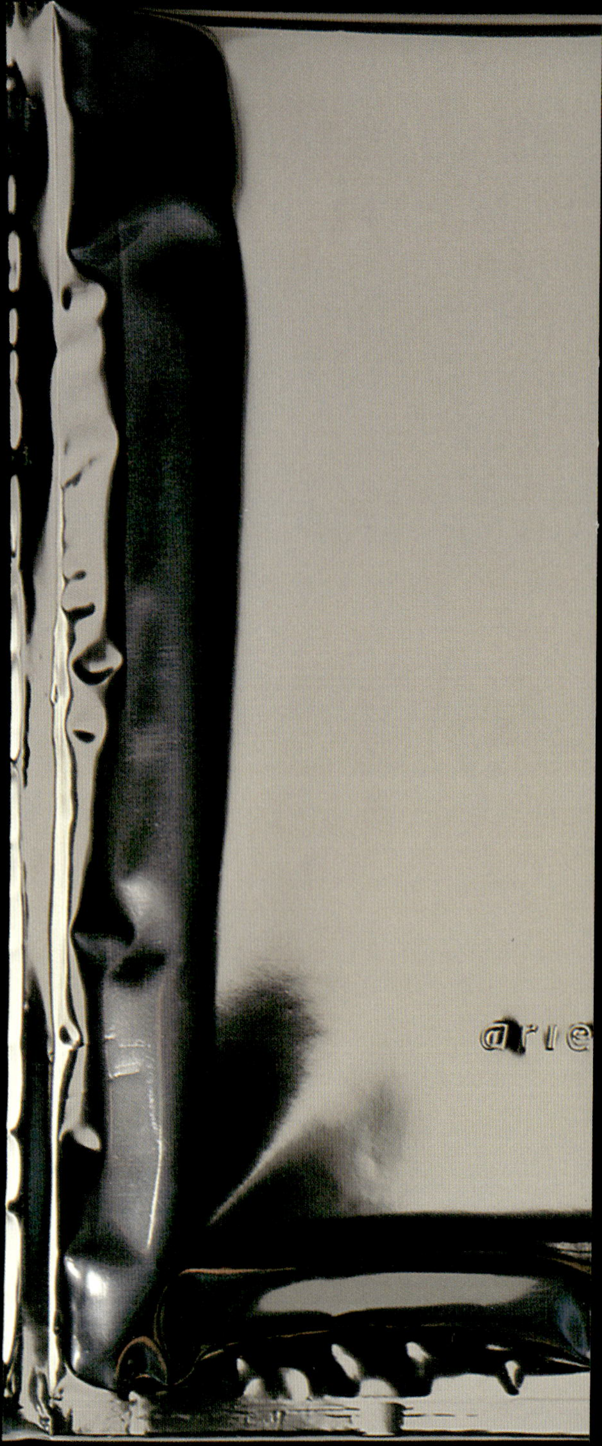
ariel

ariel

BEYOND THE WALL DANIEL LIBESKIND

A DISCUSSION OF RECENT WORK
MONDAY 24 MARCH 1997, 6.00 PM
STOREY HALL, AUDITORIUM, RMIT
SWANSTON STREET MELBOURNE
MEMBERS $15, NON-MEMBERS $20
STUDENTS $5, LIMITED FREE
TICKETS FOR STUDENTS ONLY
AVAILABLE FROM UNIVERSITIES
BOOKINGS ARE ESSENTIAL
TICKETS PROVIDED. 2 PD POINTS
RSVP BY WEDNESDAY 19 MARCH

BORN IN POSTWAR POLAND AND
NOW AN AMERICAN CITIZEN LIVING
IN BERLIN, DANIEL LIBESKIND
IS AN INTERNATIONAL FIGURE IN
ARCHITECTURAL PRACTICE AND
URBAN DESIGN. HE IS WELL
KNOWN FOR INTRODUCING A
NEW CRITICAL DISCOURSE INTO
ARCHITECTURE AND FOR HIS
MULTIDISCIPLINARY APPROACH.
HIS PRACTICE EXTENDS FROM
BUILDING MAJOR CULTURAL
INSTITUTIONS, INCLUDING
MUSEUMS AND CONCERT HALLS,
TO LANDSCAPE AND URBAN
PROJECTS, TO STAGE DESIGN,
INSTALLATIONS AND EXHIBITIONS.
HIS IDEAS HAVE INFLUENCED A
NEW GENERATION OF ARCHITECTS
AND THOSE INTERESTED IN THE
FUTURE DEVELOPMENT OF CITIES
AND CULTURE WORLDWIDE.

Andrew Hoyne
Hoyne Design

Nikki Goldstein
essential energy
a guide to aromatherapy and essential oils
Scientists at the Memorial Sloan-Kettering Cancer Center in New York have discovered the vanillalike smell of heliotropin can help reduce patient anxiety when undergoing stressful examinations like magnetic resonance imaging (MRI).
Japanese firm Shimizu deploys a woody scent to soften the mood in the banquet room of its headquarters.
Allow the patient to share his or her feelings with you. It is rare, but if you or your patient feels unwell after a treatment, or if a child swallows an essential oil, consult a physician immediately. It is always a good idea to consult a textbook to check on the dosage and toxicity of essential oils.

Andrew Hoyne's reputation will scare the hell out of you. He barrels into your boardroom, hair on fire. He insults your corporate image, trashes your logo and reorganises your life. Or so they say. This 30-year-old, Melbourne-based designer has no half-pace. He serves up his design with brutal honesty and contagious enthusiasm. His solutions are inspired. People often mistake his enthusiasm for brashness. Truth is, Hoyne is energetic. Passionate. Extremely serious about design. He hates to see a job badly executed. It's an opportunity missed. Andrew Hoyne thrives on his work. He sees everything in terms of its graphic sense. Too confusing. Wrong colour scheme. Great image. How can this be improved? What could we do to make it better? Hoyne didn't wait around to finish his course at RMIT. He didn't wait for clients to find him – he went to them. He hunted down the movers and shakers at Red Earth, Holeproof, Aveda and Esprit and hassled them for a break. Esprit became a major client. Andrew wanted to art-direct books, so he did. He sought out a chef, a writer and together they went to a publisher with *Hot Food Cool Jazz*. The book and CD set is one of several of his designs on exhibition in the San Francisco Museum of Modern Art. An innovative spirit infects the Hoyne Design studio. Just because you hire Hoyne to design a brochure doesn't mean that's where it ends. Once they start, the studio has ideas falling over ideas – everything becomes fair game for their creativity. For Andrew Hoyne, design is about communication. However beautiful, however considered, it is worthless if the message is lost. Despite its incredible success, both here and internationally, Hoyne Design is still a compact firm. Andrew is the very active head designer. He's still innovating. Still regularly presenting new branding and packaging ideas to his clients. Unsolicited. Uninvited. Unapologetic. He says he's only trying to make them look good.

A world of possibility. ANZ
ANZ's brand strategy for the 21st Century
ANZ Investment Bank Equities Division
Seeing beyond the boundaries
ONE KEY THOUGHT
ONE-TO-ONE WEALTH MANAGEMENT
ANZ Private Bank
A new world of financial opportunity
ANZ Private Bank
A new world of financial opportunity
By bringing the brand to life and talking with one voice, we can make ANZ a truly unique financial company. It's going to be an exciting time for everyone involved in

ST. KILDA IN YOUR FACE
Rinaldo Di Stasio, Jill Dupleix and Terry Durack
ALLEGRO AL DENTE
PASTA & OPERA
Allegro = lively, quick, fast - like water boiling for pasta
Simon Goh, Terry Durack & Jill Dupleix
hot food cool jazz
William Heinemann Australia
hot
A Cookbook of Mostly Asian Recipes
CHOW DOWN
Geoff Lindsay
musical notes

urban attitude
It's what's inside that counts
MADC THINK TANK
FIRST WEDNESDAY OF EVERY MONTH AT O'CONNELL'S PUB IN SOUTH MELBOURNE
Pure Body Treatments
AVEDA
Sharp looks, from 12
METALICUS
AUSTRALIA
ACCESSORIES
METALICUS
AUSTRALIA
KOOKAÏ
BODY TIGHT
fits your life
ESSENTIAL REMEDIES
homeopathically prepared essential oil remedies
LIGATOR
BRAND
maxwellrodgers fabrics
Dogs Bar
54 Acland Street, St Kilda 3182
Telephone 9534 3075

Atia Cader
Andrew Majzner
Philippa Penndelberry
Paper Stone Scissors

STAR
CHOC-BAR
SOAP
CHOCOLATE SCENTED
170gm when packed
COCONUT SCENTED
170gm when packed
STAR
CHOC-BAR
SOAP
COFFEE SCENTED
170gm when packed

The paper wraps the stone that smashes the scissors that cuts the paper. The goal is to produce a result. This well-known game provides the inspiration for a company. Same challenges. Same goal. The three directors of Paper Stone Scissors are three very different people. Philippa. Andrew. Atia. Different backgrounds. Different approaches. This diversity ensures that each task inherits a distinct vision. On one hand, it's easy to believe a design problem has a single solution. On the other, diversity makes the process of creating the solution exciting. Communication, vision and expression are the key elements of the Paper Stone Scissors approach to design. Considered discussion with the client ascertains hopes, dreams, expectations. 'We strive to produce work that is a synergy of our creativity and the unique desires of our client.' In the pursuit of inspiration, global awareness is a priority. A variety of places, people and situations. Travelling inspires. The buzz of western centres of design, fashion and business. Spiritual capitals in the Far East and the subcontinent. A sense of adventure and exploration is central to their philosophy. It is the attitude brought to each challenge, no matter the size. It is always reflected in the final product. Through travel, each one of the three has developed a greater sense of Australia's place. An industry that once relied on outside influences is now developing a character of its own. It's exciting. For Paper Stone Scissors, graphic design is clearly not a static art. Their integrated approach to design embodies an understanding of the client's objectives and a passion for exploring expression.

...true charity is the desire to be useful to others without thought of recompense.

THE PRATT FOUNDATION

URBAN PROVISIONS

URBAN PROVISIONS
good food fast

COME & SEE THE CLEVER CAR THAT WILL CHANGE THE RULES ON HOW WE MOVE OURSELVES INTO THE 21ST CENTURY
MERCEDES-BENZ • MERCEDES-BENZ • MERCEDES-BENZ • MERCEDES-BENZ

The A-class from Worrells Motors
& your partner
to the launch of the
Mercedes-Benz
A Class

very cheeky, very cute, very very smart

Friday 10th October
At Carters Avenue Toorak
At 6:30pm for cocktails
RSVP 9th October to Jenny or Monica Phone (03) 9826 0500

A class of it's own

ke a breath
you'll need it...

David Ansett
Dean Butler
Storm Image Design

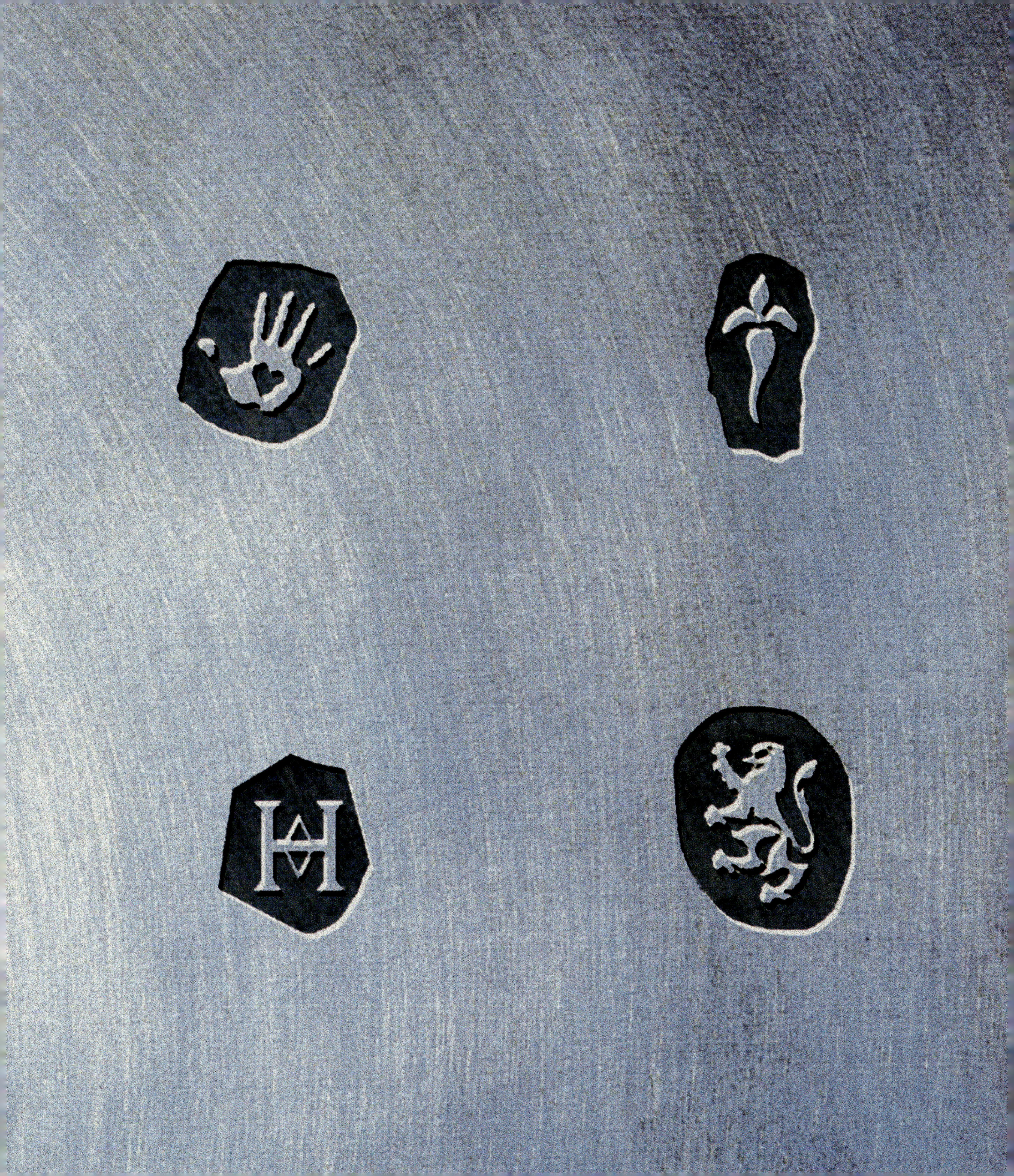

Dean Butler and David Ansett met at Swinburne University. Dean down at one end of the hall, David at the other. On a bus trip to Brisbane for Expo 88, David sang Elvis songs. Dean tried to sleep. In 1990, recession stopped many in their tracks. In the middle of the chaos, Storm began. Young. Fresh. Going places. Along the way, insight has come from unexpected sources. Oprah gave a lesson about life. Mistakes, the best teachers. People don't inspire David. Design does. His Year 10 art teacher gave him a D+. 'Best not follow a career in art.' An extreme radical lies inside Dean. A nonconformist. He's drawn to history's visionaries. Luis Buñuel. Rudolf Steiner. Ancient primitive sculpture at the Louvre. Mythical animals, half-dragon, half-rabbit. Wet-your-pants exciting. As young designers, representing their own studio, they have often worked with clients twenty or thirty years their senior. Big hurdles. It's taken time to believe in their own capabilities to provide a professional design service, even when competing with this country's most successful and experienced design firms. Storm's confidence has blossomed. Its talent is budding. Its ideas are colourful. Its work focuses on communication and concept. Design that doesn't reach its audience is poor design – it doesn't matter how good it looks. Visual ideas start with pencils and sketchpads. The finetuning of colour, form, scale and typography are the languages of visual communication. Style dates quickly. Storm defies the 'studio style' trap. A good idea will work for years. The consistent thread in Storm's design is the strength of concept and the humour. They try to create a personality in their work, not just apply an image. Their current business plan includes finding a better balance between work and home, bringing bigger projects into the studio, embracing and utilising cutting-edge technology, creating a learning culture within the studio, and finding more time to surf and play music. They are not joking. Australian design is at an extremely exciting stage in its evolution. The industry has come so far, so quickly. There is a tremendous momentum. We have to take responsibility to ensure that we now develop our own brand of effective, accountable design that is not only at world standard creatively, it delivers results to clients in Australia and around the globe.

Surface Mail

Postage
Paid
South
Yarra
3141

STORM

Hanna Cutts
Cutts Creative

GRAND ORBIT

Kng Valley, Victoria. Product of Australia. 750 mls. 12.5% alc. Pres. 220

As a child, Hanna Cutts was surrounded by the beauty of the coast of Cornwall and then central Africa. As an adolescent, her playground was the Welsh coast and then southern France. She emigrated to Australia aged 18. She enrolled in architecture at Queensland University. Hanna says, 'Don't let anyone tell you that you have to know what and where you want to be when you finish school.' She left as soon as they started talking 'bending moments' and physics. Just a diversion. She landed at Queensland College of Art and graduated in visual arts and illustration. A course big on concept and its realisation. Good training for a life in design. Keating's Federal Training Program gave birth to Cutts Creative. As Hanna remembers it, it was that or becoming an aerobics instructor. Humble beginnings. Surprisingly, clients asked few questions. Was it because she was good or were they lazy? The first label designed won the Judges' Award at the 1996 Brisbane Art Directors Awards. A label for a bottle of house red. Vampiresque teeth a feature. Along with a fairly strong use of concept, Hanna uses a lot of illustration and photography. She loves taking photographs. Take a camera with you. Everywhere. Always. Hanna Cutts makes her work a delight. She yearns for it to be clever, surprising. She designs the way the authors of her favourite stories wrote. As a child then and as a adult now, she thinks the twist at the end is the best bit.

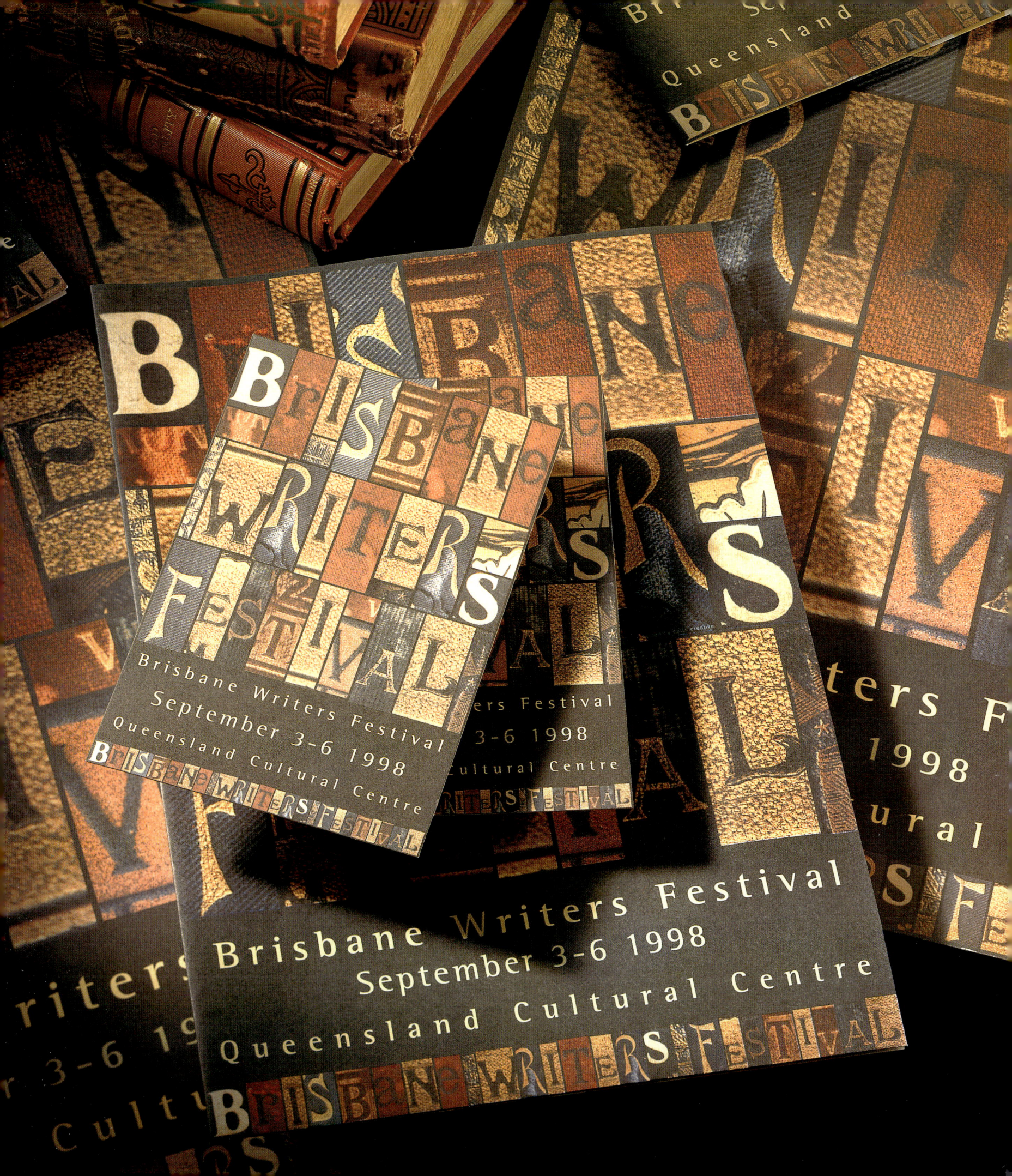

Brisbane Writers Festival
September 3-6 1998
Queensland Cultural Centre

A:
ACOUSTIC DYNAMIC CASSETTE SUPER LOW NOISE HIGH OUTPUT
RIGID CASSETTE MECHANISM
LiVid
SPEEDIE
AM/FM STEREO
RADIO CASSETTE PLAYER
Stereo
98
AUTO STOP
MHz
x10 KHz

Andrew Ashton
Rick Nelmes
Graeme Smith
Nelmes Smith Ashton

98

Col

Jim

Paul

While you sit in at the office at 8am on a Sunday getting out the annual report, these guys are out chilling their chops at Coogee Ocean Baths and have been doing so every Sunday over 40 years. Members of the Coogee Swimming Club are of all ages and come from all walks of life, some breaking records for fitness, others for sheer commitment.

AUSTRALIAN GRAPHIC DESIGN ASSOCIATION
1998 NSW CALENDAR OF EVENTS

How does the creative process work for Nelmes Smith Ashton? It begins on a computer or in a camera on a roll of film. But the idea soon takes over, transforming what began into something else, another medium, a new way of experiencing the things that surround us. A desire is to create something much more meaningful than a bunch of paper rectangles covered in nice-looking words and pictures. A serious connection is sought, a connection between things the world may initially have assumed were unconnected. What results? Beautiful objects. Captivating images. Type as illegible texture. Exquisite words. Objectionable ideas. Irreverence. Nelmes Smith Ashton will not shy away from slaughtering the occasional sacred cow. Intense pleasure comes from moving people's perceptions. Anything to do with career enhancement comes after this. It's automatic. The myth of the graphic design rock star is obsolete and irrelevant in the world of Nelmes Smith Ashton. It is a partnership of three. Three individual viewpoints. A common focus. Where do such thoughts about design come from? A background of odd clutter. Inherited working-class ethics. A rich imagination. A fast pushbike. Hundreds of hours in bushland. Little respect for the education system. A broken family. Reclusive tendencies. Excessive habits. Friends. Lovers. Precious stories. Nelmes Smith Ashton tries to incorporate the richness of the everyday – even the outright banal – into its work. Great food. A good book. Bumping into people who influence a whole life. Finding some piece of nothing in the bin, scanning it, turning it into a piece of design. Surprise! Sometimes Nelmes Smith Ashton's best work comes from an intuition. Other times, it's the desire not to be bored. They wonder if we need logos for everything? They sense we are surrounded by a lot of variation but very few ideas. Are ideas too risky for marketing people? What the world needs is more emotional connection, more interesting ideas. Examples of their work is viewed in isolation. Detached from its full meaning as graphic design. The audience will see shapes, colours, texts. They will not see the origins of interesting ideas. Nor how they enriched the working experiences of the people who created them. Nor will it be seen how many of them enriched the bank accounts of the people who paid Nelmes Smith Ashton to create them. But what is that, anyway? Simply an affirmation of principles often proposed but too seldom implemented.

suits ~~type~~

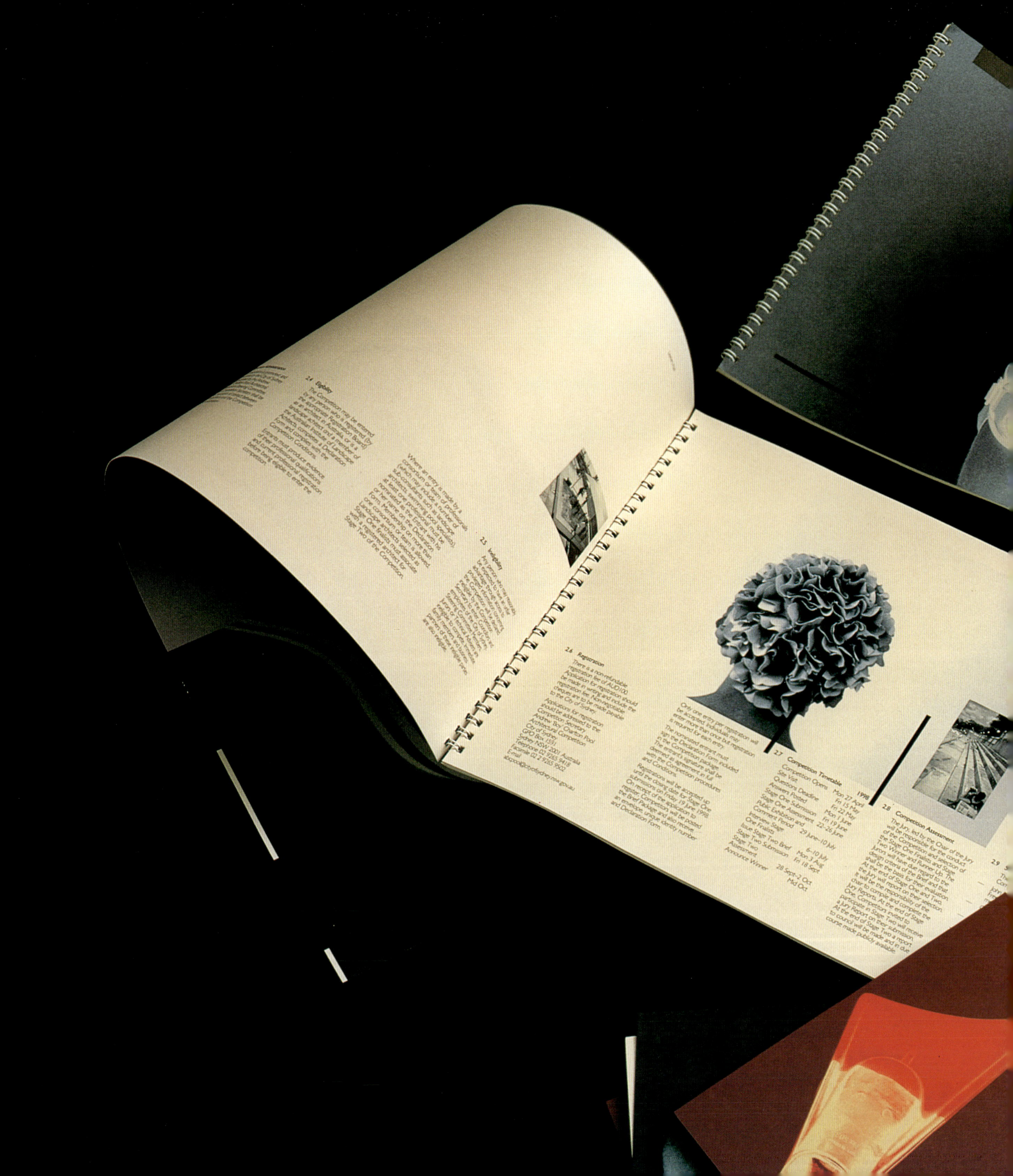

POOL
BUOY
LARGE

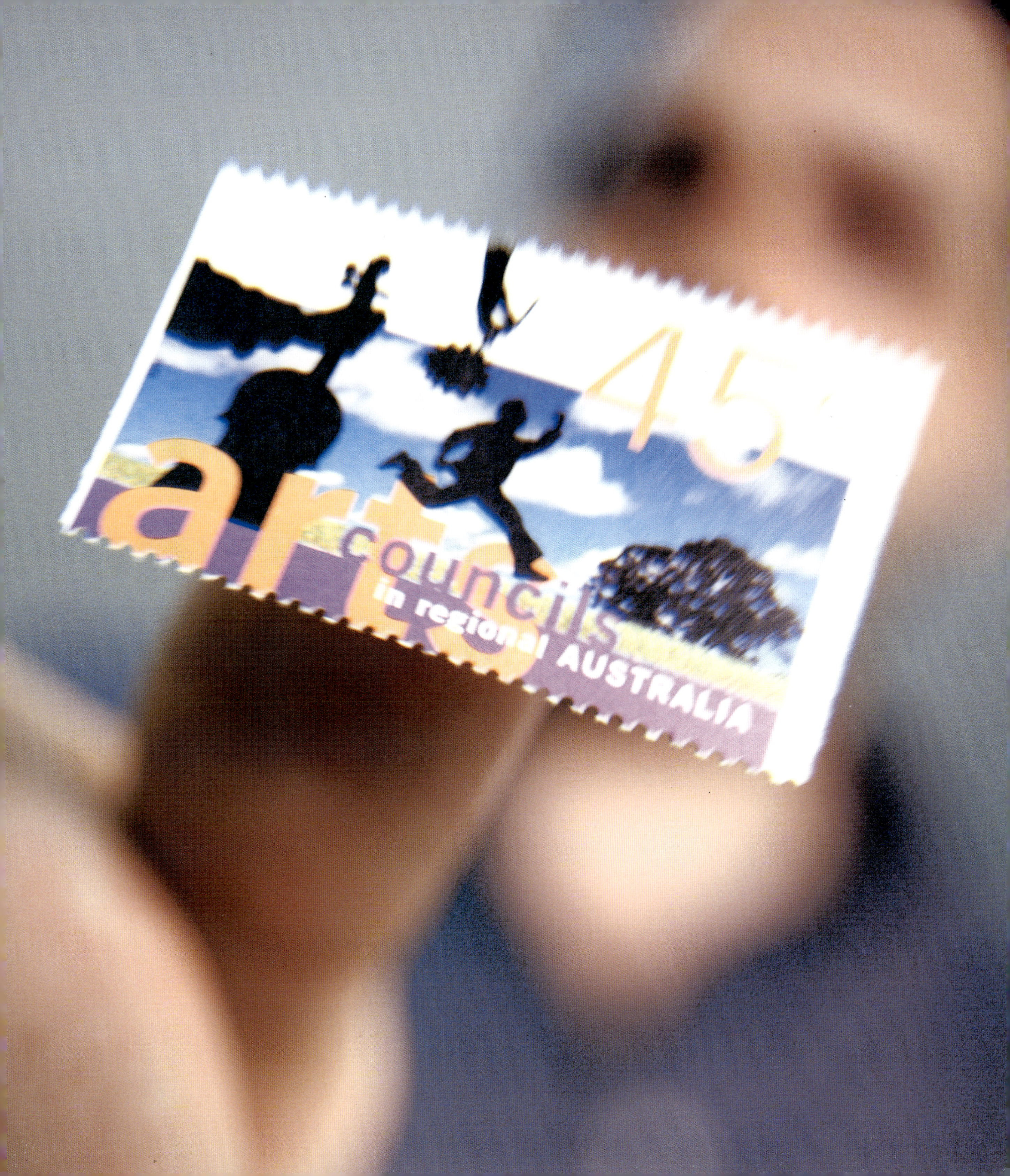
45
arts
councils
in regional AUSTRALIA

Ashley Durrans
Dean Hastie
Nova Design

Craft Australia

These guys are honest. They'll tell you they don't have all the answers. Not yet, anyway. They're headed in the right direction, though, and having a great time getting there. A career in design is a journey. Ashley Durrans thinks rationale. Dean Hastie thinks concepts. Sometimes the lines cross. Responsibility is shared. Seeking new experiences, new clients, new opportunities becomes a challenge, not a chore. They're both from the UK. They like it better in Australia. They miss the humour of UK design. Should Australian clients learn to laugh more? In this business, there is strength in numbers. Two is better than one. Complementary skills. Stronger ideas. More talent. More provocative outcomes. It takes time to build courage, to know you have the experience, the passion, the ability to make an impact. Confidence generates attitude – the necessary cunning to challenge a client's view. It makes you want to push them to new heights. It gives you the freedom to find your own way of doing things. Nova Design aims to produce work that has meaning. It should differentiate the client or product from the rest of the market. Inspiring solutions that exceed expectations. It's an attitude that has afforded creative control and financial viability. Nova Design has recognised the necessity of strong business skills. Absolutely vital. The future of Australian design will be fostered by those making the business decisions. More examples are needed. Clients must see how vital design is to their business.

integra
information systems

Desperately seeking Canberra...

paddock
spoiled...?

After almost one hundred years of grazing, agriculture and mining, the decisions to build the national capital resulted in the resumption of many local landholdings. This displaced many of those who had earlier displaced the indigenous peoples.

New social
landscapes:
a 19th century view

Relationships with the land underwent radical transformation from the 1820s. 'Rude wildernesses' were seen as opportunities for profit and pleasure.

There was a time when the
phrase 'art' in Canberra seemed
a contradiction in terms. It was
thought that public servants
lived in Canberra, not artists...

Michael Desmond, *Contrast*, (catalogue) 1995

It was an unhappy
combination of small
town atmosphere, stuffy
suburban attitudes,
imposed bureaucratic
snobberies, the
bewildering arc of
streets... and a rather
colourless prettiness
like the polish on
a veneer.

George Johnston, *The Australian*, 22 August 1964

People from all around
the world who have
visited it claimed they
didn't know how
beautiful Canberra was
because other Australians
had tried to talk them
out of going. It is
another case of the tall
poppy syndrome.

Bill Simpkin, *Canberra Times*, 17 October 1966

This country
bin lose 'm
dreaming...

packag1ng & b3yond

Nearly twenty years ago, [Andrew Lewis] saw a gap in the market for a specialist packaging design firm. He had no experience in running a business, but convinced by the idea, he registered Andrew Lewis and Company and opened for business 24 July 1979.

The work was heavily brand and FMCG orientated with clients such as Master Foods, Procter & Gamble, Kelloggs and Penfolds Wines. Although profitable, it was certainly no designers' haven.

Enter Mike Staniford, a Creative Director of considerable experience and Clio Gold awards winner. Mike had the mandate to improve the creative standards, to diversify the business into other multi-disciplinary areas and to balance the challenge of producing results-orientated projects with award-winning work.

The company has now been relaunched as Lewis Kahn Staniford with a new strategic direction. Mike's talk will demonstrate the secrets of powerful design solutions that work, by fulfilling the client's marketing objectives and the designers' hunger for creative excellence.

VENUE
Australian Museum

East Sy[dney]

...pm
...mbers
...mbers $15
...1000+ digital press

USE BY
JUNE 1
1998

2 DESIGNERS

talk & walk the walk

packag1ng 2 p3y

AUSTRALIAN GRAPHIC DESIGN
...JUNE 9... / MIKE STANIFOR[D]

Industrial Design

Simon Christopher
Celina Clarke
ISM Objects

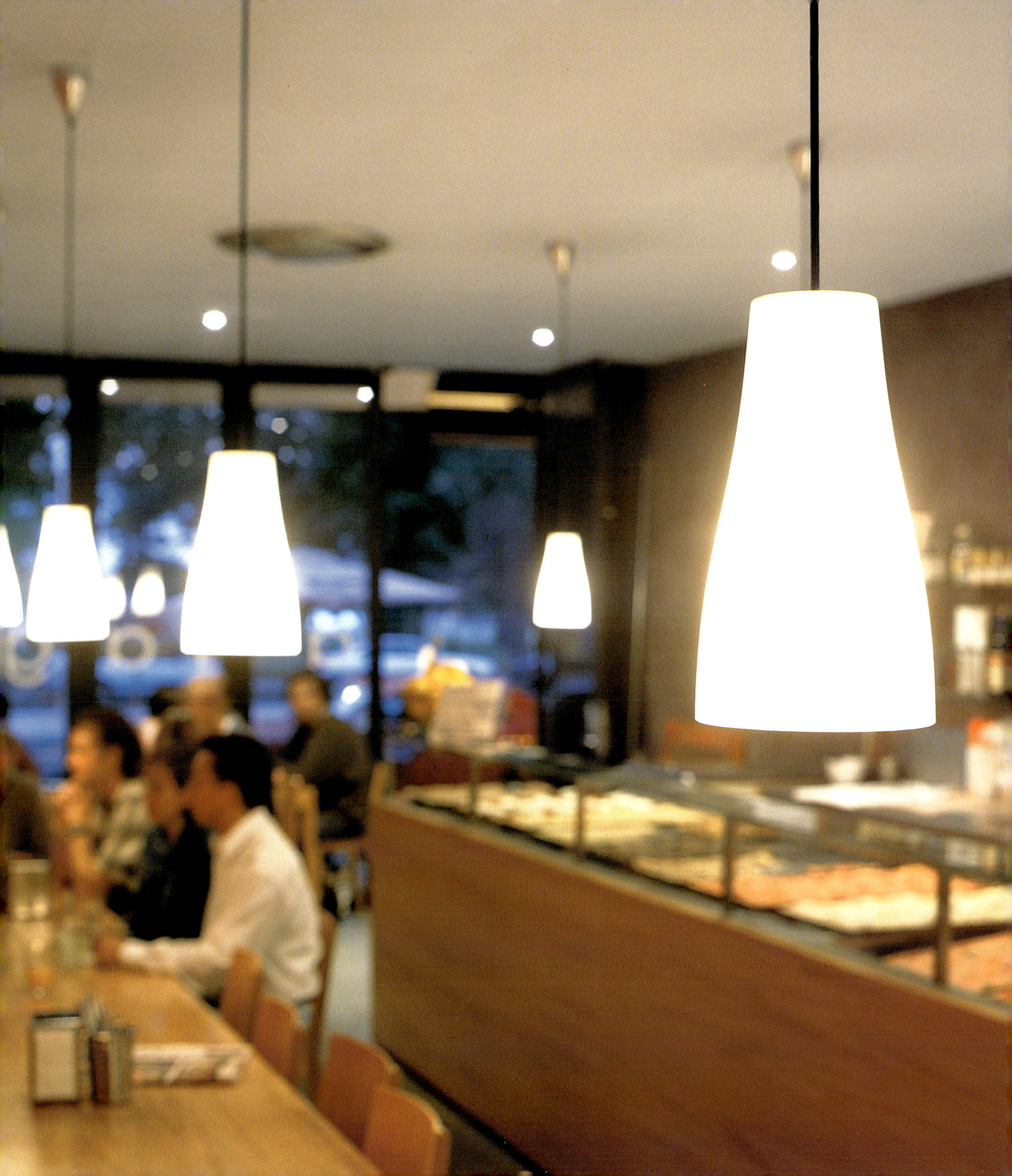

They got together in 1990. Celina Clarke and Simon Christopher as ISM Objects. Their aim? To design and market quality furniture and lighting at an international standard. Their mission? To design, produce, market and distribute each of their own products. Celina and Simon both hold degrees in industrial design. Their specialty is custom-designing to their client's particular specifications. Big projects. Small projects. All challenges. In conjunction with Daryl Jackson, Perrot Lyon Mathieson and Bates Smart, the team worked on Melbourne's Crown Casino, developing and supplying numerous light fittings for the main gaming areas, restaurants and eateries within the complex. ISM Objects fittings can also be found at Radisson Hotel, Flagstaff Gardens in Melbourne, Couran Cove Resort on Stradbroke Island and the Sussex Centre in Sydney. Celina and Simon feed their passion for design with constant research. Their development of ideas through the latest technological processes and materials has led to an extensive product range. They have a reputation for quality and durability. Their market includes exclusive retail outlets nationwide. Their success? The company has won seven major design competitions and received two grants from the Australia Council for the Arts. Their work has been featured in *International Design Yearbook 1994* and *50 Lights: Innovations in Design and Materials* by Mel Byars. Their lamp, Madam Ruby, is touring the world in an exhibition organised by the Arango Design Foundation called *Re(f)use, good everyday design from reused and recycled materials*. The Museum of Modern Art, New York, has also included ISM Objects works, in *Mutant Materials in Contemporary Design*. In its current collection, ISM Objects presents furniture and lighting solutions focusing on practicality and maximum space exploration. Elegant. Simplicity of design.

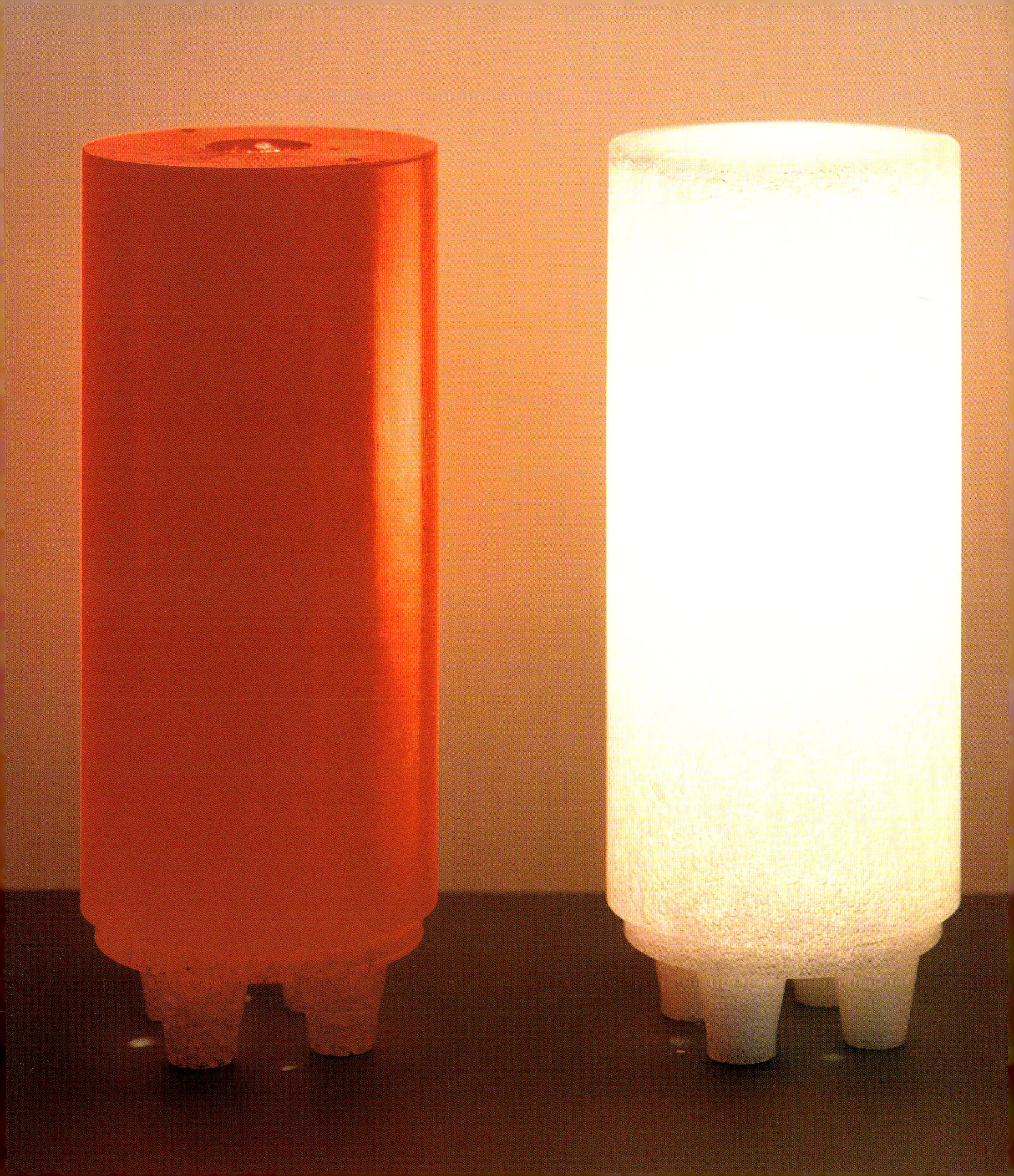

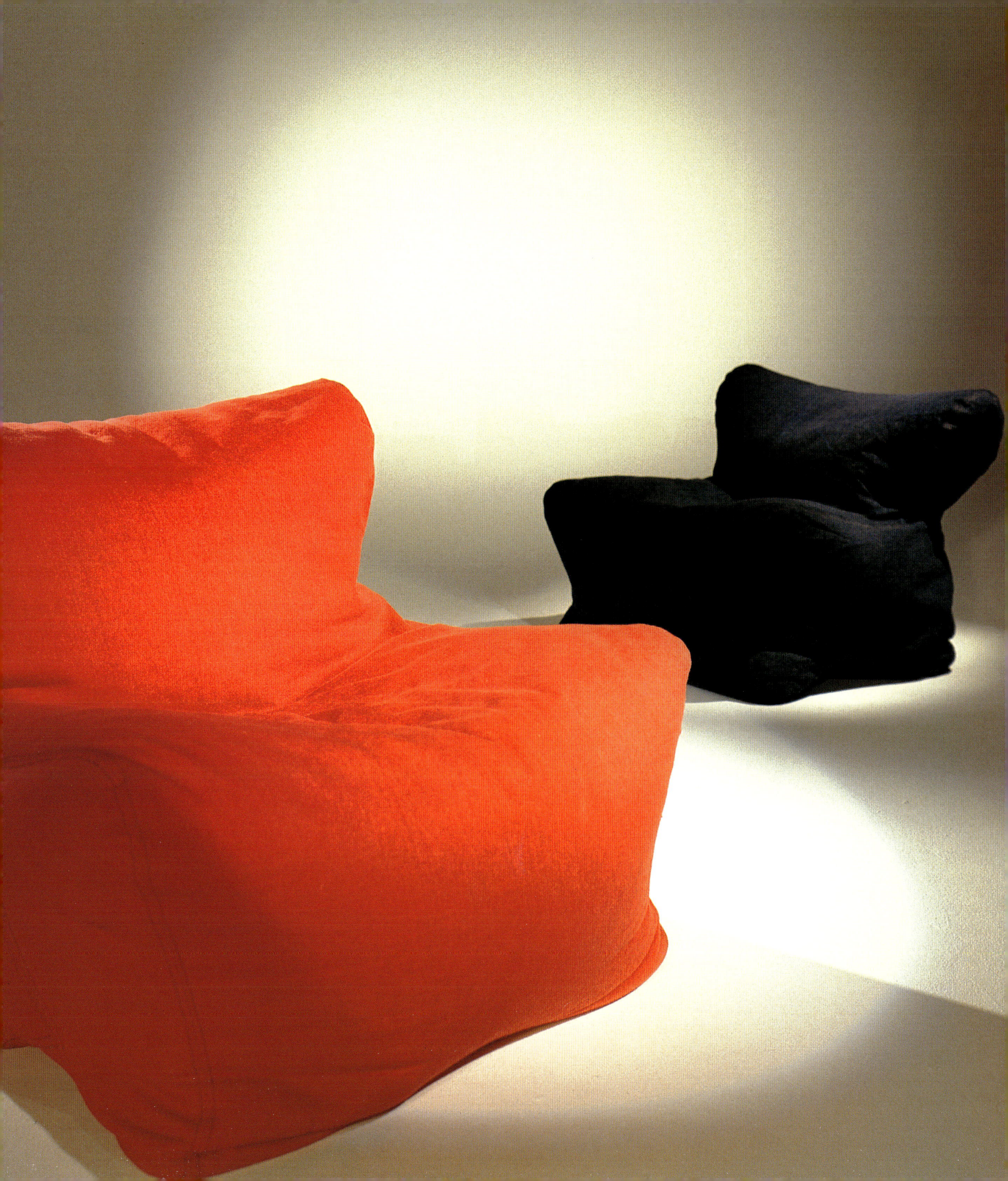

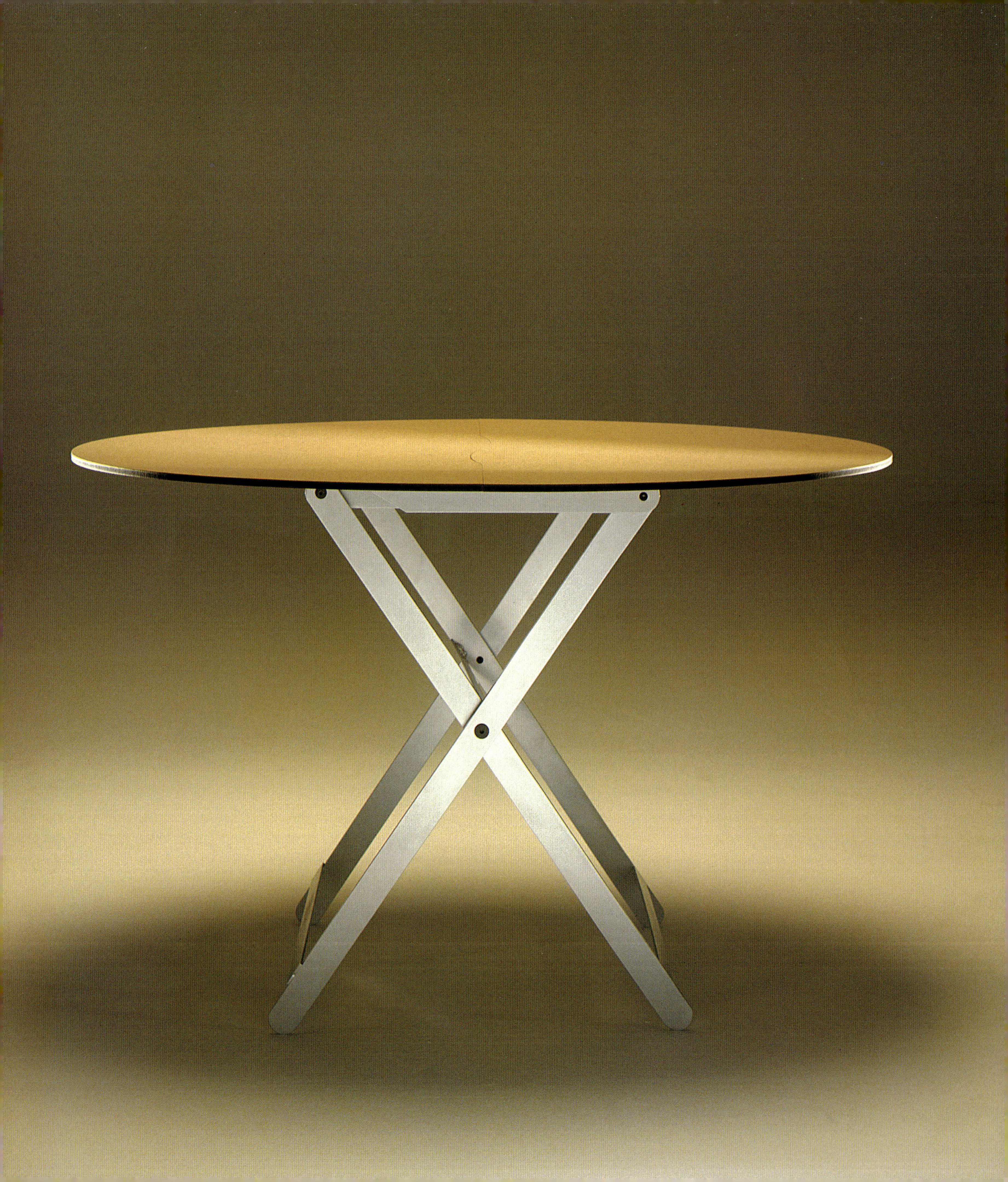

Marc Pascal
M2 Products

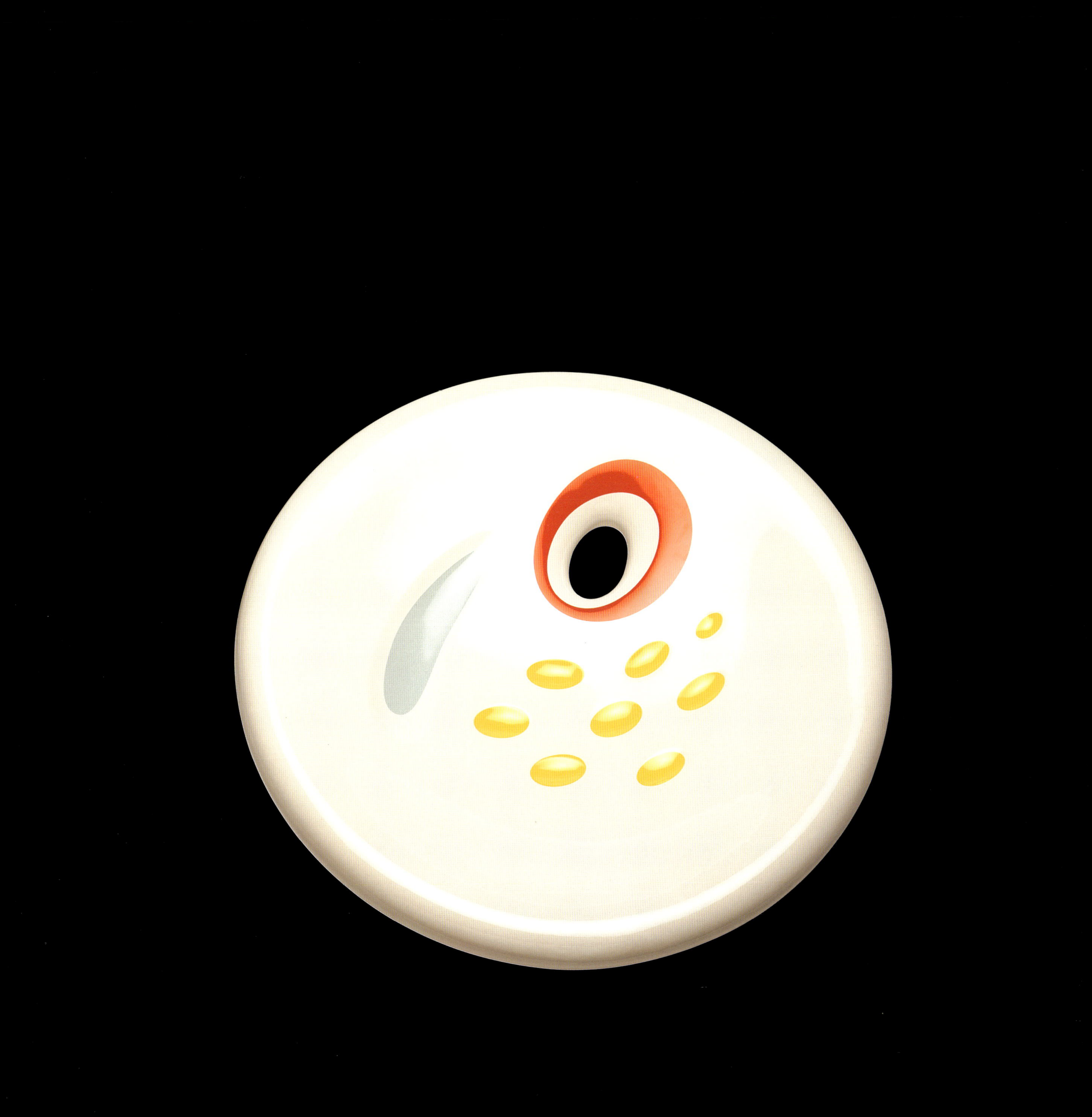

M2 Products is the design label of Marc Pascal. It appears on a range of original and innovative objects designed and produced at his studio in Melbourne. Marc's work is the hybrid result of formal training in industrial design and an ongoing interest in artistic practice. His marketing identity grew out of the success of his first solo exhibition. An event made possible by the Australia Council and Arts Victoria. They funded the development of a coherent range of objects presented to the Melbourne public in the early 1990s. Interest from Marc's exhibitions has fostered a growing national and international demand for his work. Marc Pascal creates objects of intense character. Their anthropomorphic quality adds spirit and interest to any space. His inspiration is found in juxtaposition. The strictly practical considerations of market requirements and the laterally creative adaptation of the swooping elegant form of a palm frond turned into a Frond Light. Early exposure to European culture through his French father sustains him. It gave him the gift of a sense of dual heritage, a combination of identity that produces work that is refined and sophisticated, yet fresh and energetic. The interplay between fabric and form fascinates him. Marc constantly experiments with new materials. His objects give you an irresistible urge to touch, to play. Useful, practical domestic objects perform that most difficult of artistic statements – they depict and engender happiness in a way that is complex and profound.

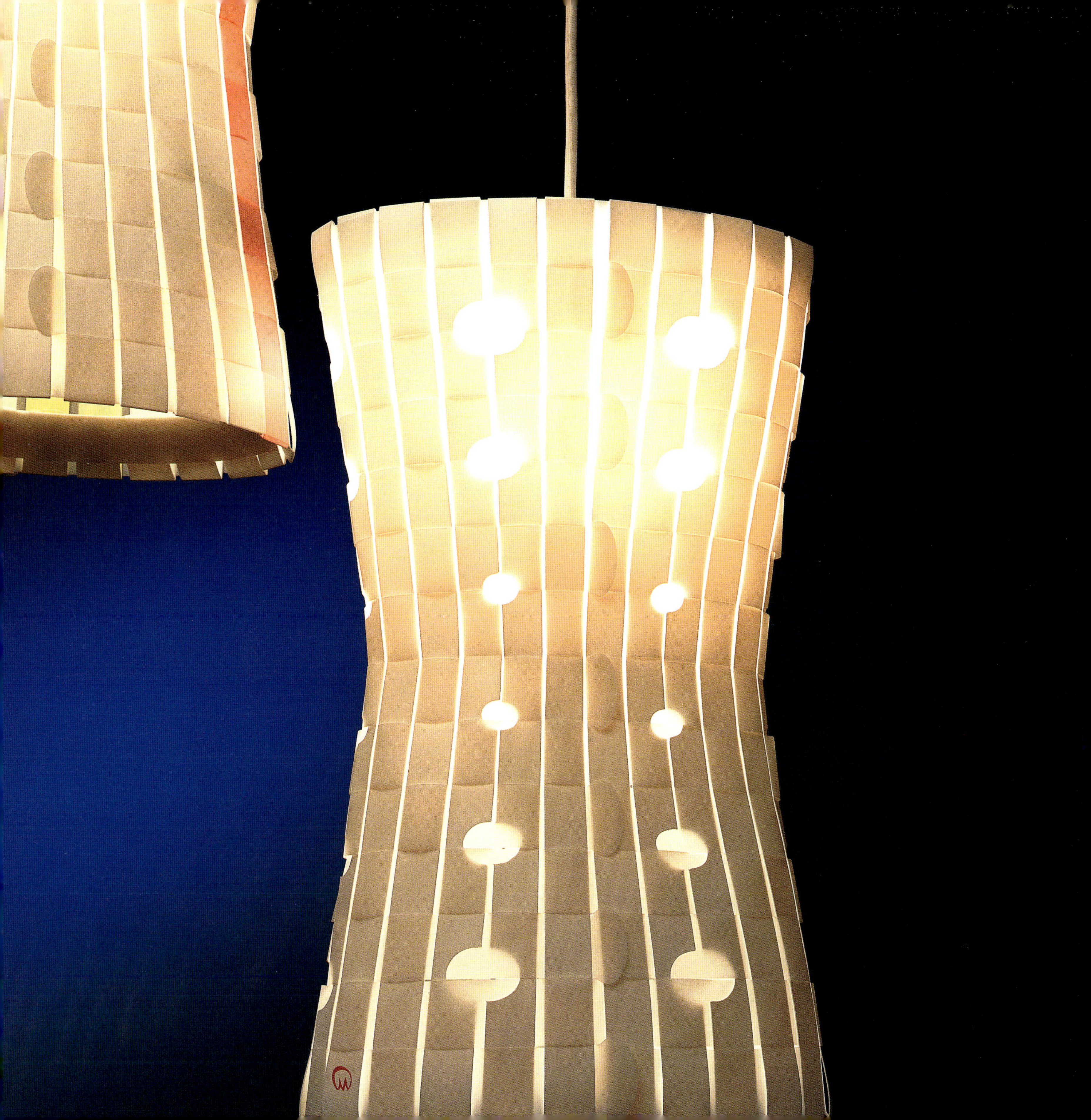

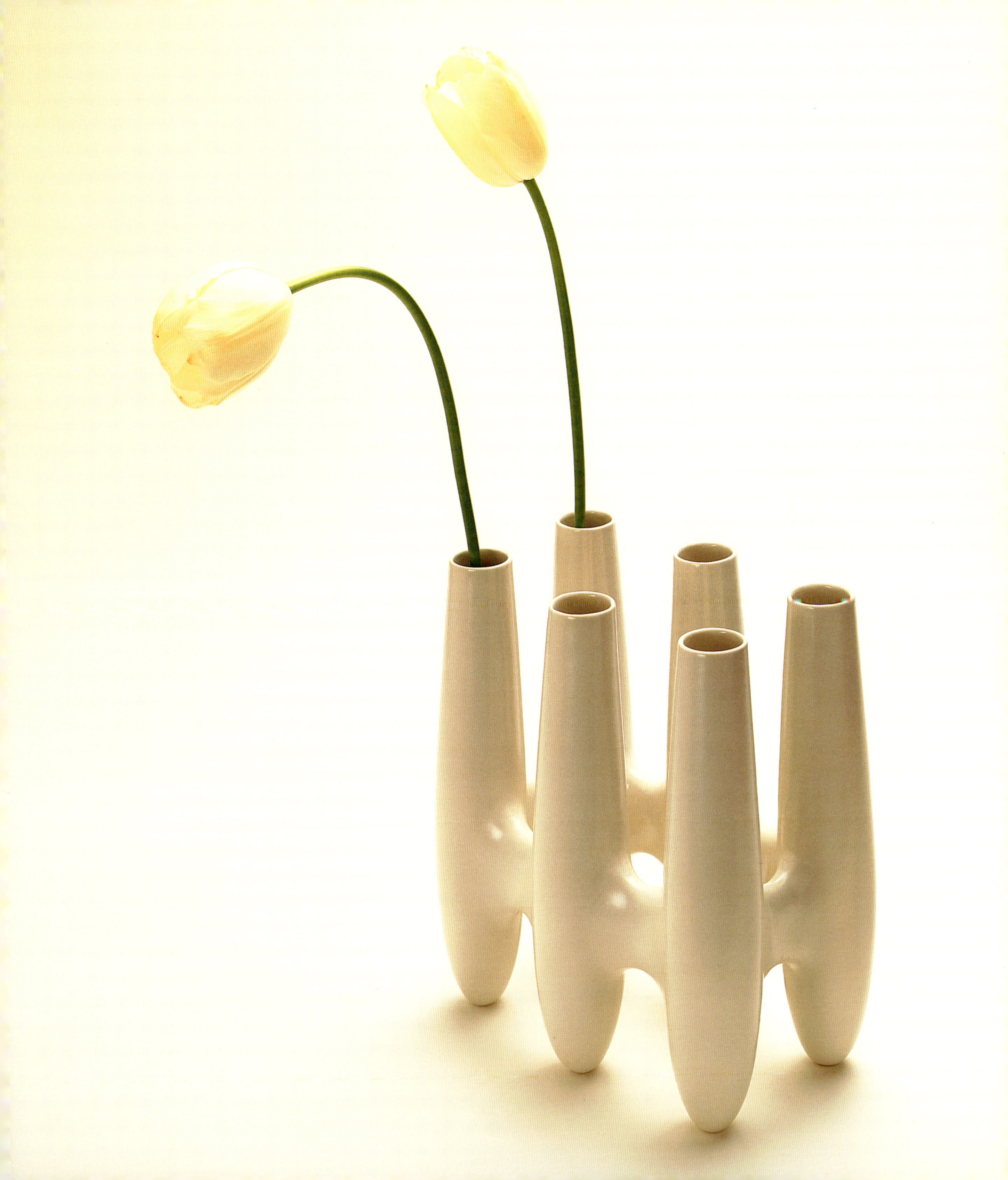

Hugo Davidson
Catalyst Design Group

ptt telecom
ALARM 1
ALARM 2
DAY/NIGHT
AUTO ANSWER
CALL DIVERSION
Extension
1
Option
2
Auto Answer
3
Hot Line
4
Speed Dial
5
Day/Night
6
Alarm
7
Call Bar
8
Miscellaneous
9
Profile
0
Function
SCROLL
ENTER
CLEAR
homevox
universal

They're ideas he gleaned from overseas. Relatively simple. Powerful. Get engineers to engineer and designers to design. A team of designers working together is more effective than any individual working alone. Target clients who recognise the benefits of good design. Balance innovation with market understanding. Work globally to better understand other cultural needs and product functions. Try to forecast trends and fashions. Do not follow them. Develop special interests related to the work you do. Understand your clients' history, then help them translate that into the future. He returned to Australia in 1983. Learned and wise. Unemployed. It was the end of a recession. Starting his own business seemed like a good idea. Hugo set up shop with his architect father. The Catalyst Design Group. A company born of the concept of working with like-minded, multi-disciplined designers. They drew together industrial designers, architects, product engineers, graphic designers and interior designers. Technology has become a key player in Hugo's design methodology. Concepts are now explored in virtual 3D space in real time. Forms are now far better resolved. Design is no longer limited by the straight edge of a T-square. Rapid prototypes can be generated overnight. This industrial designer now sculpts the previously impossible. His tools of trade broadcast his work to the world in an instant. With clients as far afield as Europe, Japan, the US and South-east Asia, Hugo attributes only half his work to Australian-based clients. Hugo has been joined at Catalyst Design Group by two other directors and a team of sixteen designers, engineers and architects. The open-plan office is conducive to collaboration. Communication. Better solutions.

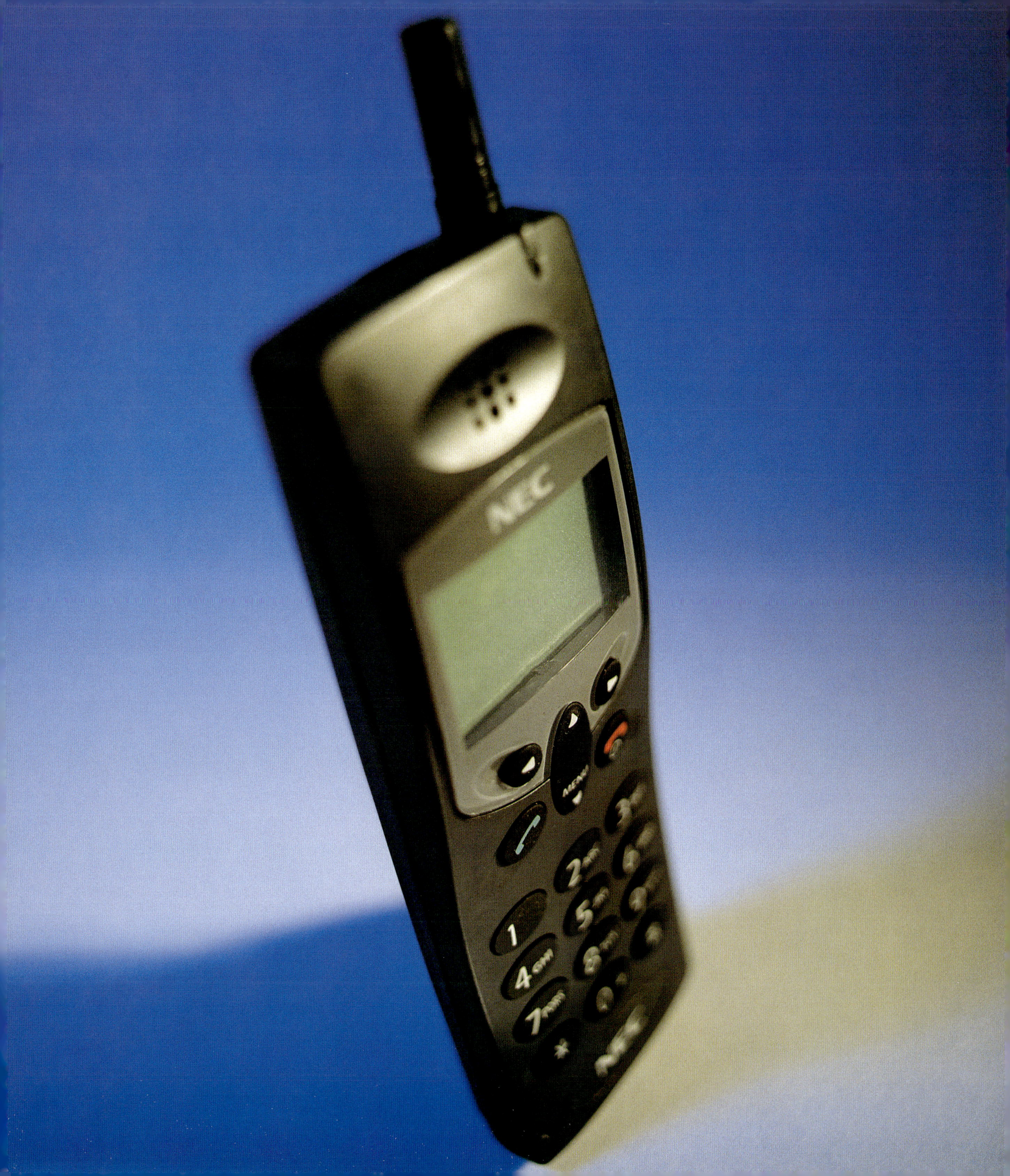
NEC

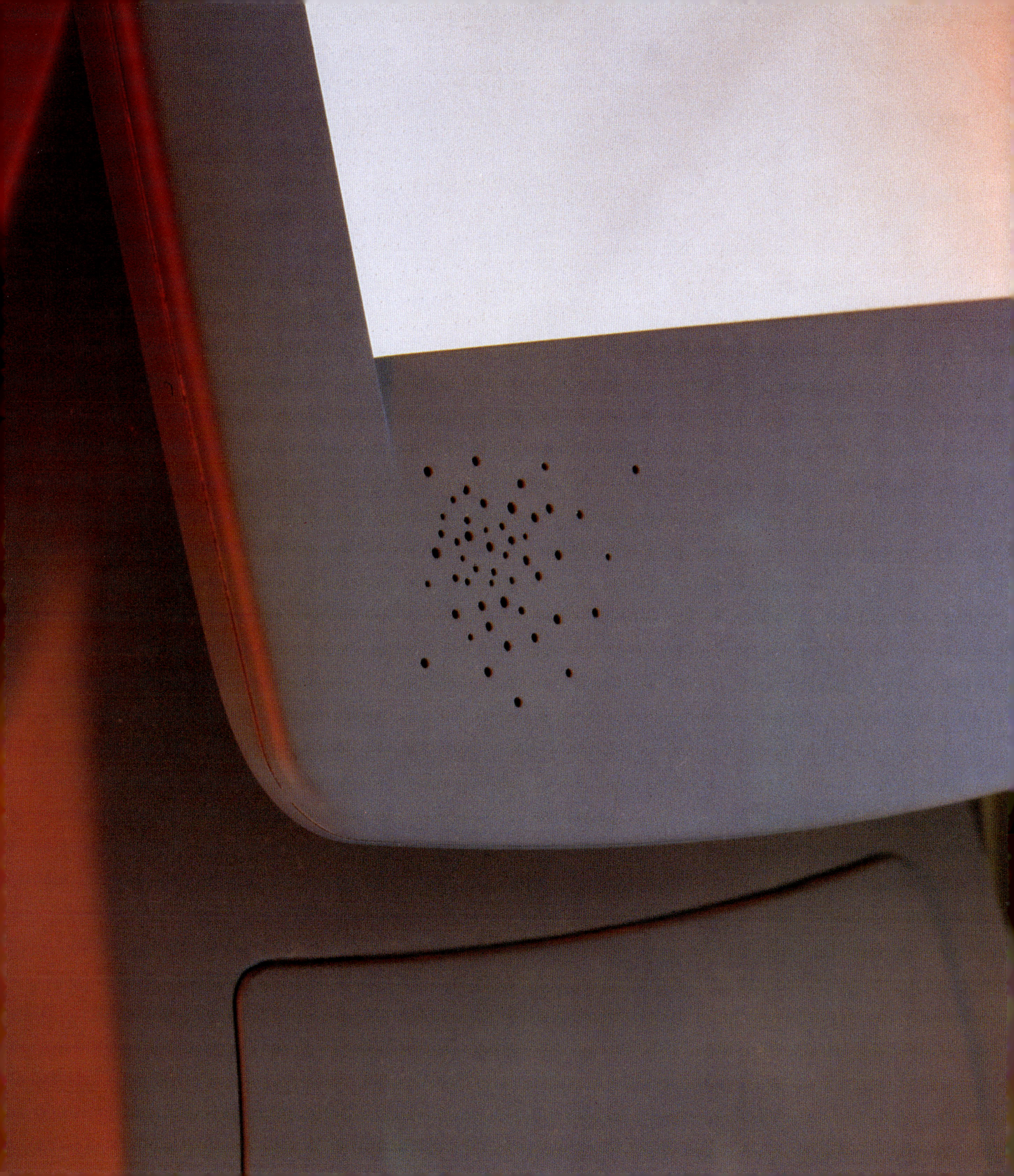

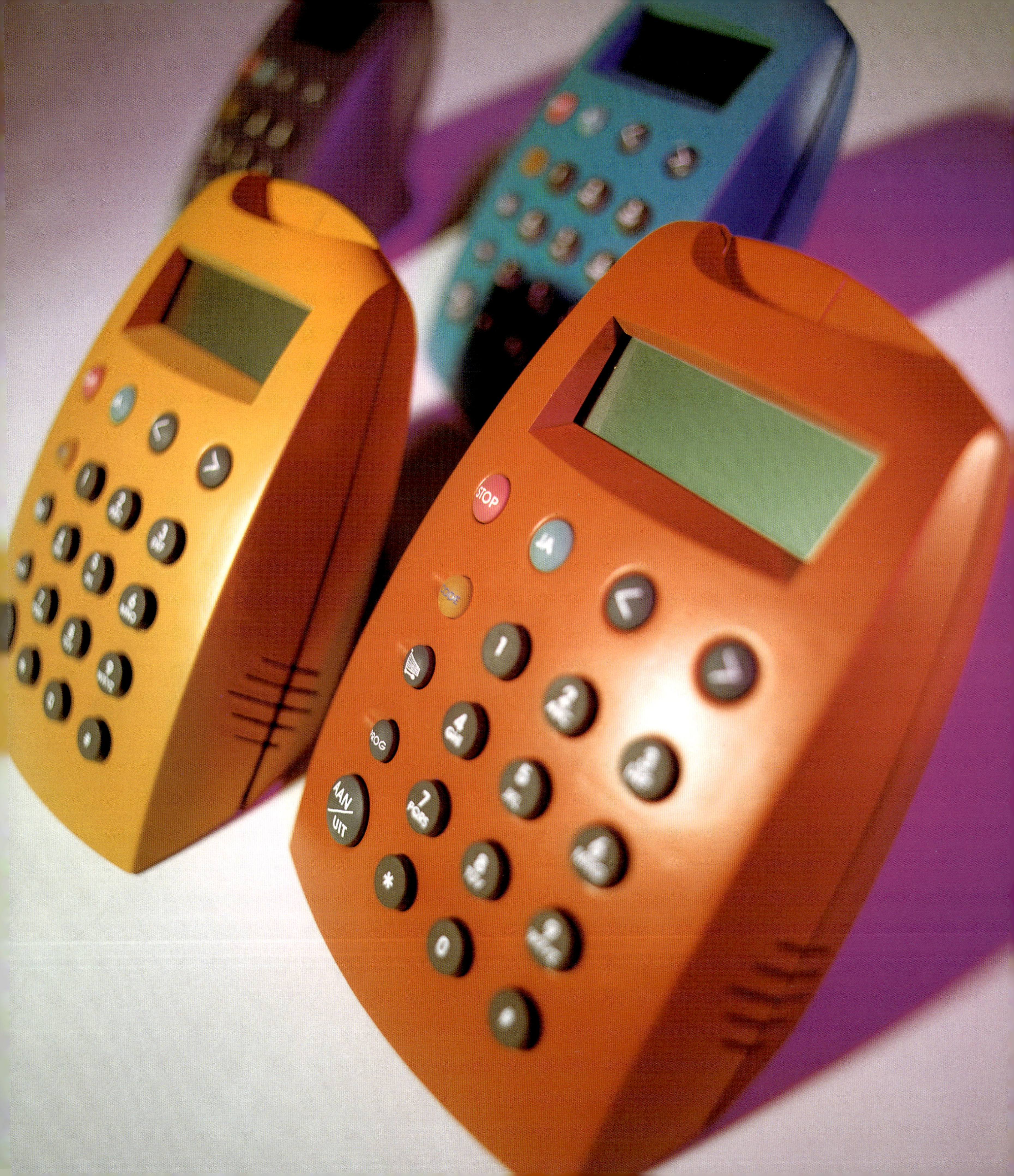
STOP
JA
PROG
AAN
UIT

Malte Wagenfeld
Studio M3D

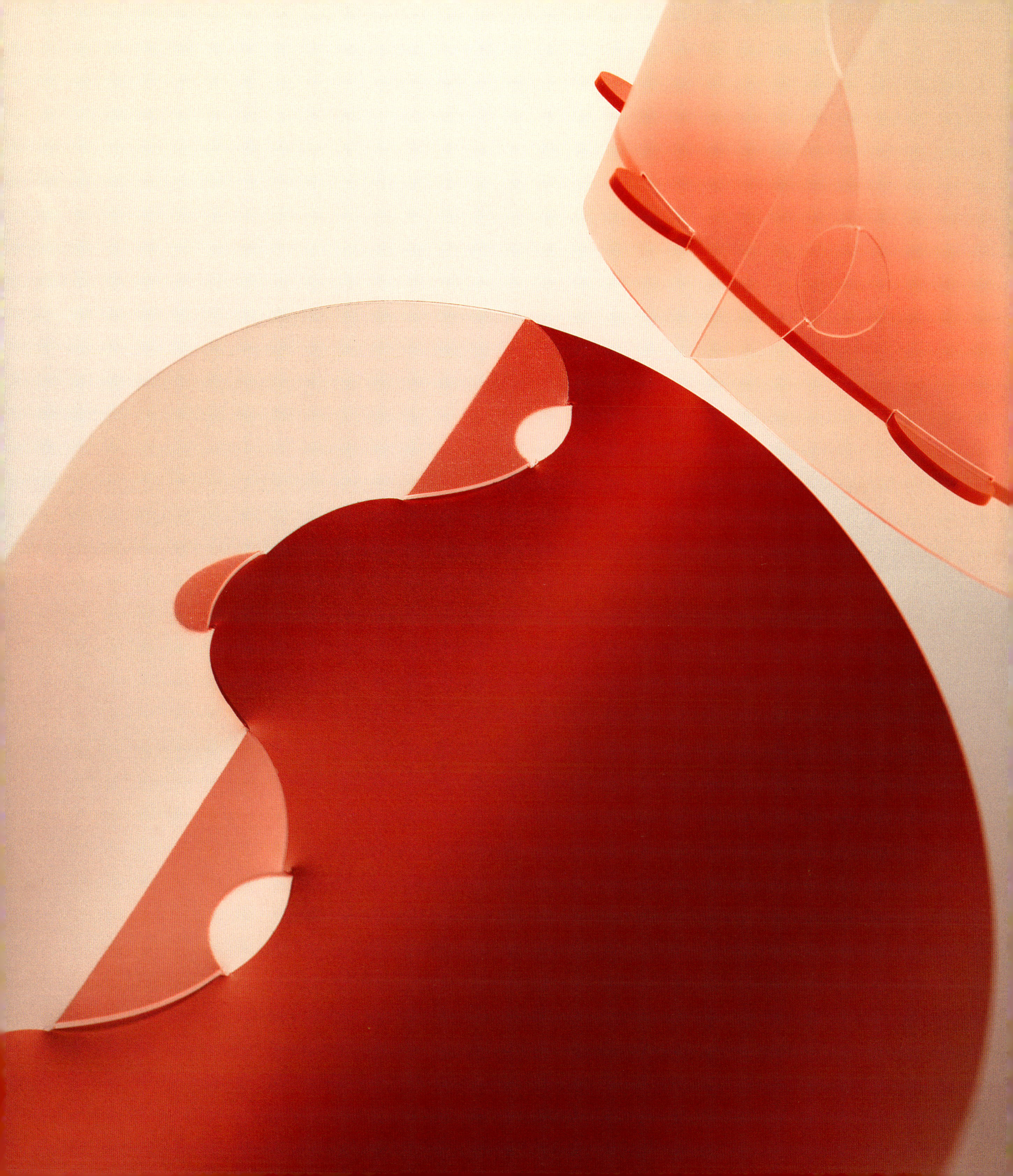

It is important to Malte Wagenfeld that his work has a lasting quality. At heart, he is very much a contemporary modernist. Instead of a family religion, he was brought up with the Bauhaus teachings of modernism. His grandfather the teacher. It is in Malte's blood. The influences on his life are difficult to pinpoint. An inquisitive mind covers a wide field of interests. Ideas come from books, articles, old objects. Malte despises the 'throwaway' mentality that determines the value of objects in today's consumer culture. The economics are obvious. The implications are not. He is convinced such behaviour is not sustainable, either environmentally or culturally. He pursues an alternative solution in his work. Malte's design methodology can best be described as an interaction between sketching and testing in three dimensions. He simultaneously explores an idea on paper, on the computer and through experimental models. It is an essential process. It is not the answer. Sometimes, the material suggests the solution. He now teaches the lessons learnt in his career. He attributes his approach to the time he worked at Aero in Melbourne. In particular, the notion of being a designer–manufacturer. He also holds the work of German lighting designer and manufacturer Ingo Maurer in high regard. Malte is an adventurous designer in his own right. He believes Australian industrial design is much more significant than is commonly understood. He sees a lack of interest in high-end design. It is both crippling and liberating. It forces young designers to make their own future.

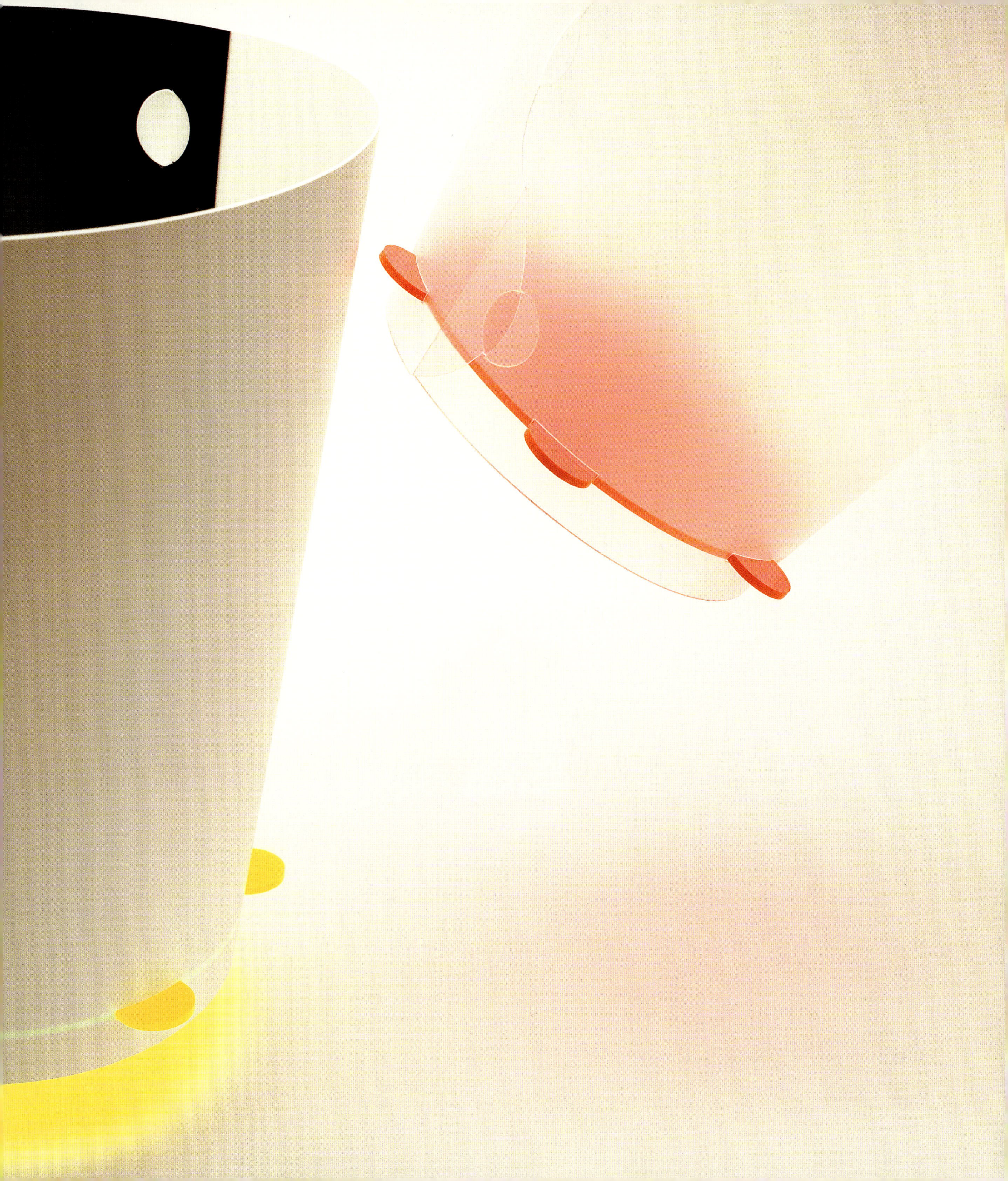

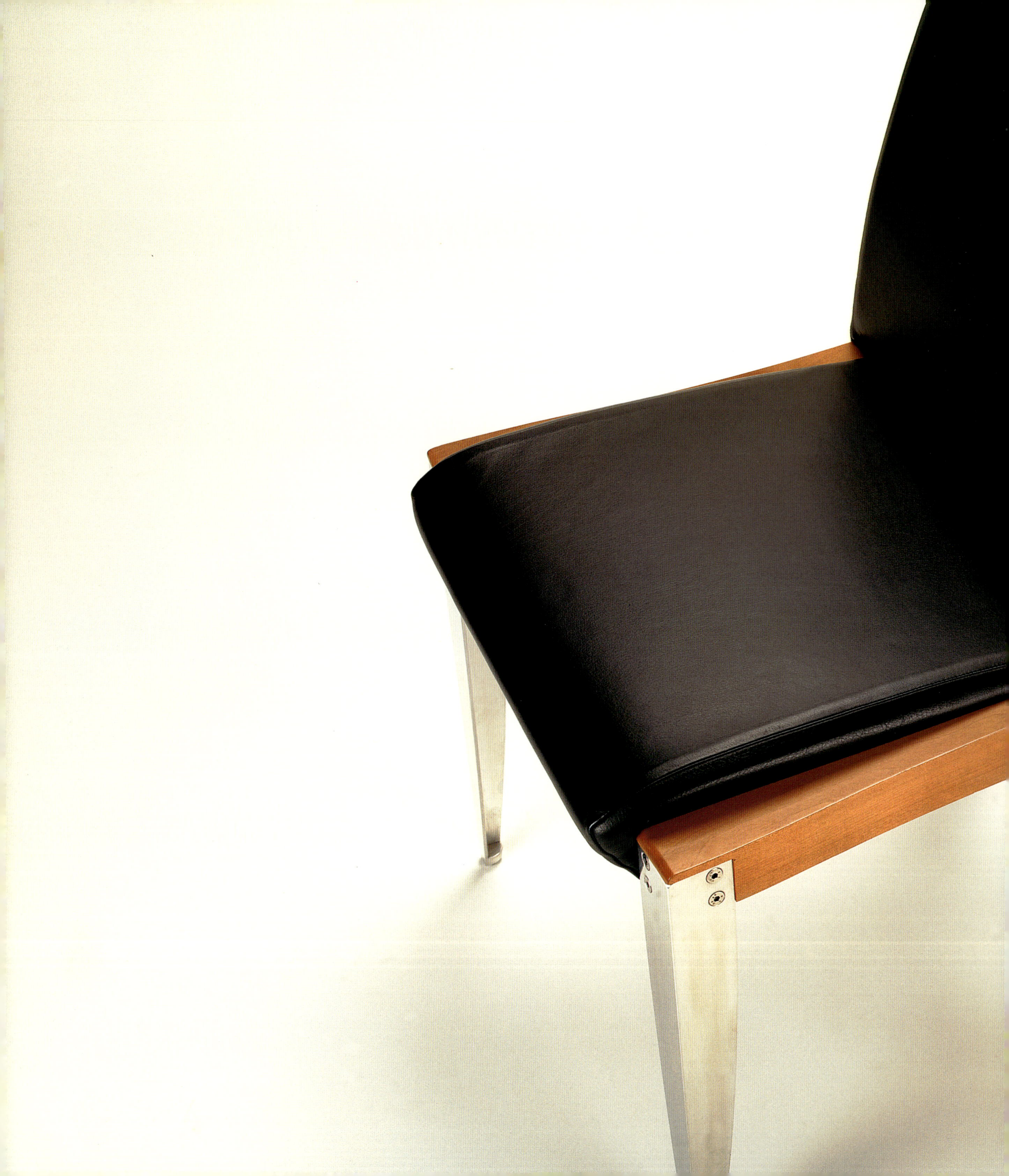

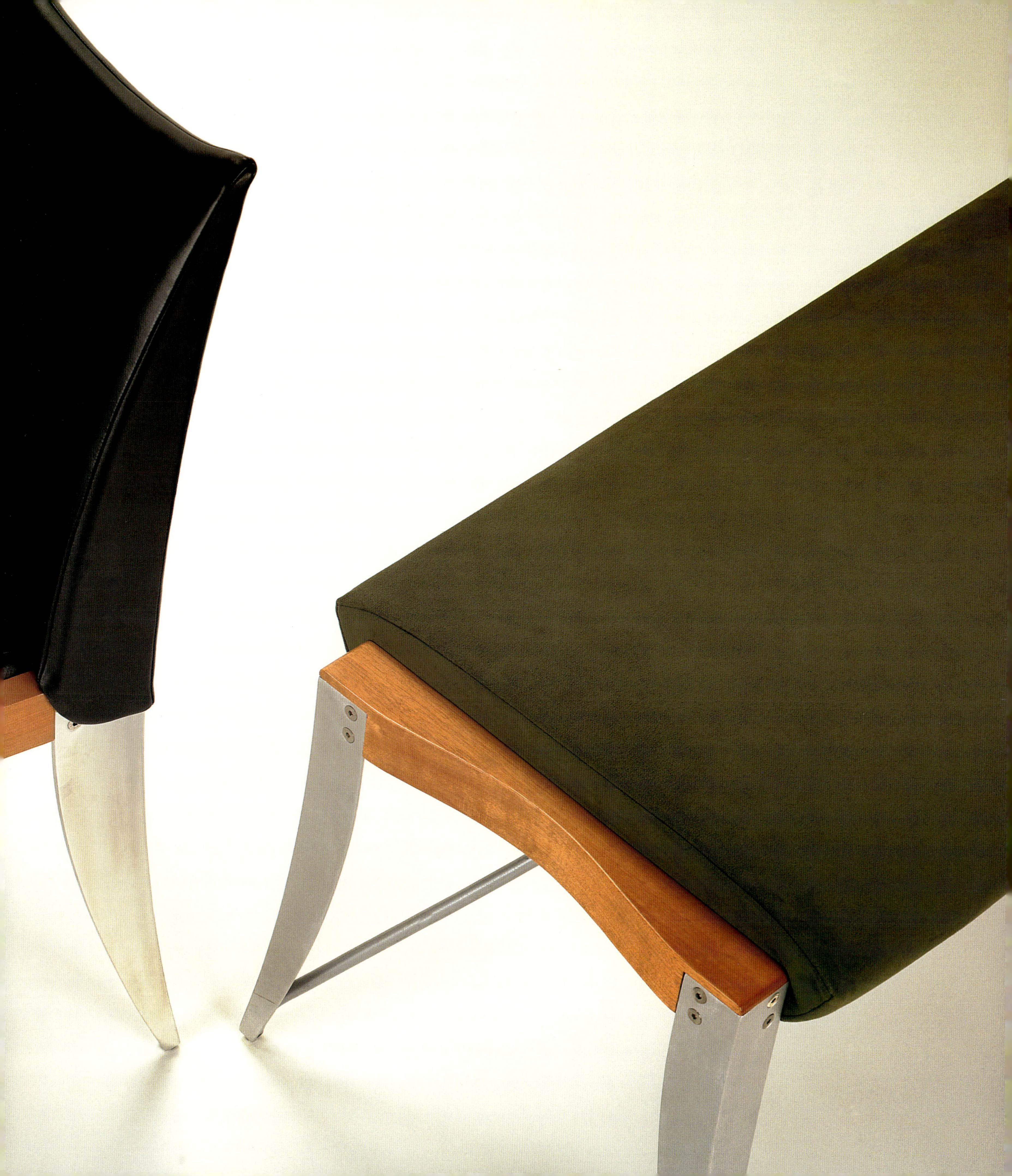

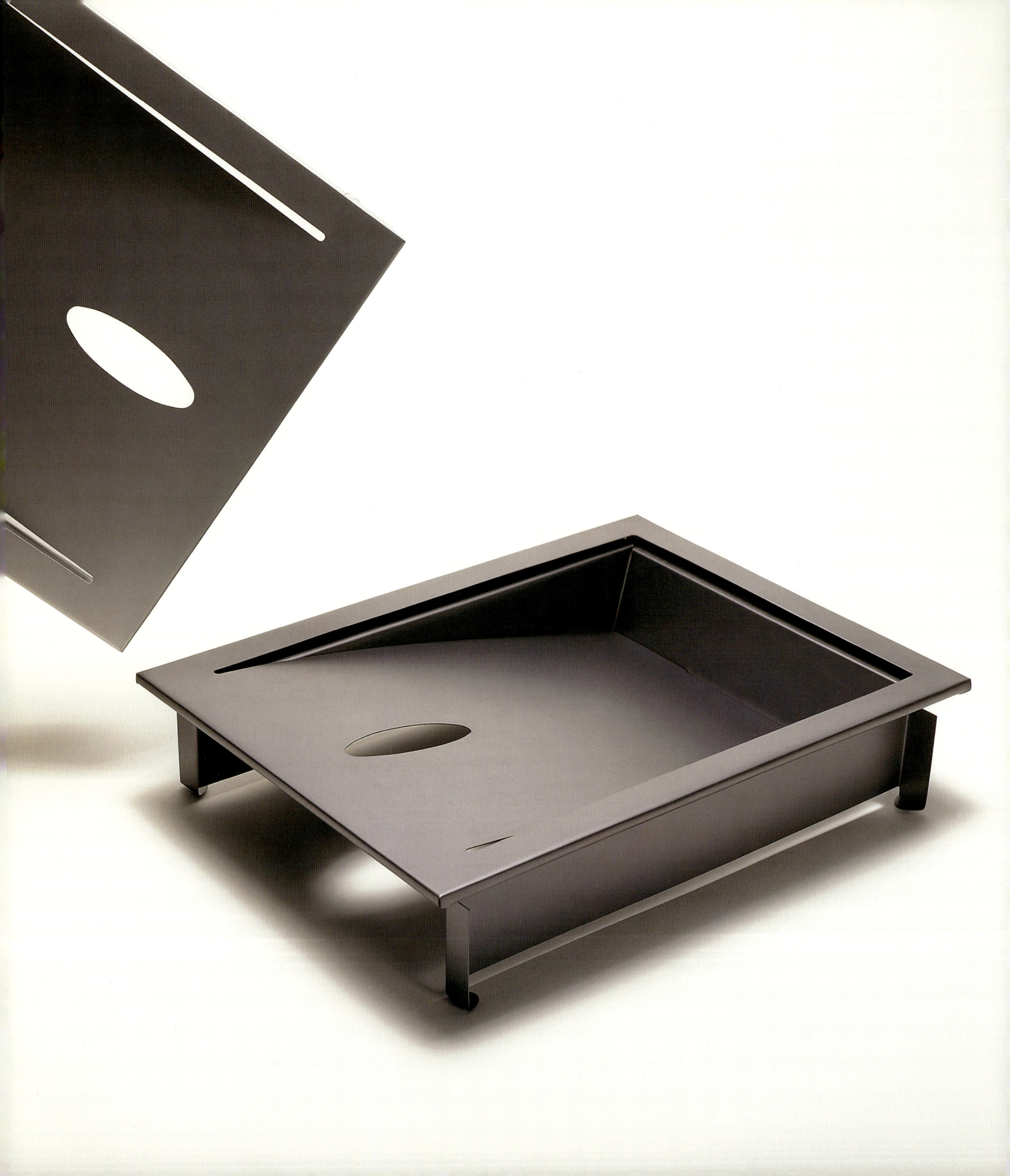

Mark Armstrong
Blue Sky Design

PHILIPS
INDEX
STOP
STILL
CLEAR
TIMER
SELECT
PLAY
INDEX
STILL/JOG ON
STOP
COUNTER
INSTANT
VIEW
MONITOR
PHILIPS
PHILIPS

After graduating from RMIT, Mark Armstrong was recruited by Philips Australia as a junior industrial designer. A typical path for a new graduate. But this was not a typical new graduate. Mentors watched him. Inspired him. Robert Pataki imparted the importance of efficiency and guided him through the lessons of corporate decision making. Robert Blaich developed Mark's strengths in corporate strategy and gave lessons on the use of design as a tool to enhance business. Good industrial design is about more than aesthetics. In 1984, he teamed up with Cameron Robinson to form Blue Sky Design. The company has become one of Australia's leading exponents of good design. What influences Mark? Talent. The diverse and interesting. Philippe Starck. Santiago Calatrava. The lessons learnt at Philips were learnt well. Mark adheres to a proven approach and methodology. 'High design' is an enriched approach to design that integrates basic and traditional skills with a multi-disciplined design-related expertise. It's about responding creatively to the world's increasing complexity. It's about tailoring products to the real needs and characteristics of the end users. Ability. Skill. Vision. There is not one particular piece of work that can represent the style of Mark Armstrong, or in fact of Blue Sky Design. The promotion of one style would be myopic. Mark believes that each product has a unique character that leads to the correct solution. The true style of any design results from the ease of use, appearance and success in its marketplace. The future? Blue Sky Design will continue to develop, broadening its client base into Asia and introducing new services. Diversification. Utilising new technologies and multi-disciplined global offices. Mark has seen the world. Impressions of Eindhoven, Manila, Milan and the Asia Pacific region influence and inspire him. He has seen problems, too. Ignorance is a problem – not just for Mark but for others, as well. An ignorant public unable to grasp the essence of good design. Is awareness coming? Slowly. But the truth remains to be discovered fully. Design has very real marketing implications for each product and for everyday life.

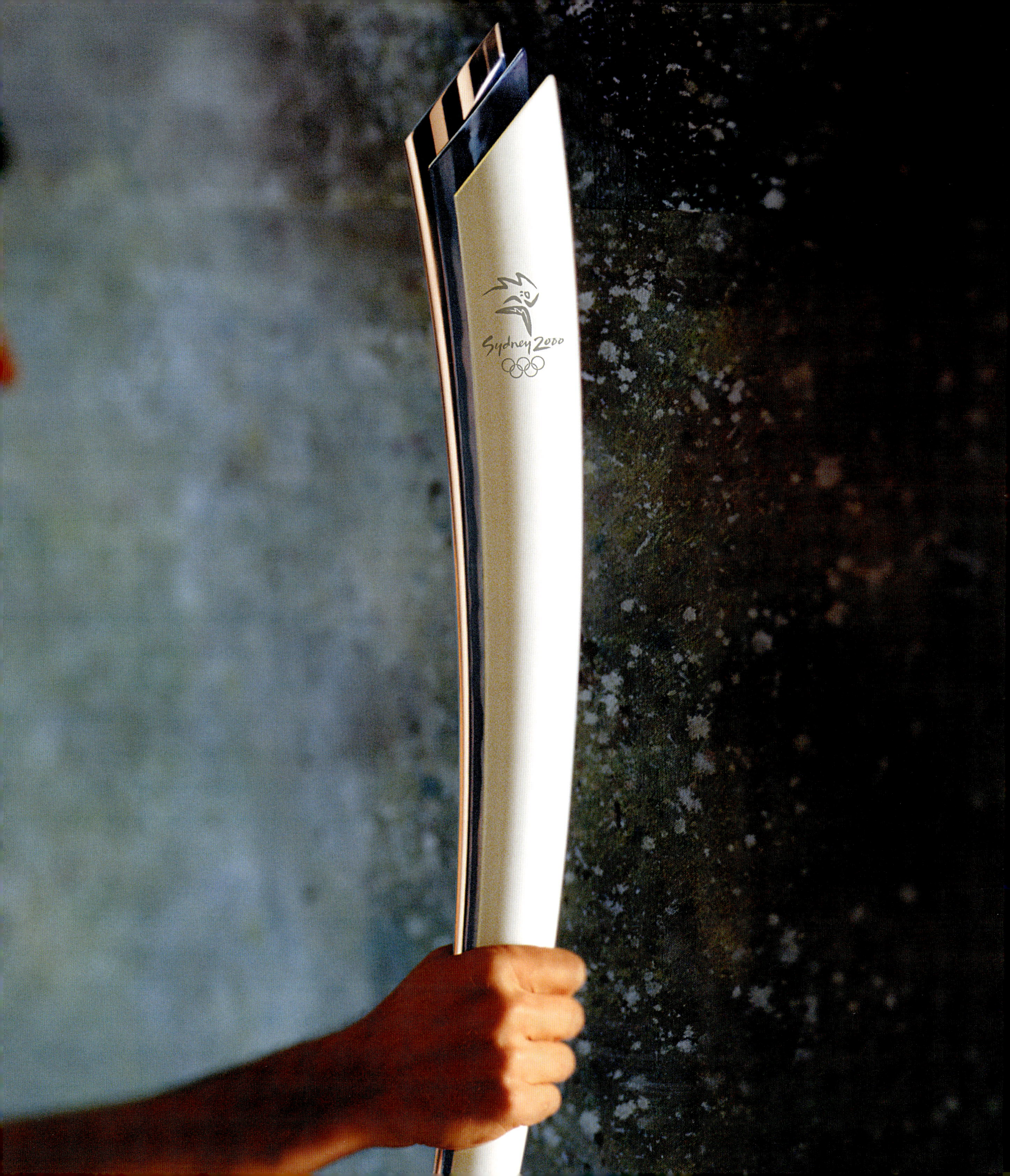
Sydney 2000

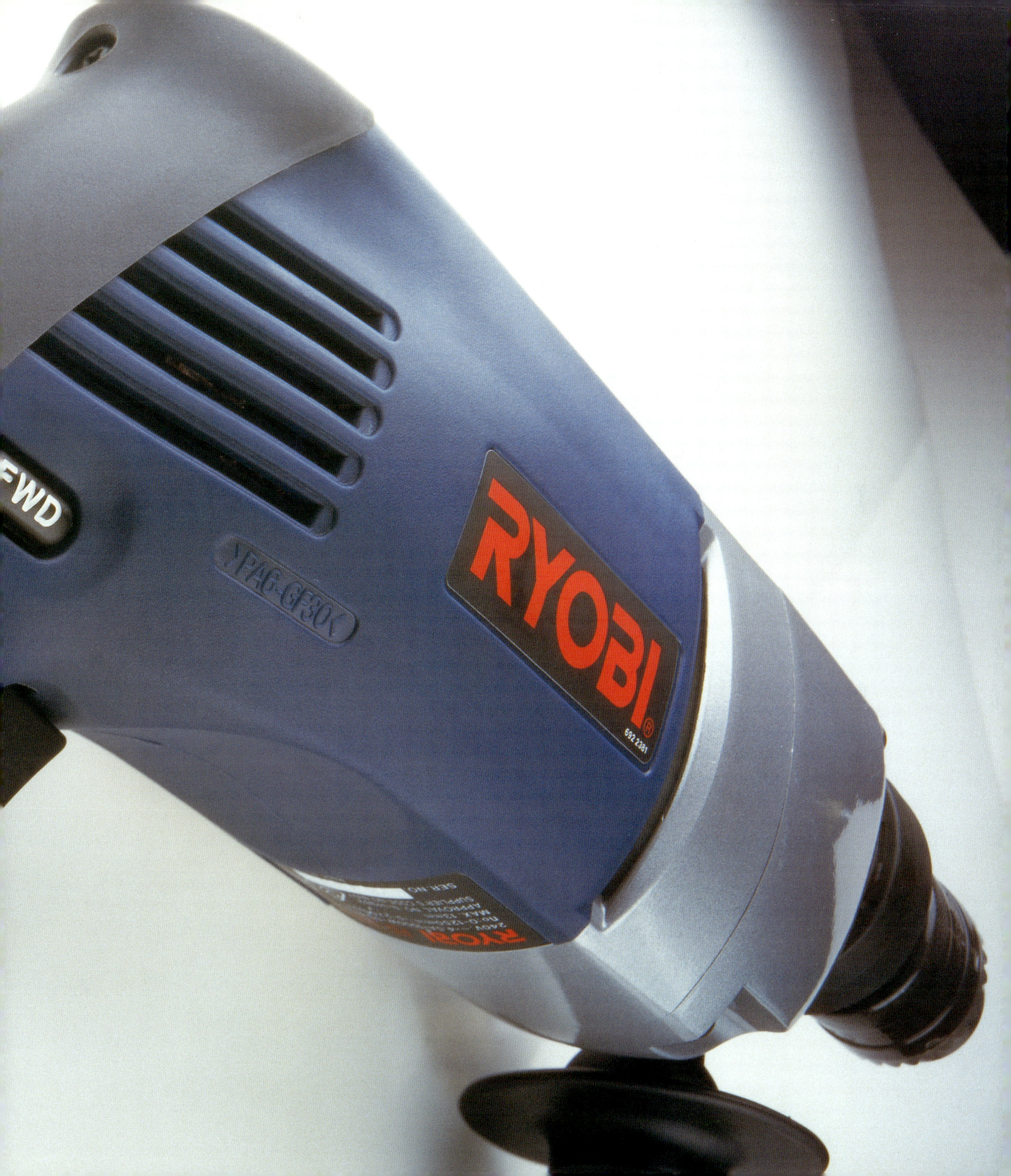
FWD
RYOBI

Pots
Normal
Conserv
Fast
Program
or
Clear
35
Start
or
Pause
Eco
Half
Delay

Peter Cooper
Stephen Neil
Konstrukt Design

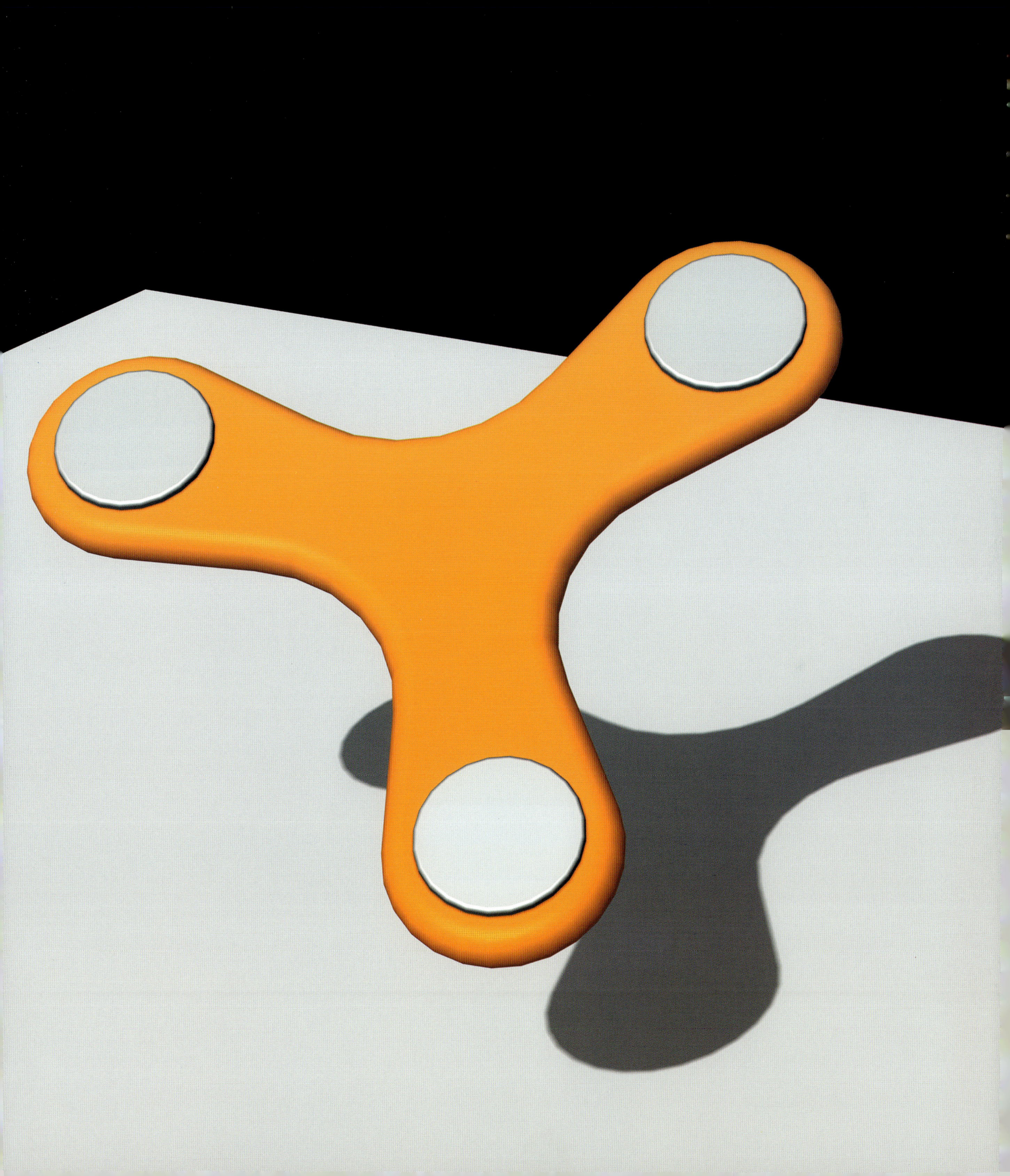

April Fools Day. 6.30 a.m. London. Peter Cooper receives a call from Stephen Neil. A friend and former colleague. 'Want to form a new consultancy?' The suggestion is genuine. Too many lengthy international phone calls follow. A few weeks later, Peter Cooper boards QF001 bound for Sydney, Australia. A new company is born. Who is Stephen Neil? A graduate of Sydney University and Sydney College of Arts. His career is depicted in a collection of industrial design solutions and interactive museum exhibits. Peter Cooper is a graduate, too. Of University of Canberra, University of Technology, Sydney and Domus Academy in Milan. When a founding member of the Konstrukt Design group left, an opportunity arose for Stephen and Peter to pick up where he'd left off. Having worked for the company earlier in their careers, they were already familiar with the projects and clients. An opportunity too good to miss? Probably. They moved in. Konstrukt Design was a renovator's delight. Great name. Good reputation. Well established. Complete with staff, premises, equipment and a significant debt. An interesting way to start a new partnership. Konstrukt Design (Version 2.0) was launched. Since then, Stephen and Peter have built on their inherited reputation, producing distinctive work with a strong aesthetic component while retaining the technical edge the company has been known for. With the first products of the new venture now entering production, Konstrukt Design is re-emerging, this time as one of the leading product design consultancies on Australia's eastern seaboard. The future is an opportunity to explore.

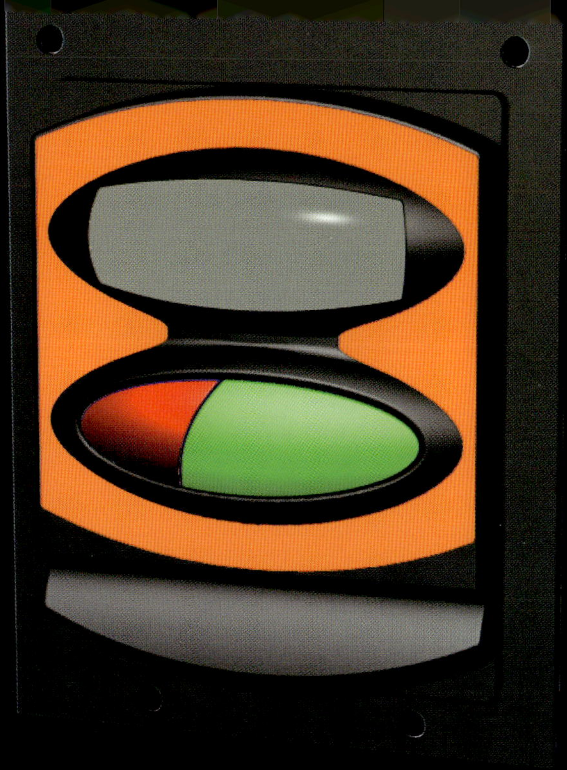

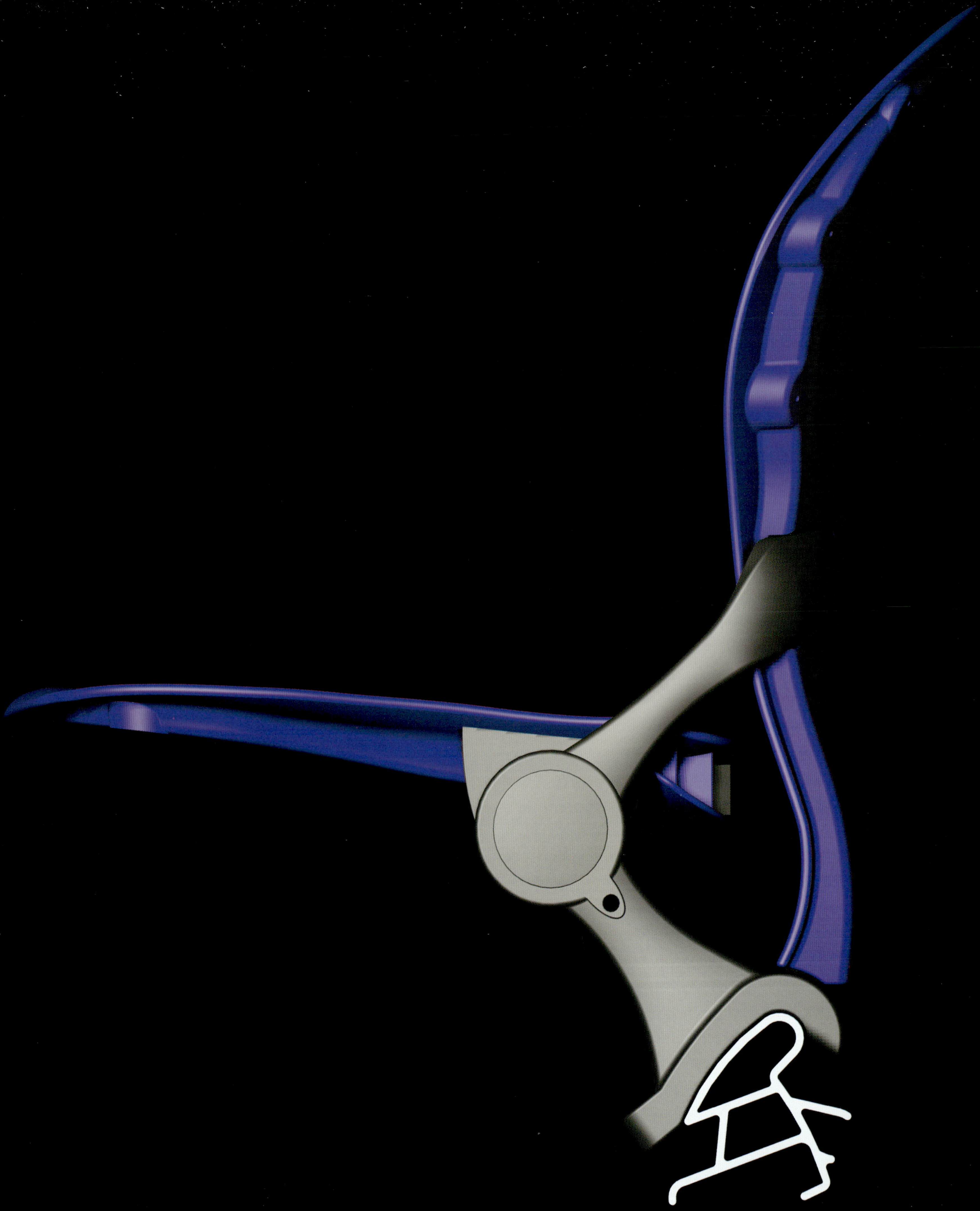

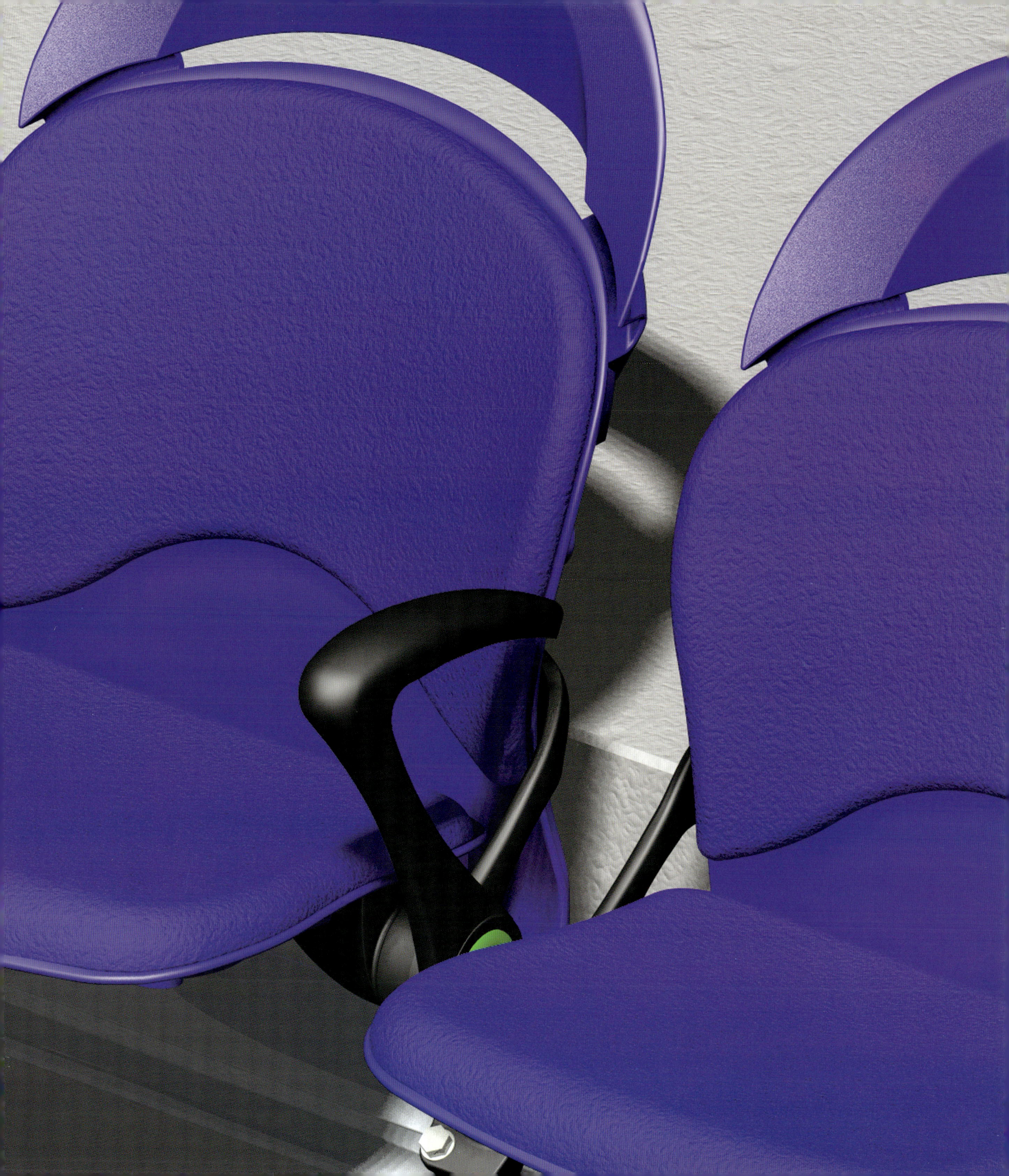

Interior Design

Nik Karalis
Woods Bagot

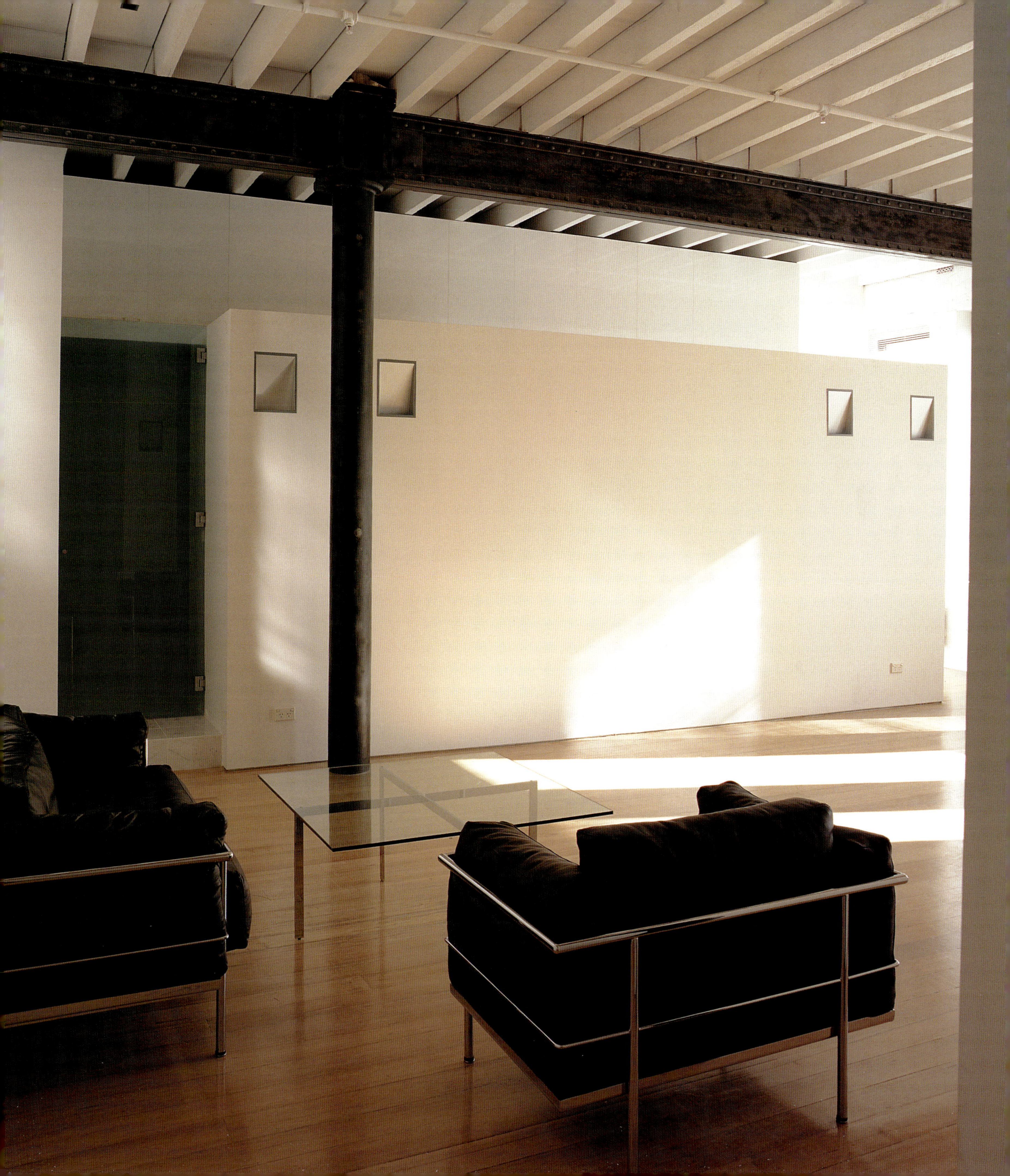

The lively academic culture of Adelaide contradicts its perceived reputation as a small town. It generates a dynamic tension. Charles Sturt's vigorous logic of modern planning is embodied in the streets and landscapes. It was a frontier for Sturt and a frontier for Nik Karalis. The city's optimism spurred Nik's own journey into the field of built environments. Nik's career began at Inarc Design. A young firm practising modern architecture in a domestic environment. Not easy. The corporate sector accommodated such thinking more generously. David Chipperfield's suspicion of ideology and functional determinism inspired. Nik applauds experimentation with material, form and figure. His projects deliberately attempt to avoid the standard. He believes architecture and the built environment should force people to readdress typical notions of surroundings. Uncomfortable clients do not distress Nik. 'Too loud.' 'Not bright enough.' It is of no concern. Interiors should allow a predetermined function and incite emotion. Both are important. The challenge, irresistible. For Nik, design begins with an understanding of the true essence of the brief. What are the innate fundamental complexities to be unravelled? His design methodology is driven by the exploration of space, form and material. Fashion is irrelevant. Non-linear relationships develop. It's a complex process. Contradictory. At the end, everything fits perfectly. Nik focuses on doing as little as possible, reducing things to their absolute essence. The rich potential of design is not limited by the selection of media or palette of colour. Design dialogue and collaboration with other design disciplines create new opportunities. The outlook for Nik Karalis is a broadening horizon of potential media and expression. He believes such cross-fertilisation is essential if Australia is to realise its true self. A unique Australian design experience in a global context.

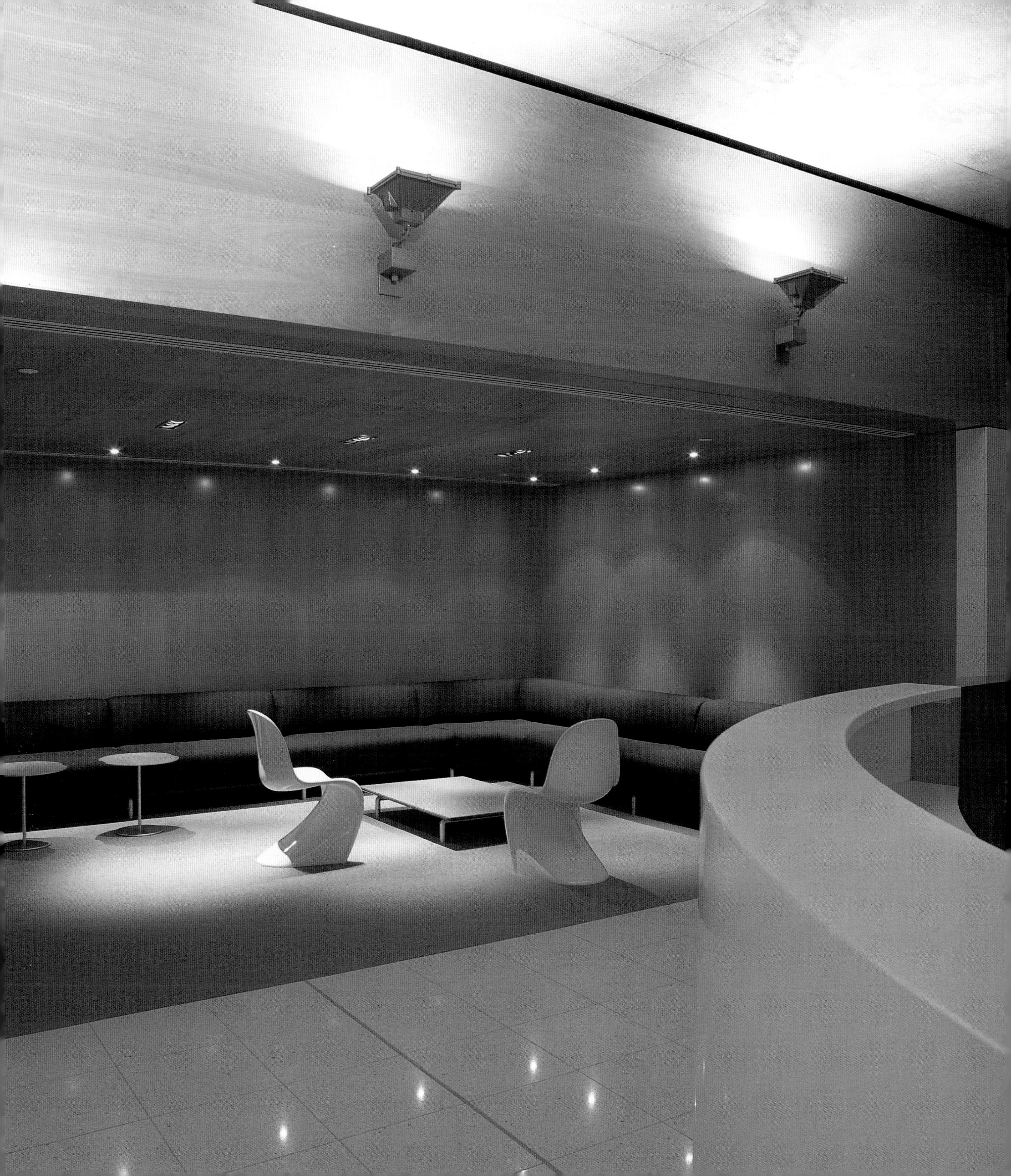

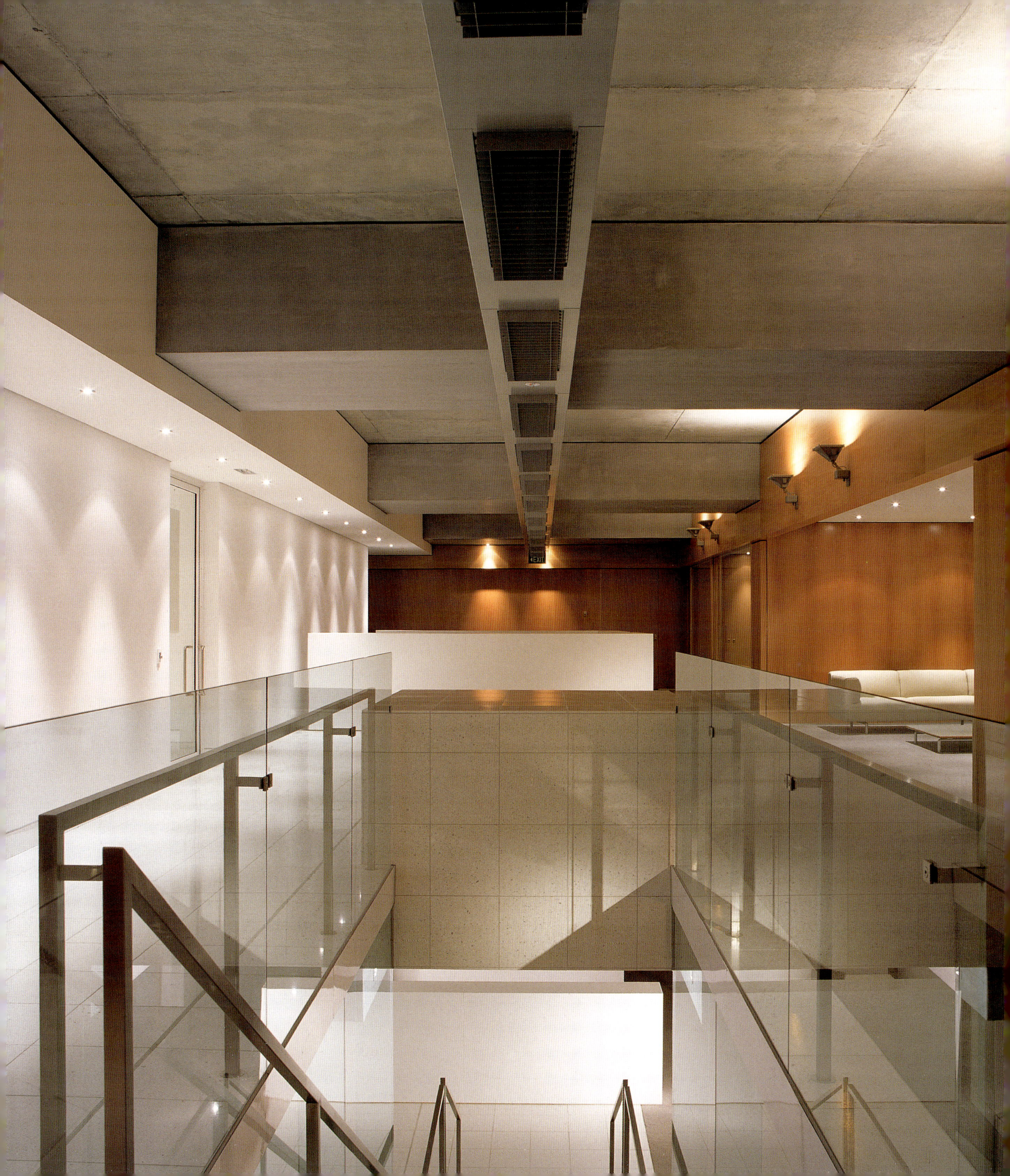

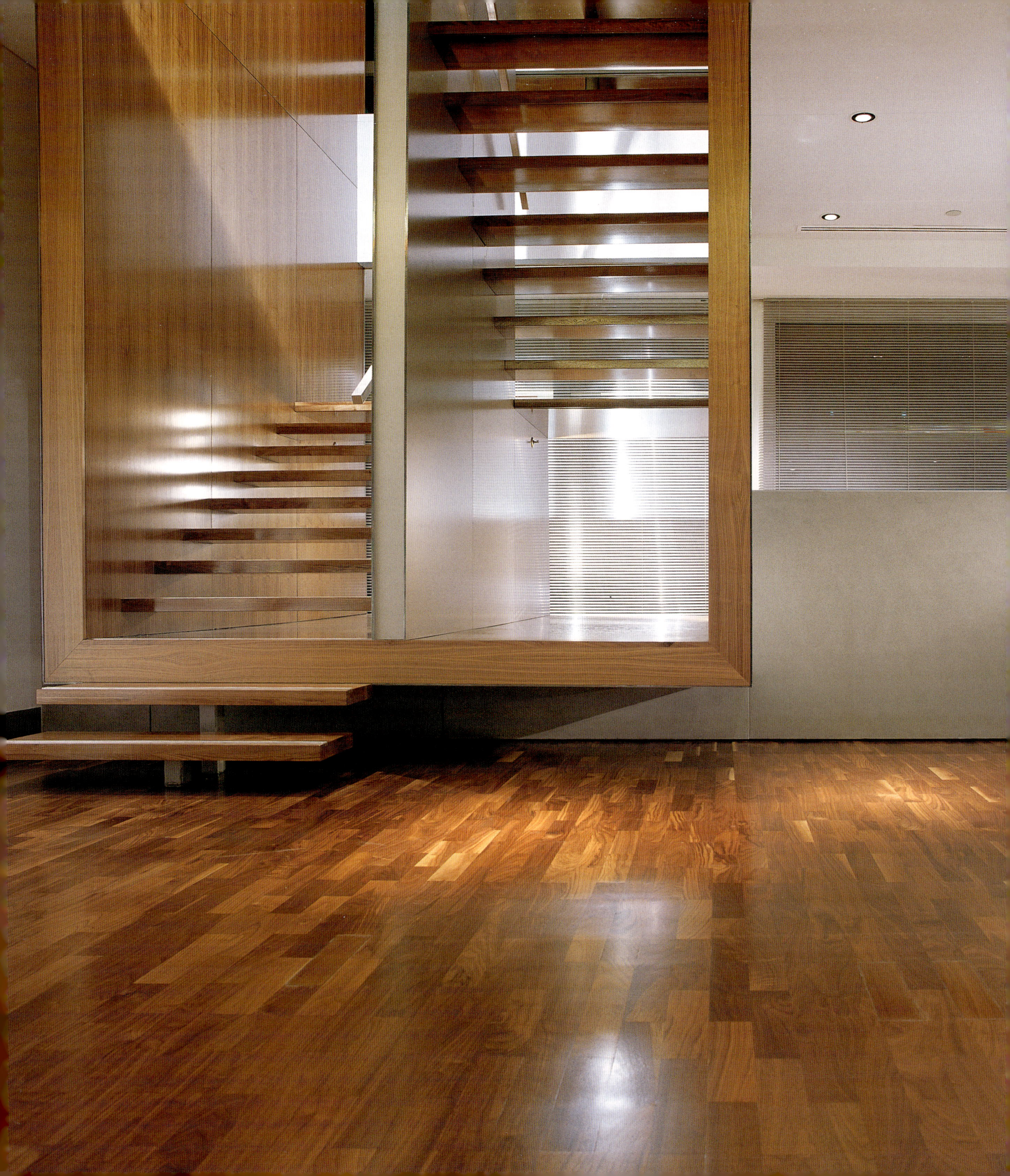

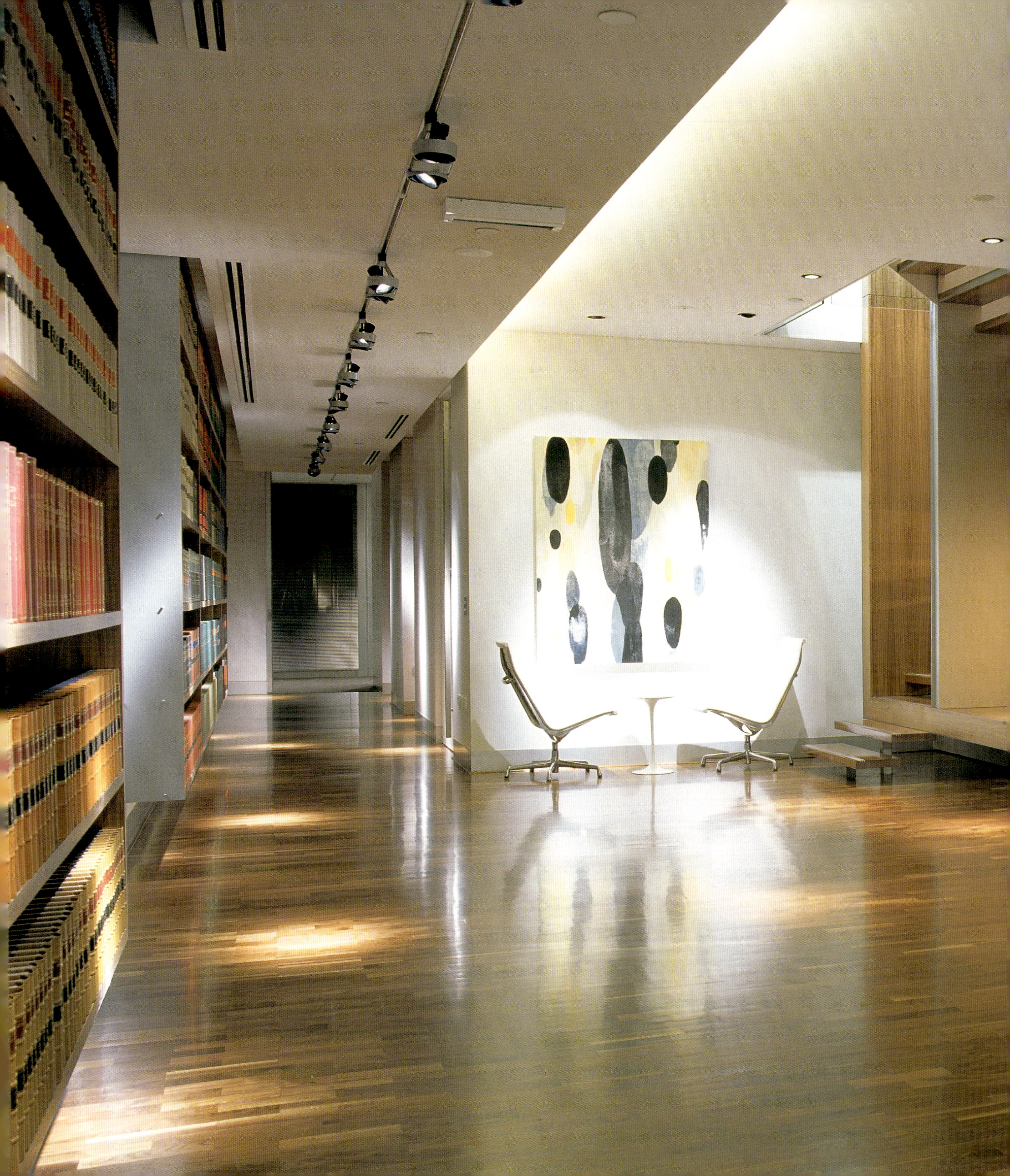

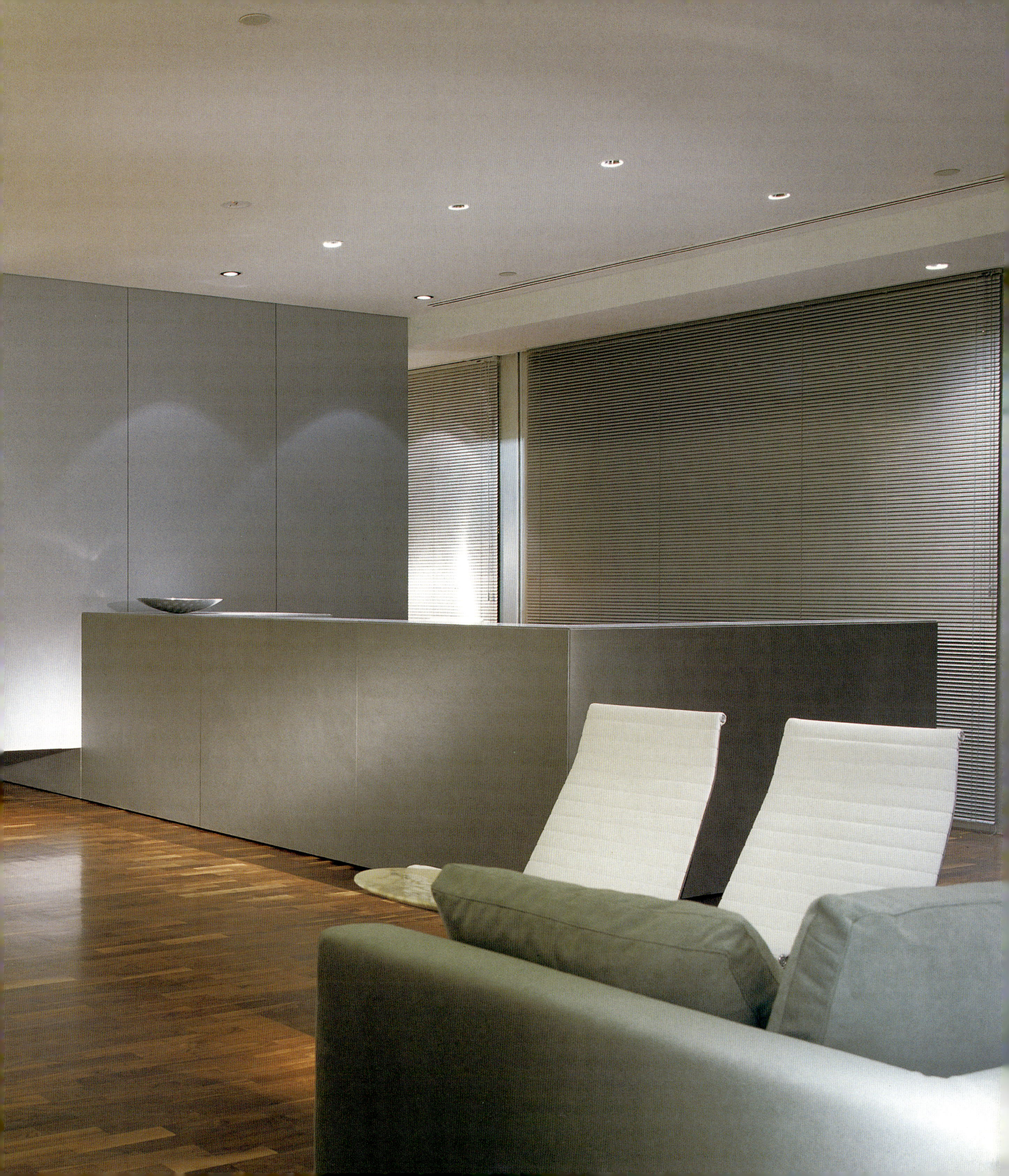

Andrew Parr
SJB Interiors

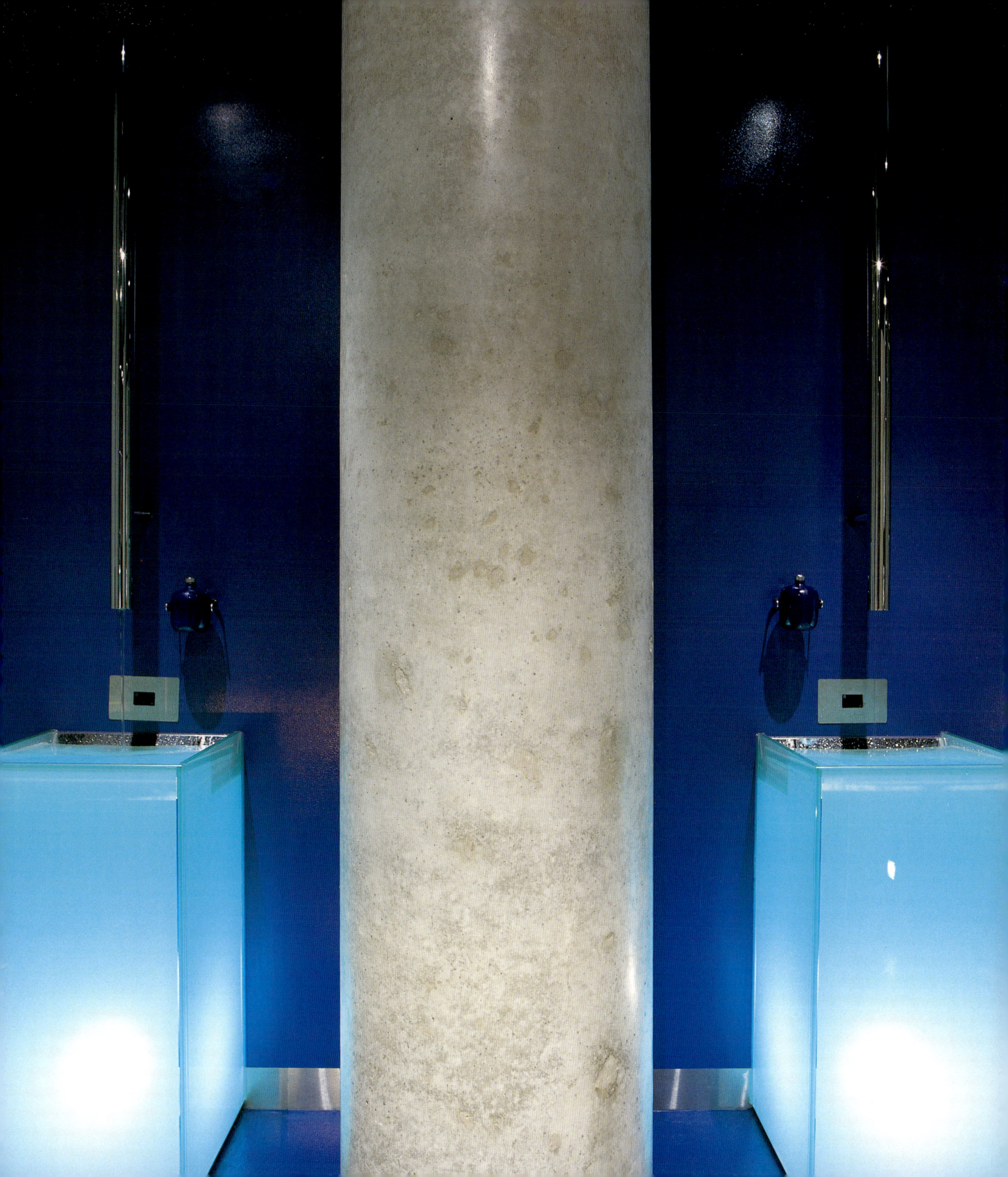

Mies van der Rohe, Andre Putman and Luis Baragan. Their work inspires. But why? It is not easy to articulate. It just does. Andrew Parr believes contemporary can mean comfortable. A statement defending his modernist heart? No. Simply the basis of his approach. Clean lines. Linear forms. Colour. Texture. Form. He begins with these elements. The finished product is a culmination of his creative response to the brief, the client's own input and ultimately the expression of Andrew's own ideals for the measure of good interior design. His designs ignite questions. Where's the logic? What's the strategy? For each piece of furniture, each finish, each piece of joinery and each colour. Andrew's response is clear. A memorable interior cannot be attributed to planning or strategy alone. It is in the designer's translation of instinctive concepts. Instinct takes years to formulate. Years of experience to control. Many years to understand. The impact an interior can have on a company image is significant. Andrew insists on using the interior space as part of an overall brand strategy. The interior must capture the customers' imagination. Influence. Make the decision. Commit. Andrew constantly surprises himself by challenging his own perceptions in his search for new solutions to client problems. Evolution is inevitable. Response will change. The lifestyle revolution will drive a new century of designers.

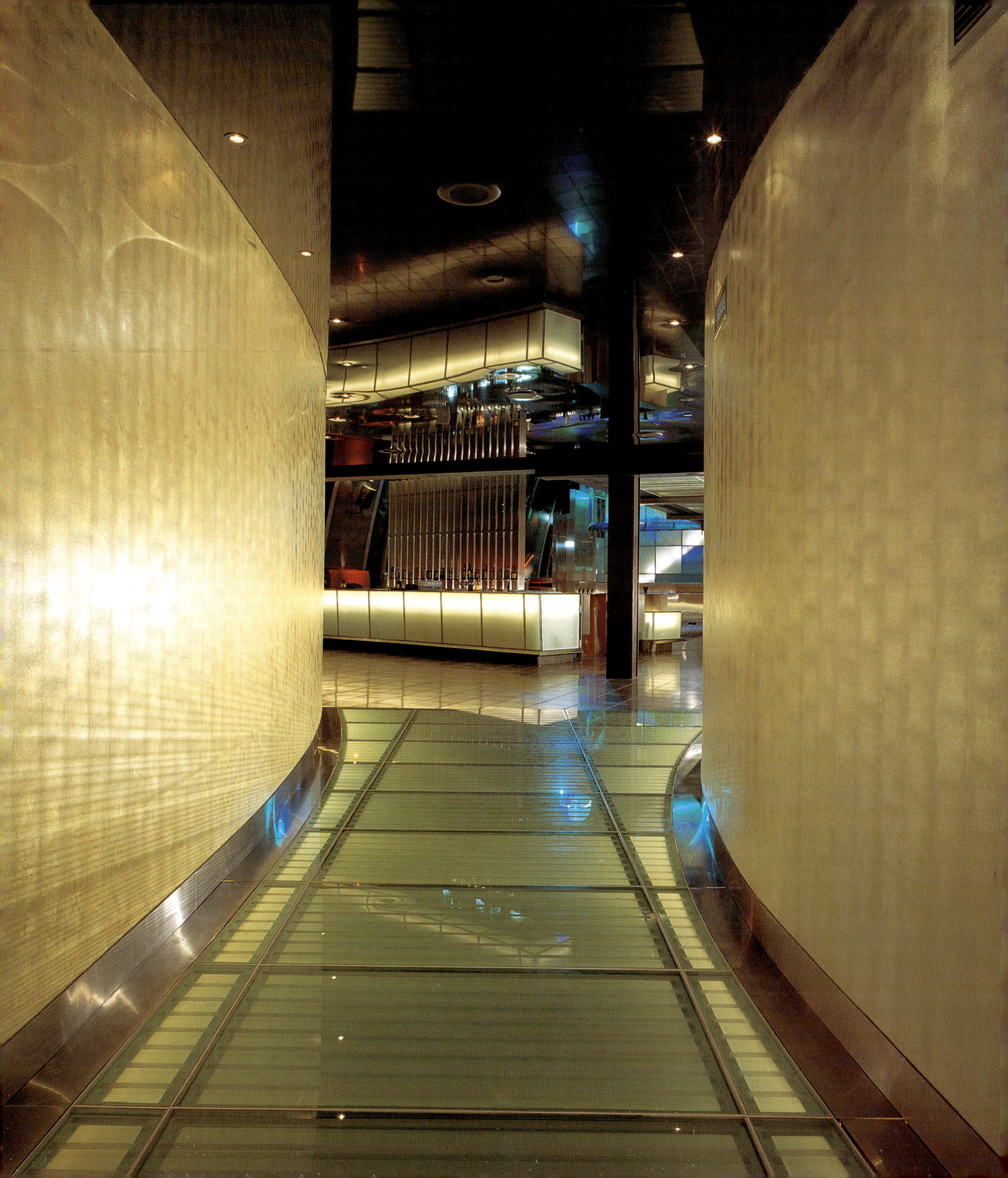

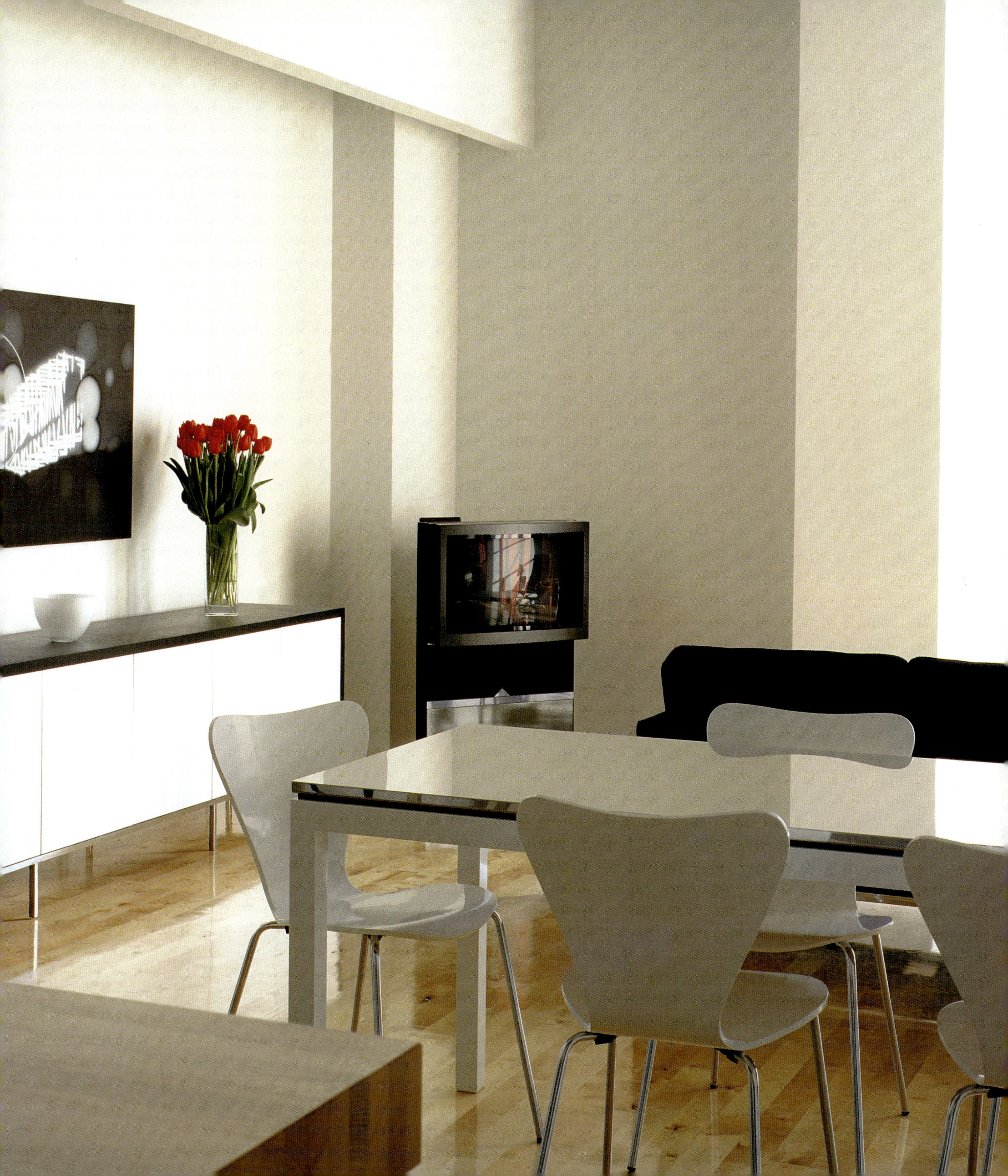

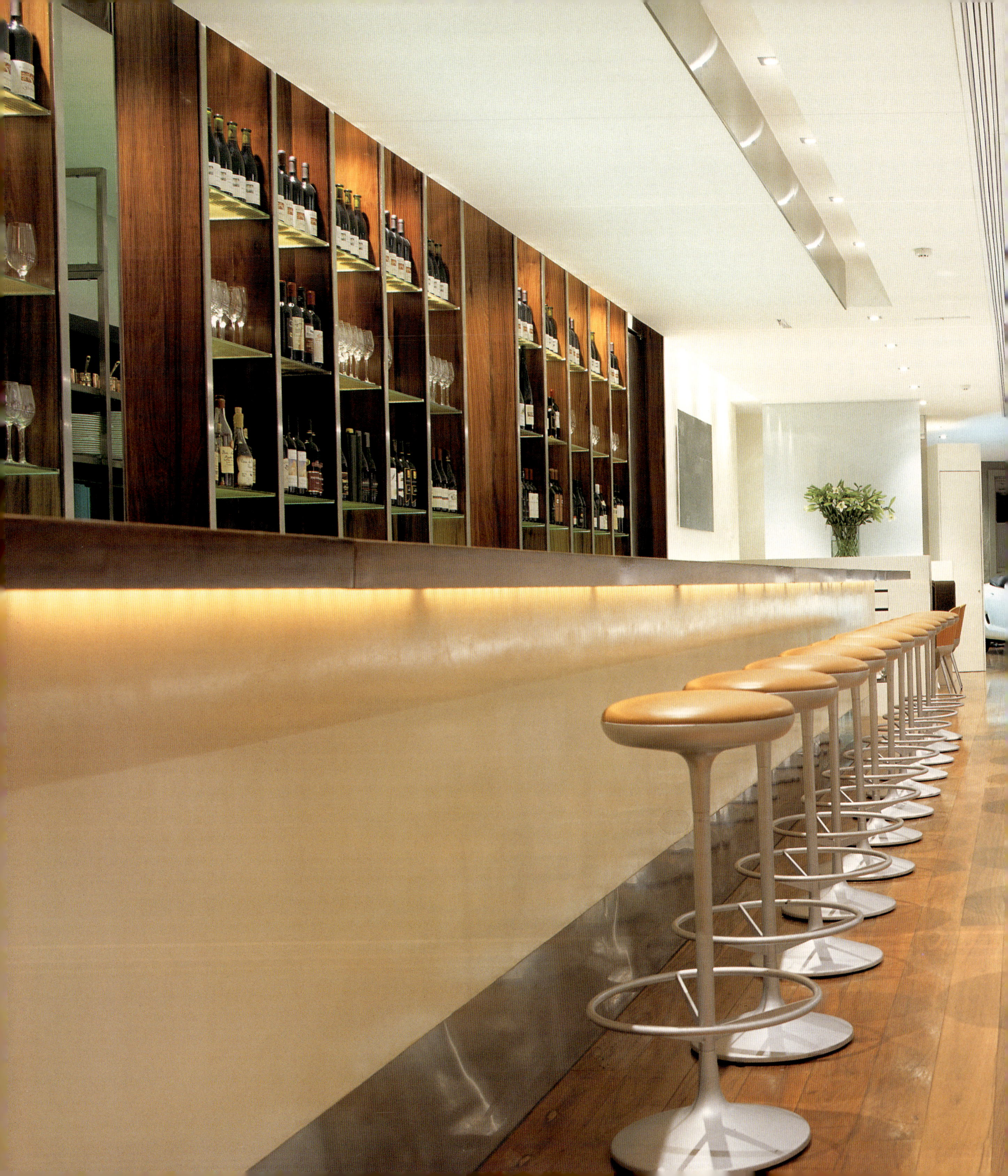

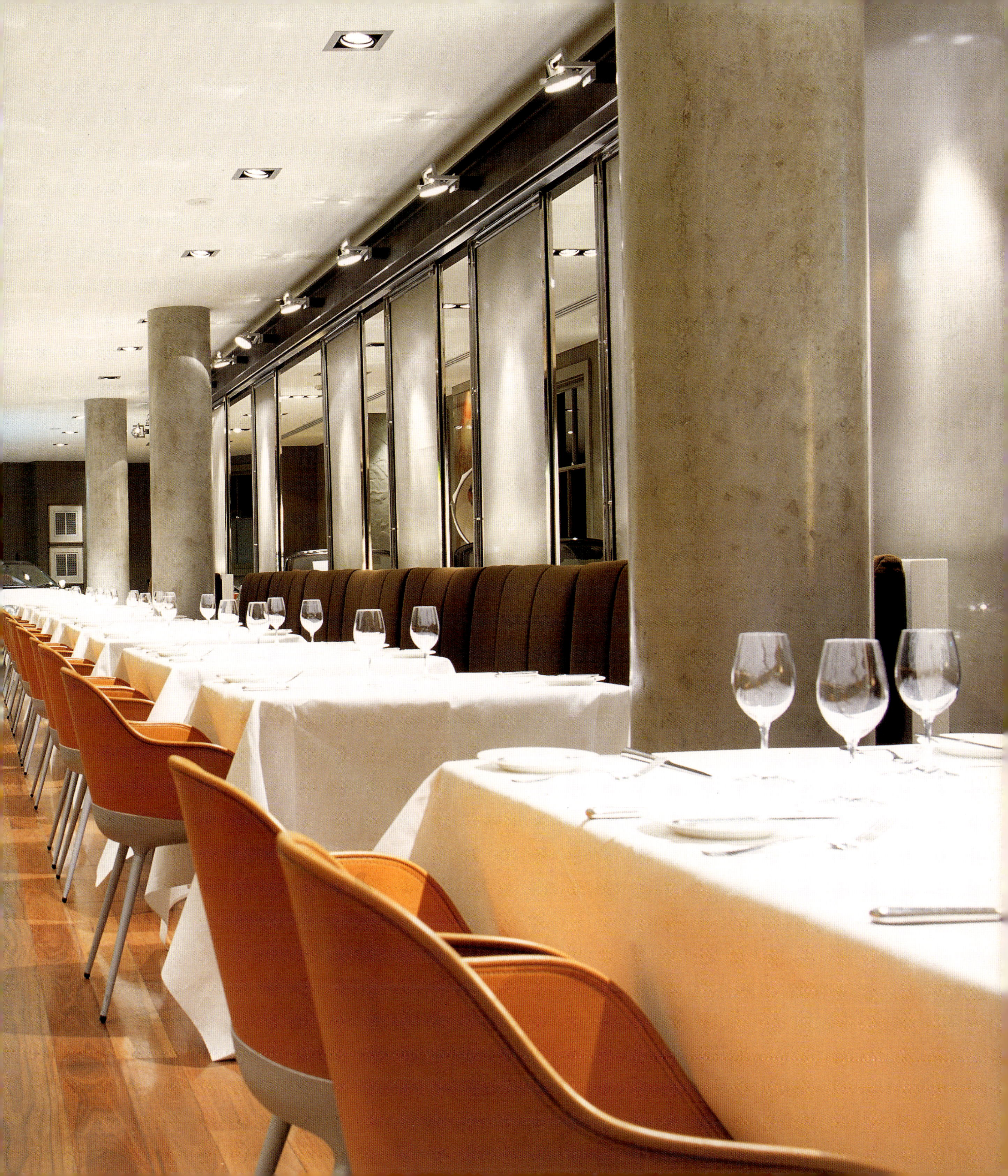

Jackie Johnston
Bates Smart

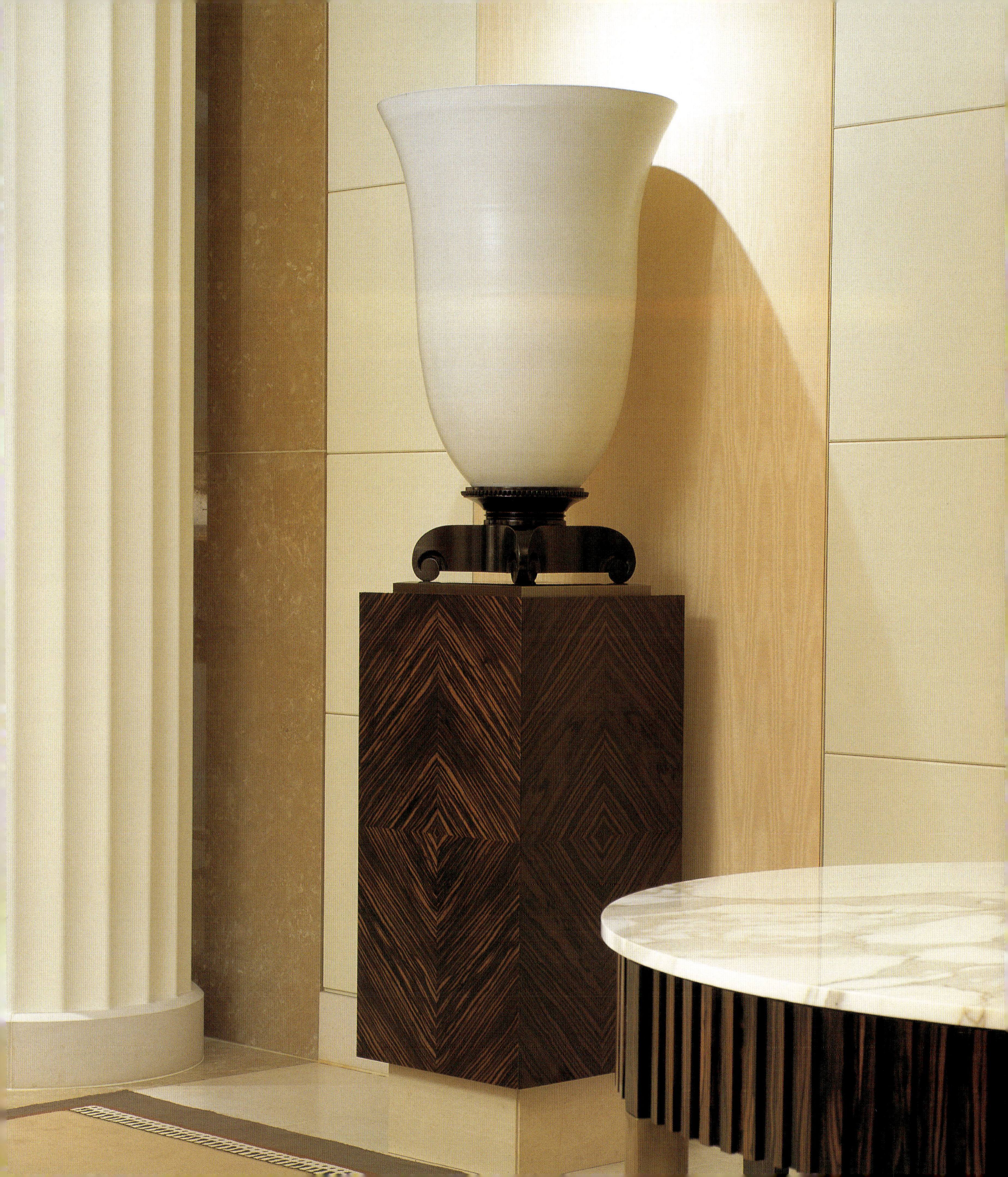

Born in the Year of the Dragon. A lucky sign in the Chinese horoscope. Born towards the end of February. Pisces. Creative and imaginative by nature. With this profile, how could Jackie Johnston fail as an interior designer? Her background in design is broad. Extensive. Projects have included office fit-outs. Institutional and medical, hospitality and domestic. Working partnerships have included Andrew Reed and Associates and Daryl Jackson Architects. After time in the UK, Jackie came back to Melbourne to join the Crown Project Group. Three years of work covering all aspects of the project. The primary concern was the five-star hotel, a precise design exercise. Complex client and public requirements. The aim: a level of quality and luxury that meets the common perception of what a high-quality hotel is all about. The style achieved is uniquely 'Australian'. It indicates our cultural preference for casual, comfortable surroundings. Christian Liagre and Andre Putman were pivotal design references. The creators of the Hotel Montalembert in Paris were inspirational in the detailing of Crown Towers. A style for living. Jackie's favourites from the world of hotel makers are Kerry Hill's The Chedi in Bali and Peter Muler's The Oberoi in Lombok. She is excited to see the boundaries of hotel design being challenged by The Hemple in London. Now in her thirties, Jackie feels her apprenticeship is complete. Finally. She is currently working with Bates Smart. She's on the brink of the next millennium with new technology at her fingertips. The immediate future is an exciting prospect for young designers who are inherently unhappy with the status quo. New ideas, new challenges are always on the horizon. A future ambition is to design a range of furniture or household items with mass appeal. As a child, Jackie's mother predicted she'd end up on stage. Jackie's not sure where she's ended up. This feels more like a beginning.

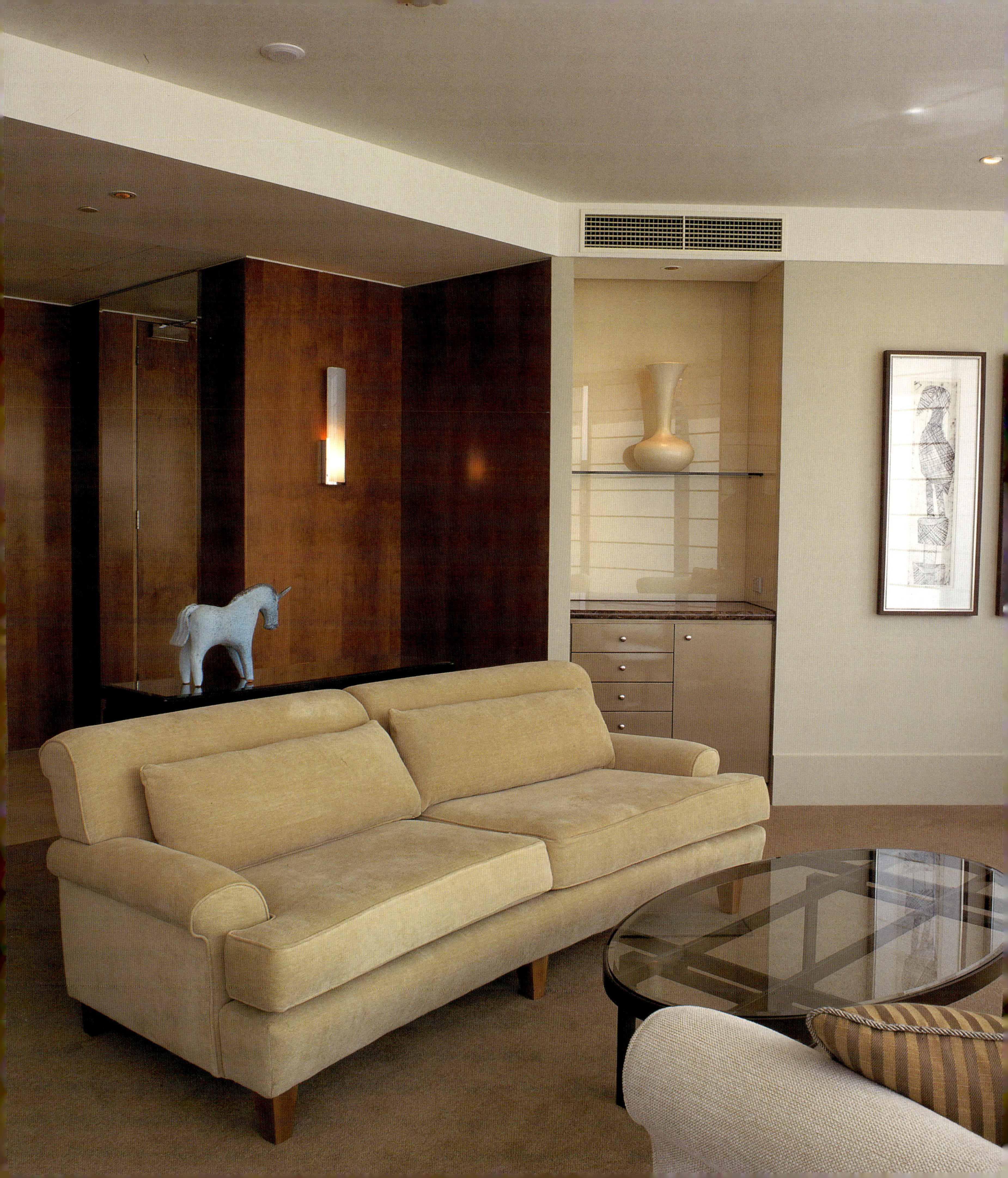

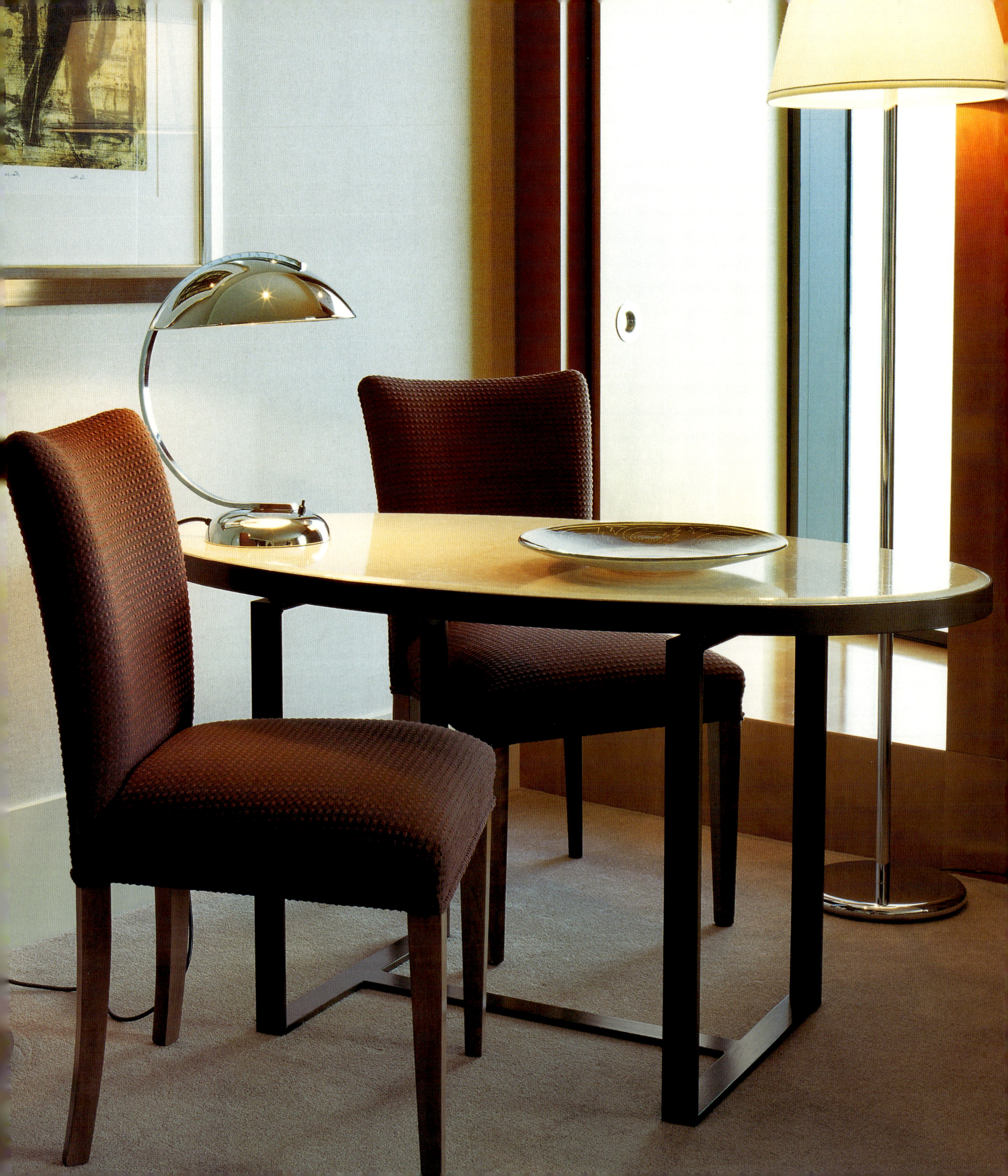

Paul Hecker

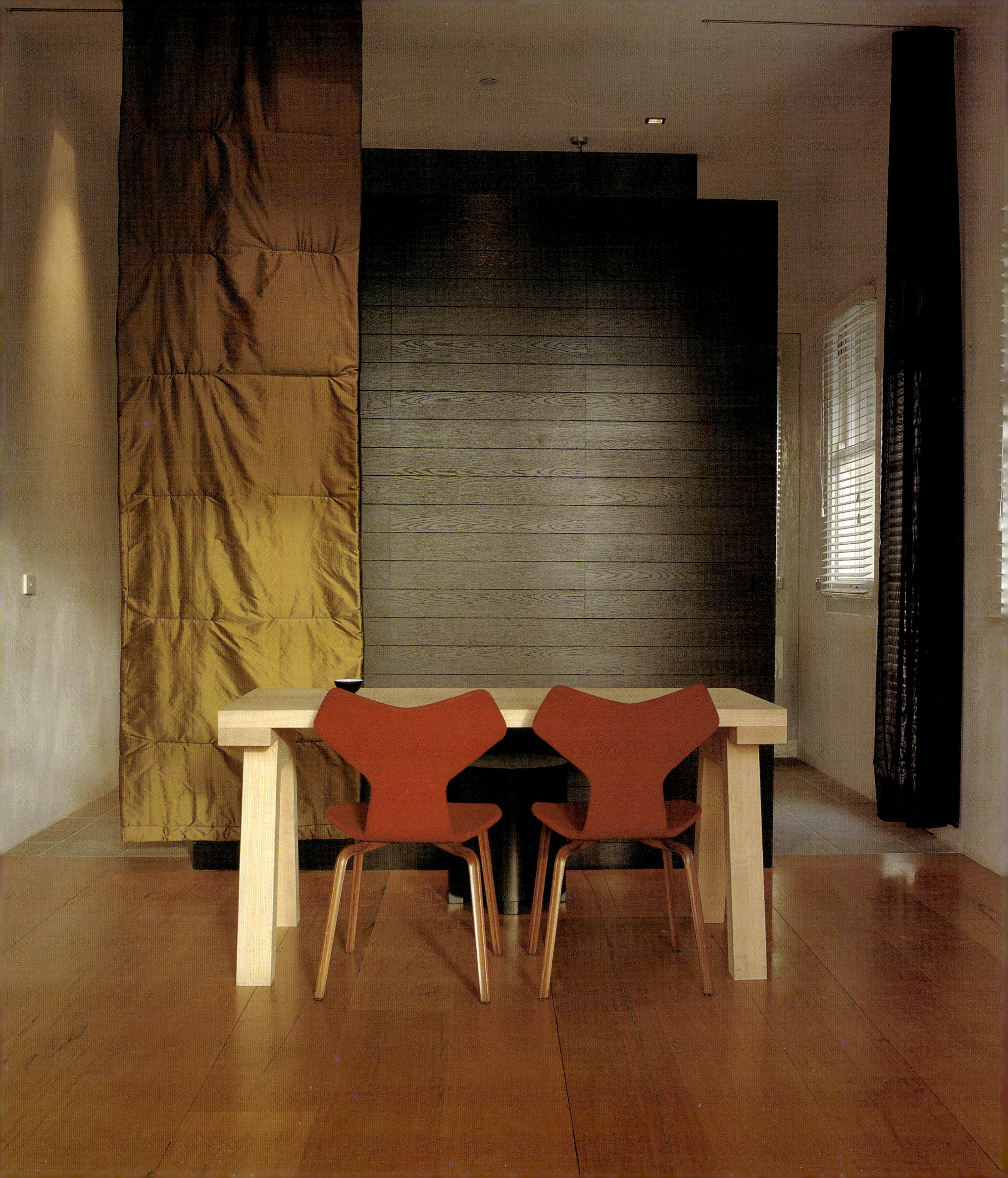

Thirteen years of working as an interior designer. A lifetime to go. Isn't interior design just like any other profession or job? Do it long enough and it becomes second nature. Do it with your eyes closed. You know what works and what doesn't. Reasonable results come without much thought or effort. It's acceptable. Clients are easily convinced. You're giving them the right solution. It might even be new. Exciting. Thirteen years of working as an interior designer. Paul Hecker is clearly not settling for anything like 'acceptable'. His passion and enthusiasm for design is unrelenting. Paul contemplates the next thirteen years of his career with heightened expectation. How does he do it? His enthusiasm and freshness of approach are treasures to be nurtured. A process to be embraced. There's no room for complacency. Smug is not a word to describe Paul. He maintains a critical eye when reviewing his own work. With the other, he watches the world. This designer does not live in a vacuum. His world envelops popular culture, new ideas, change, questions. Paul's favourite question is 'Why?'. Why do we like it? Why do we not? Why do we do it? Why can't we? There is no design bible dictating the terms in Paul Hecker's life. But he believes it is imperative to approach the process with ability and discernment. Don't be seduced by the whimsical or banal. Don't give the client what they want. Too easy. A real sense of achievement and satisfaction comes when you advocate a design you are passionate about. Design that reflects the most progressive elements of the moment in which it was conceived. Risky? Sure. Essential? Absolutely. It is for Paul Hecker. A lifetime is a long time to be a designer.

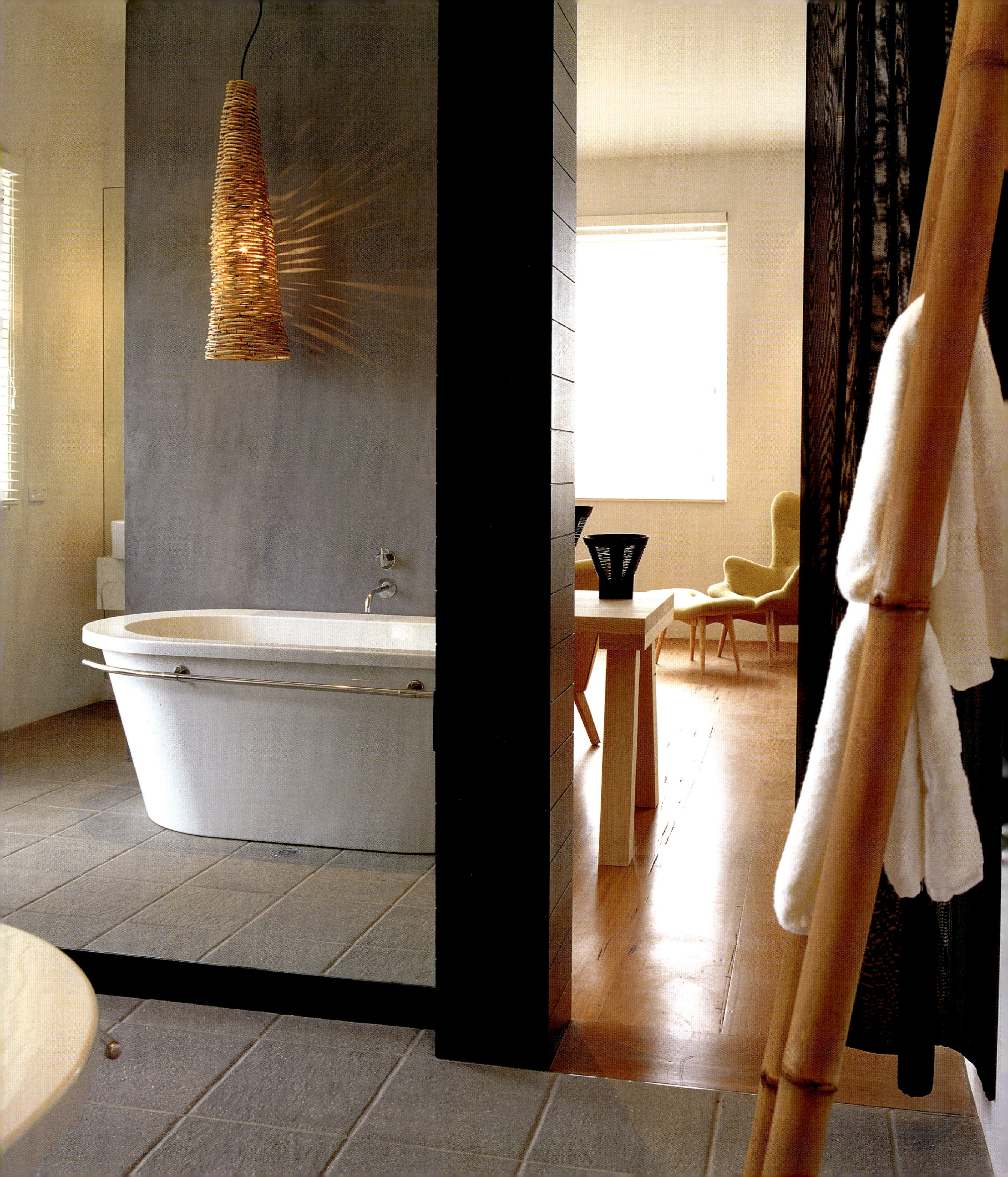

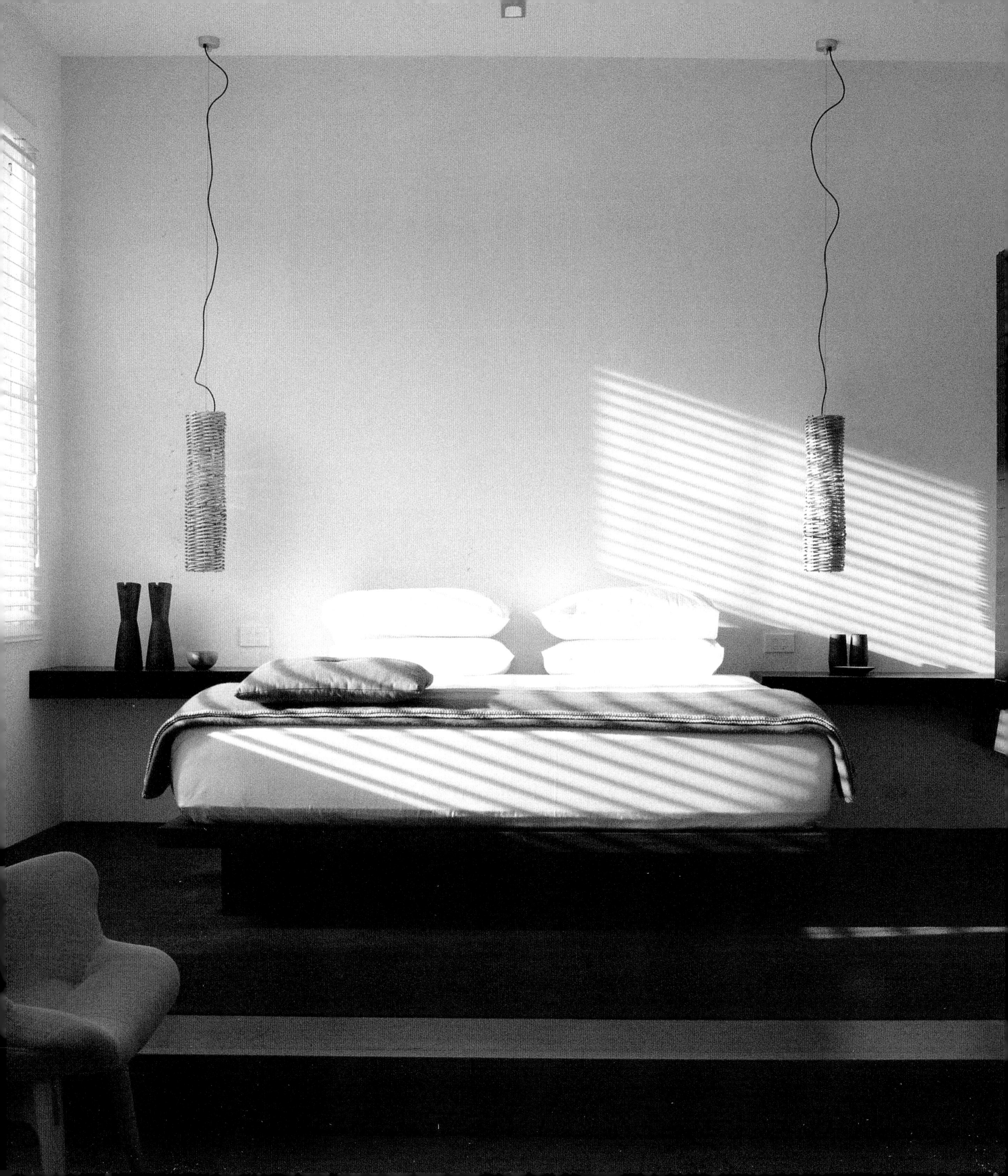

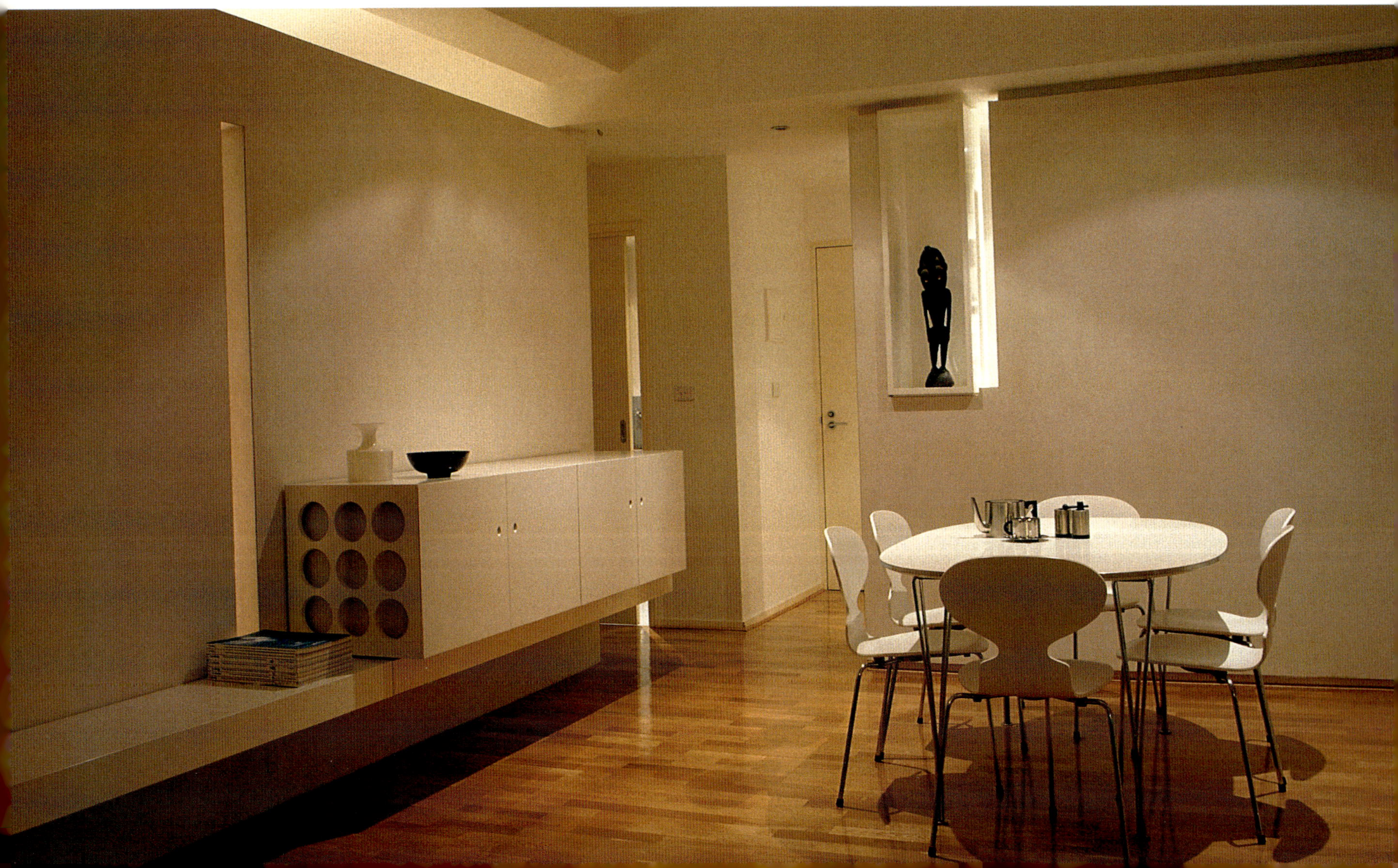

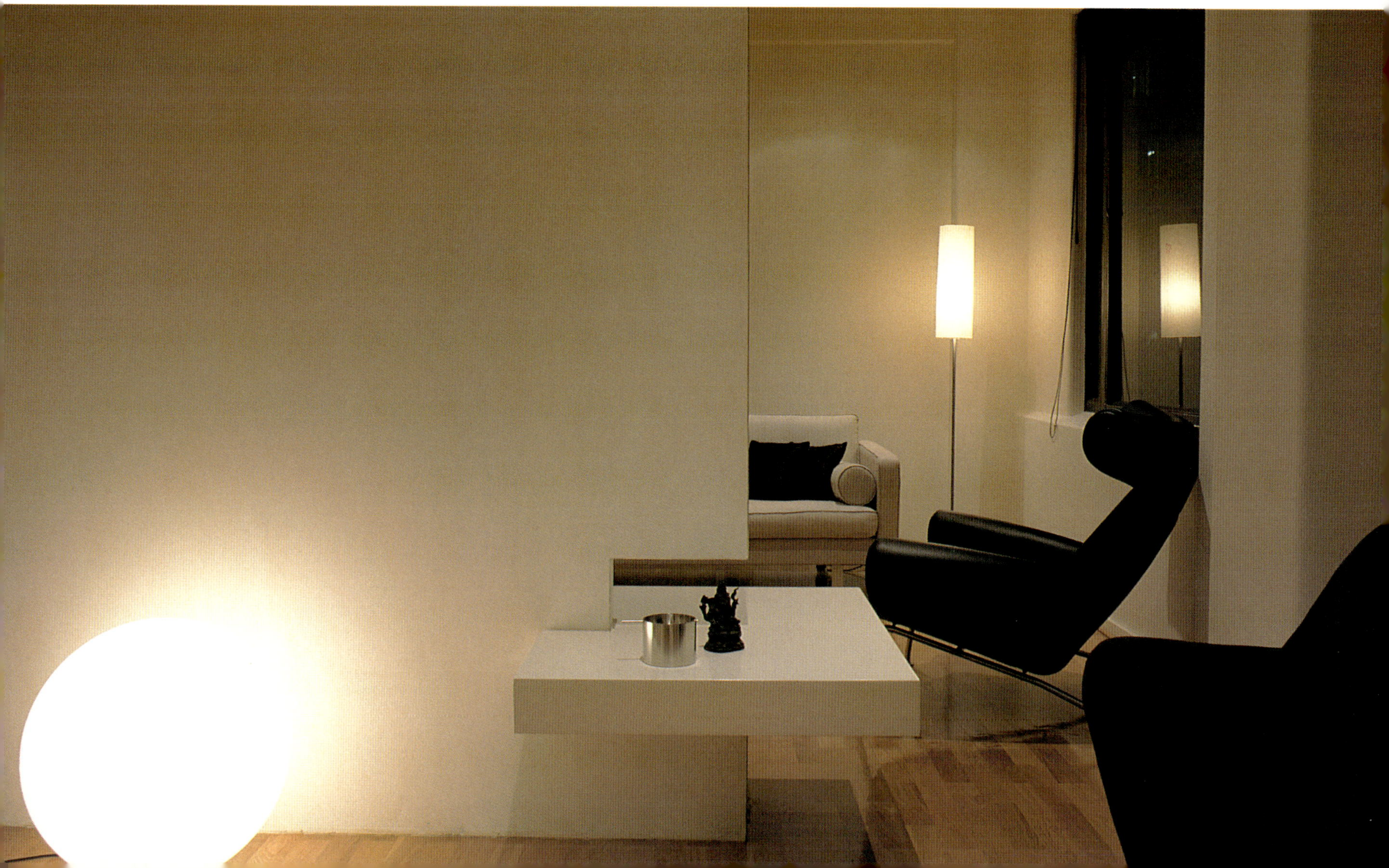

Kerry Phelan

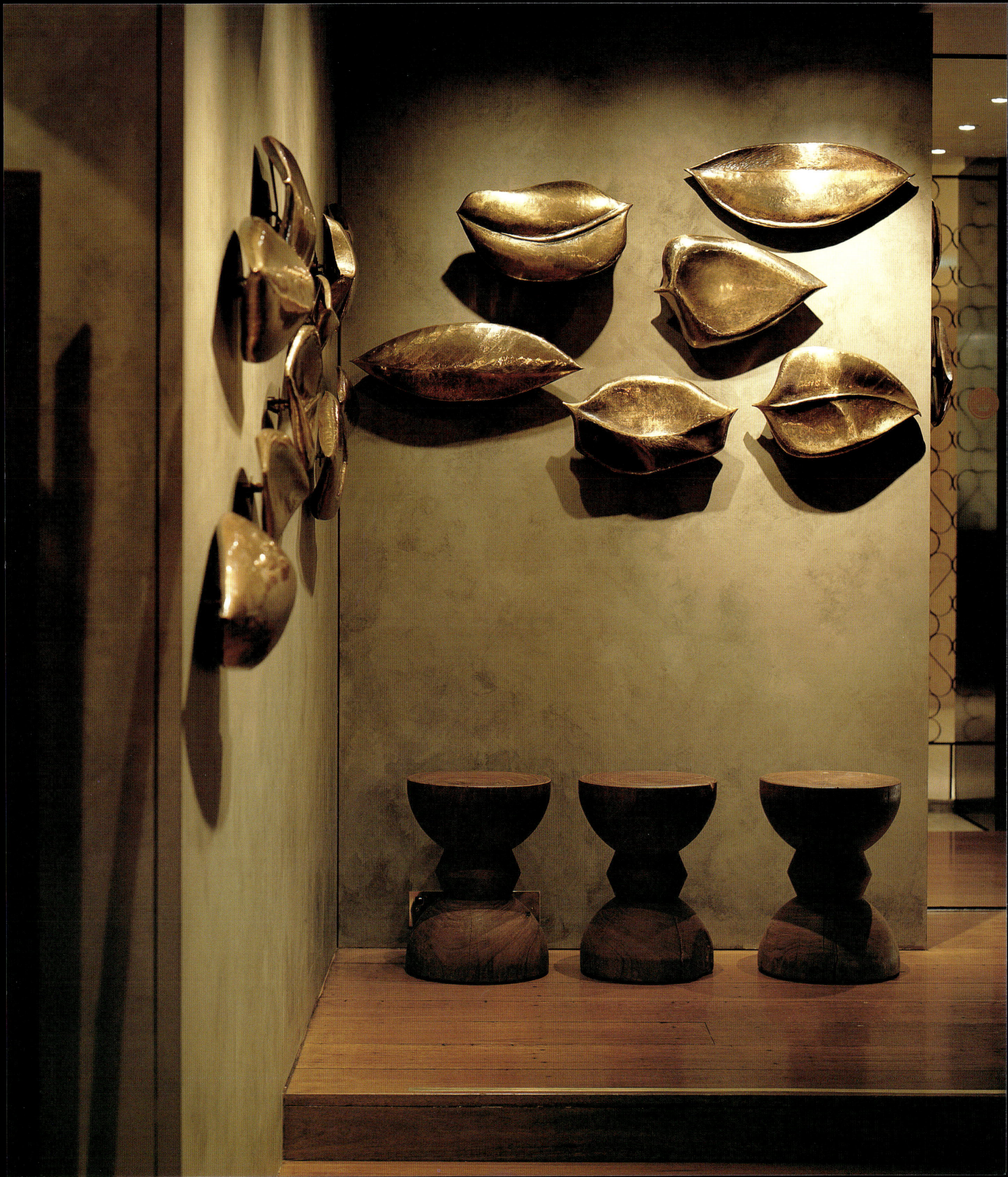

An indecisive Kerry Phelan enrolled in art school in the late 1970s. A foot in both camps. Art and graphics. Kerry soon realised she had a definite absence of the SELL, SELL, SELL attitude. Entry into the advertising world was definitely out of the question. Instead, she went to work in her father's interior design office. Making coffees. Running errands. Drafting the best she could. Thought she'd be there five minutes. She was there for seven years. Heavily based in retail. Ironic. What happened to Kerry Phelan in the 1980s? Lots of hair products. Fancied herself as a New Romantic punk. Decided Mod was far more stylish. Melbourne fashion finally caught up with her. Power dressing by day. Working at DCM. Discos by night. Shoulderpads always. Synthetic clothing. Synthetic music. Nothing wrong with synthetic! Strange geometry and acid wash soon came to an end. The retro visit to the 1970s in the 1990s brought back her mum's frocks and her dad's afro. Anything goes. Kerry believes design these days is like a big umbrella. It covers everything from fashion to architecture to lifestyle. Even books have a groovy cover design. She thinks Australian design is becoming more European. Kerry is uncomfortable with the trend to brand everything. Labels, labels, labels. Then there's the label with nothing on it. Minimalism to the excess. Does minimal mean clarity of mind and pure of essence? She answers the question with a question. What's minimal? Japan. Mies. Ame. Lightness. Being. It's not new any more. The fuzzy thinkers are all doing minimal. The casino work was minimal, a series of layers with gorgeous materials. Kerry wanted texture and gloss. She loves glam. Please! She's just bought a new silver frock.

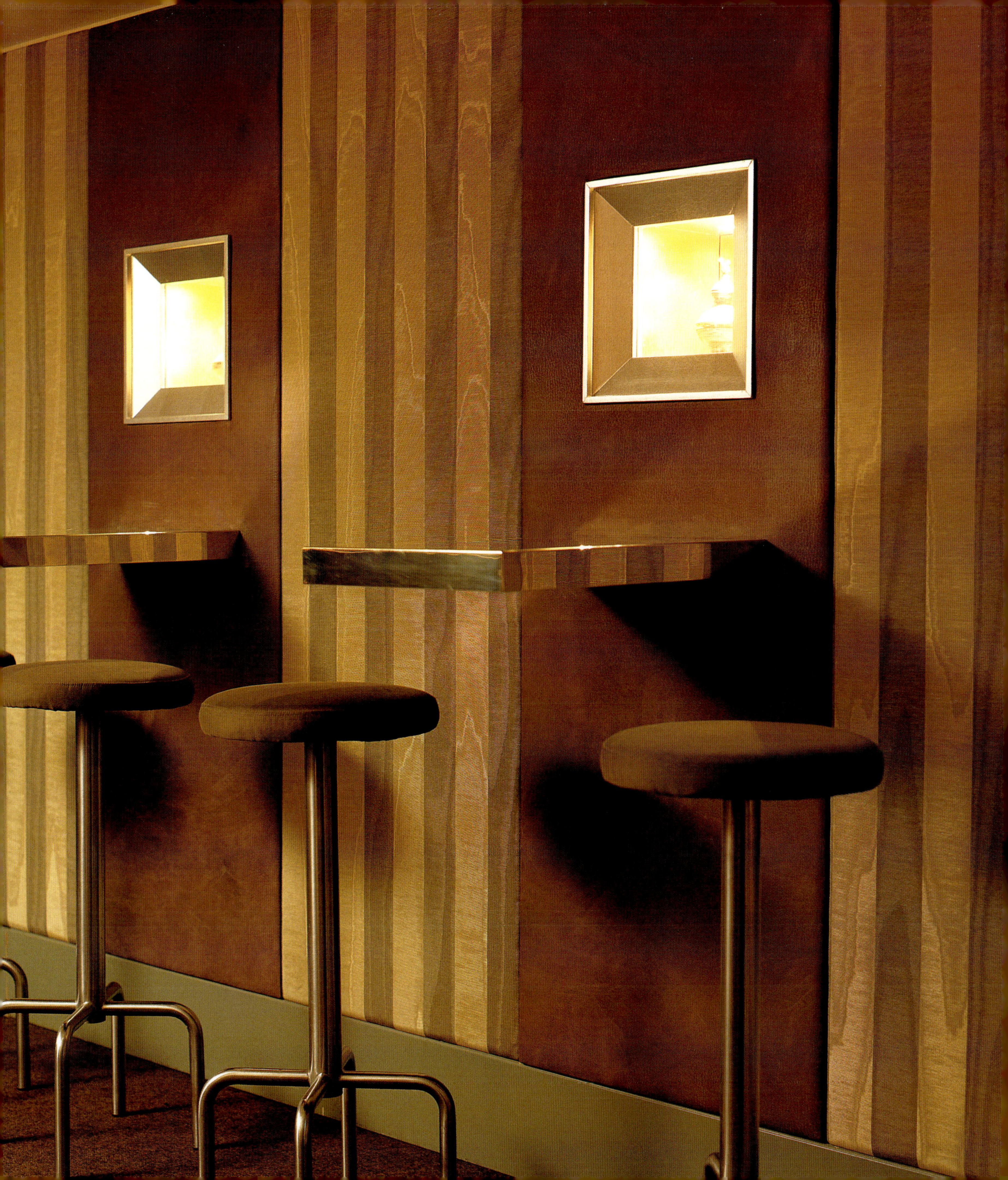

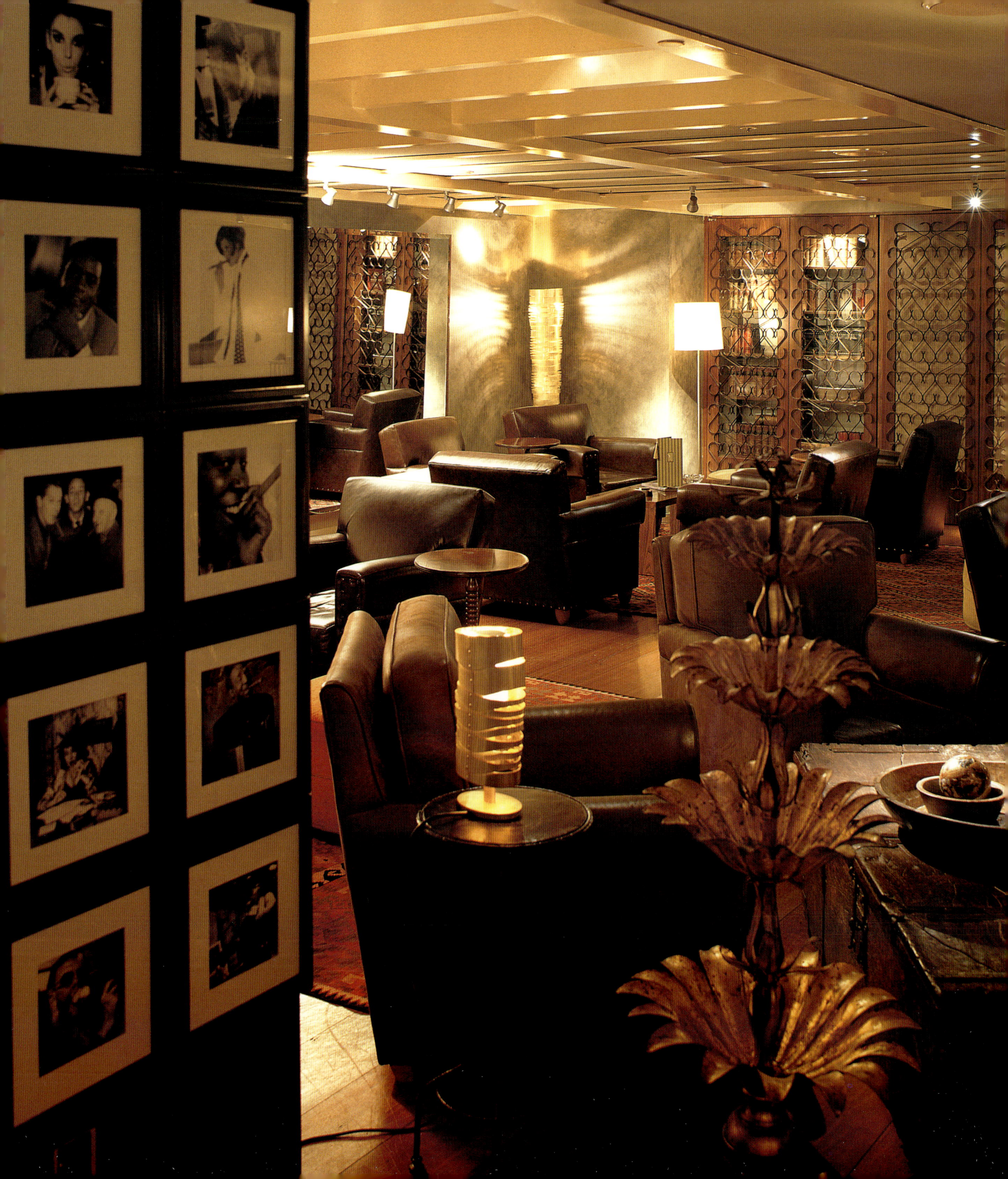

伊勢屋

cream ice-cream

Jeffery Copolov
Bates Smart

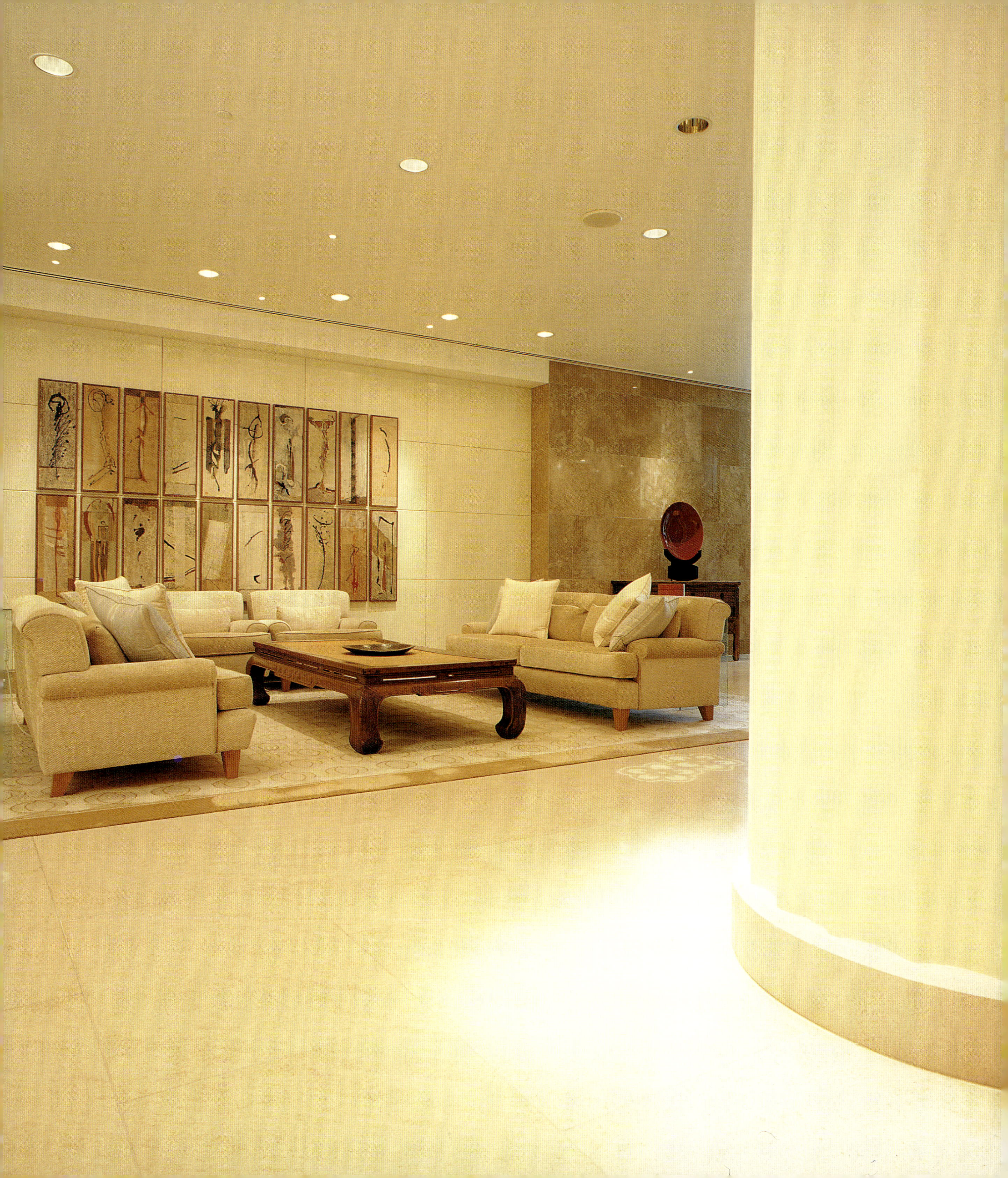

Jeffery Copolov grew up surrounded by designers and their works. Precious childhood moments watching his grandfather fastidiously sharpening his draughting pencils to a needle point, testing the point by pressing the end of his pencil against his cheeks. Jeffery loved the papers, the large swivel draughting stool, the drawings. His grandfather was the child of silversmiths, specialists in the design and manufacture of contemporary light fittings. Born in Vienna at the turn of the century. The dawn of new modernist sensibilities in design and a turning point in the history of art. Jeffery's mother, an award-winning textile designer. Memories of countless tubes of poster colour paint, white porcelain mixing dishes, graph paper. The way she conjured up new colours by blending others was mysterious and magical. Before stowing her rinsed brushes, she would run the sable hair through her lips, bringing them to a delicate point. Was design Jeffery Copolov's destiny? After graduating, Jeffery joined Bates Smart and McCutcheon, a firm with similar design ethics to those imbued by his grandfather and his mother. Attention to detail. Integration. Completeness. Minimalism. The work of Sir Osborn McCutcheon inspired. One of the greatest exponents of the modern movement in architecture in Australia. ICI House. Wilson Hall at Melbourne University. A thoroughness of thought and an overriding concern for detail. Rising to meet the challenges of design, Jeffery draws on all his skill, training, influences and experience. The interiors of the Crown Entertainment complex were a rewarding project. It provided interaction with an immense range of specialist designers and craftspeople, all experts in their fields. Jeffery's greatest personal challenge when faced with the genre of 'casino architecture' was in finding the balance between minimalism and decoration. Like a conductor before an orchestra, he wove together the collective talent to create a harmonious, fully integrated interior. The result is a design even his grandfather would approve of.

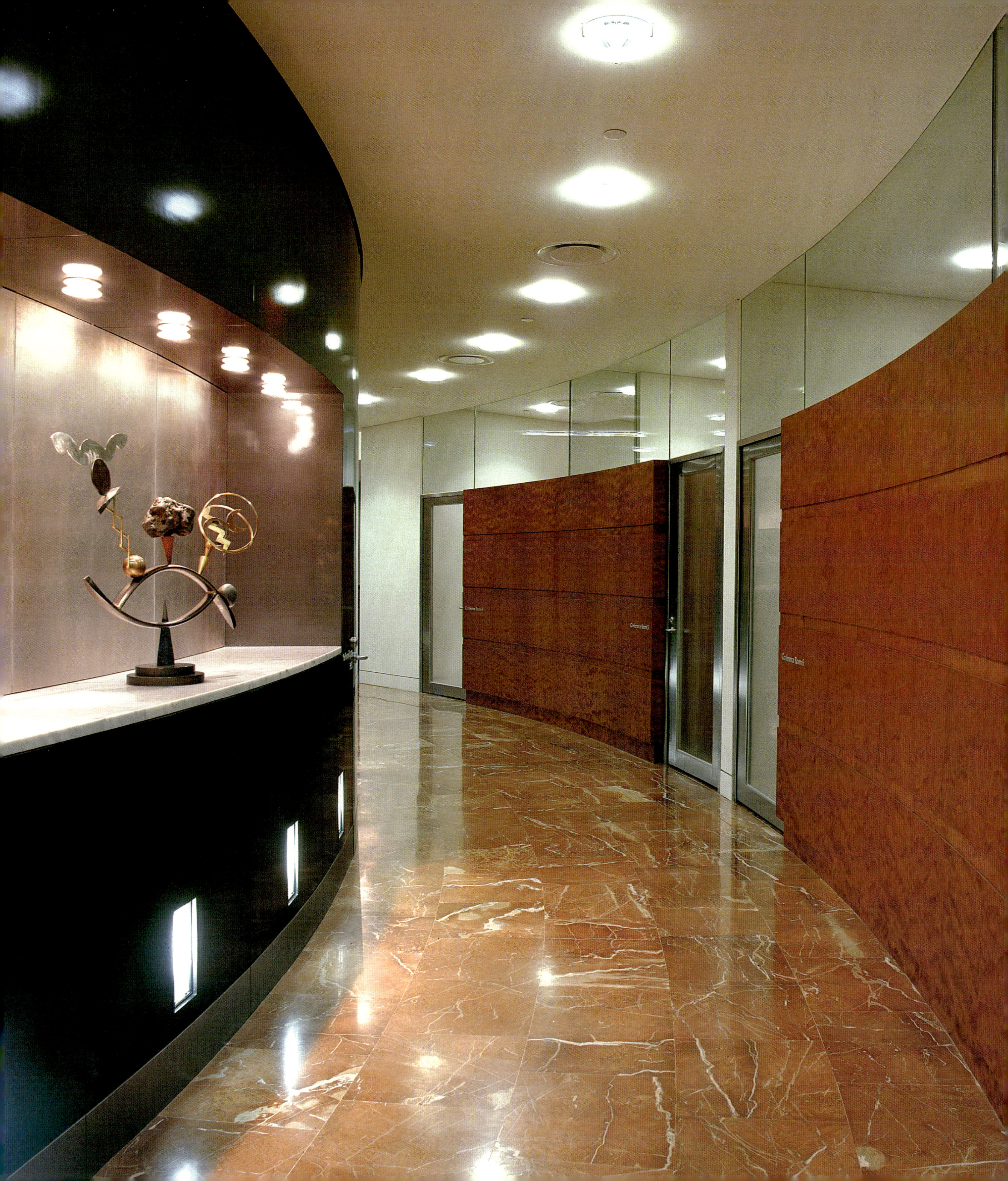

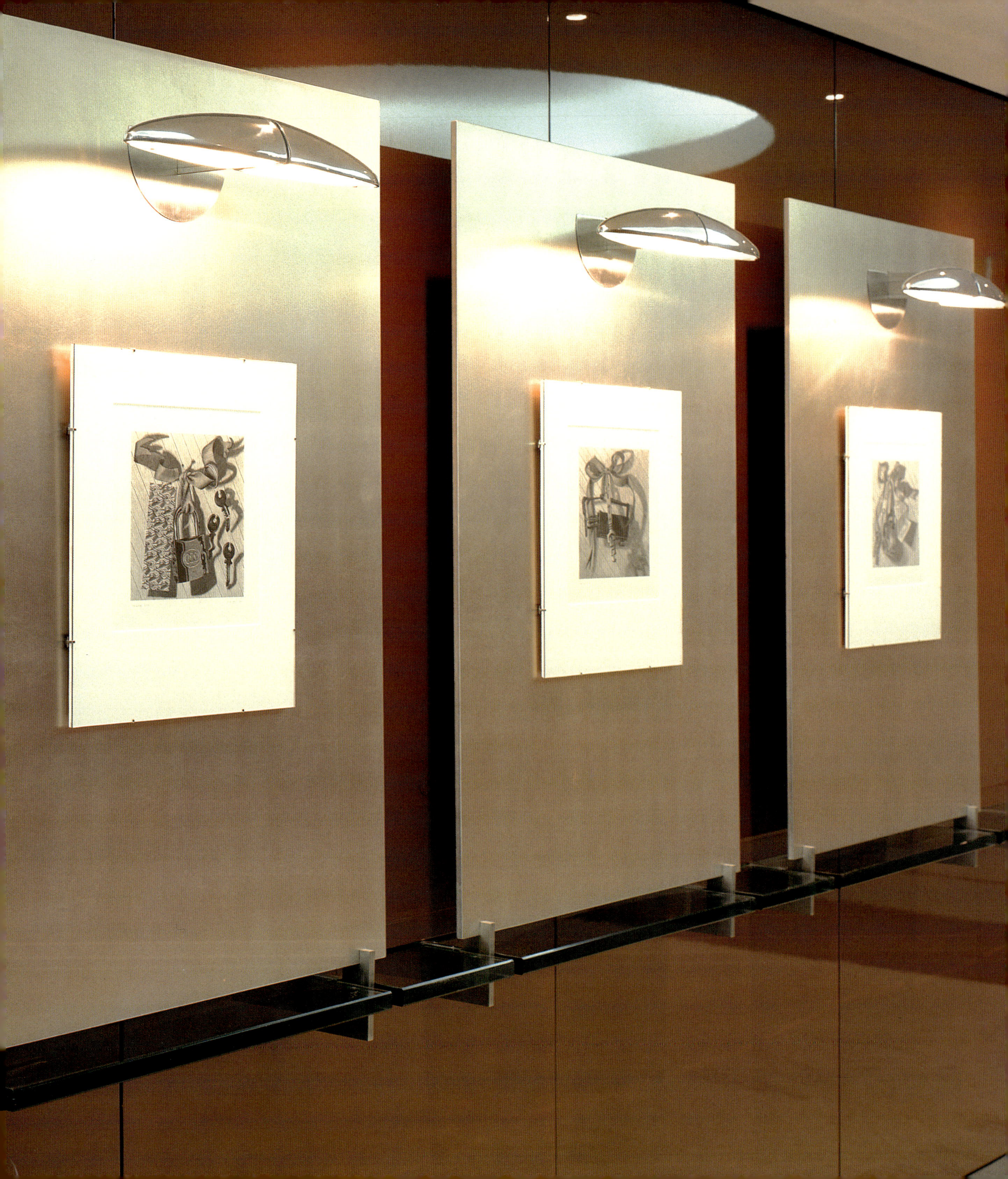

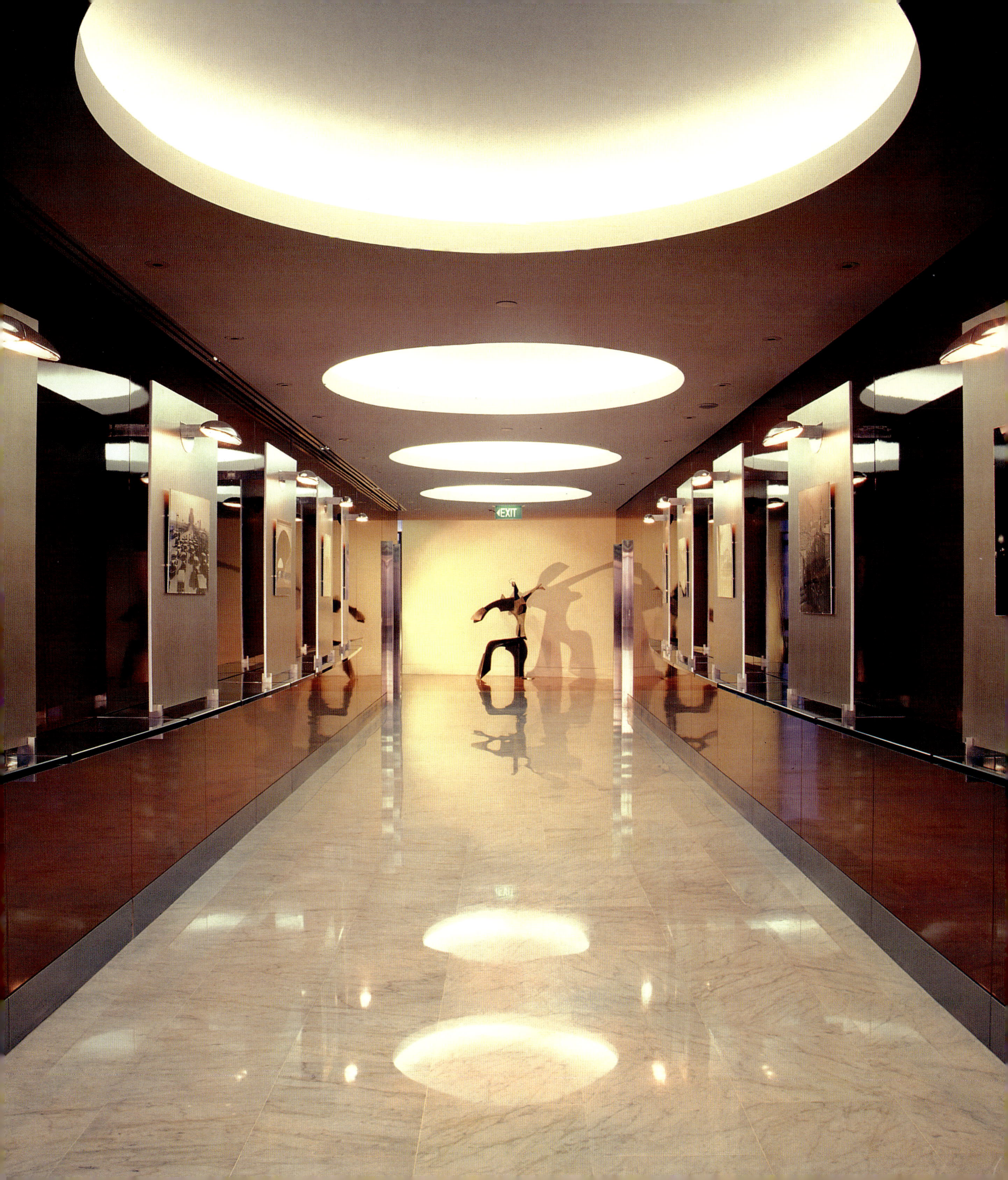
EXIT

Hamish Guthrie
Kate Hart
Olivia Jackson
Rowan Lodge
Jane Mackay
Geraldine Maher
Daryl Jackson Interiors

TIMES OF MEALS
BREAKFAST 7 AM - 8 AM
MORNING TEA 9 AM - 9 AM
DINNER 10 AM - 2 PM
TEA 2 PM - 5 PM
SUPPER 6 PM - 10 PM

THE CAFÉ

Demand creates supply. Daryl Jackson Interiors was formed in 1995 as a response to client demand. An extension of Daryl Jackson's architectural service. The complete resolution of interiors. This integrated service produced recognised success. New commissions based entirely on interior design soon followed. This group of young and energetic designers came from the same source, RMIT Melbourne. Similar ideas on design have been influenced by a strong cultural and urban base. Influences come from such architects and designers as Gae Aulenti, Alvar Aalto, Louis Khan and Hans Sharown. Innovators who place great importance on interiors as an integral part and natural extension of architectural form. Daryl Jackson Interiors believes in substance rather than style. Its work is an expression of light, form and texture. Timeless. Design that goes beyond the clients' expectations. Research, ideas, workshops, refinement, prototypes and testing are the processes that lead to the built form. Travel and design in various parts of the world has produced urban context and a layering of different design and cultural languages. Daryl Jackson Interiors believes it is imperative to educate others in the positive contribution design makes to many aspects of both personal and professional life. From its viewpoint, Australia is maturing as a country, recognising and appreciating leadership in design rather than just following established design trends. Daryl Jackson Interiors aims to work with a diverse range of clients on projects that enables the team to explore new challenges and be recognised as having made a significant contribution to their clients and the design industry worldwide.

Cornwell

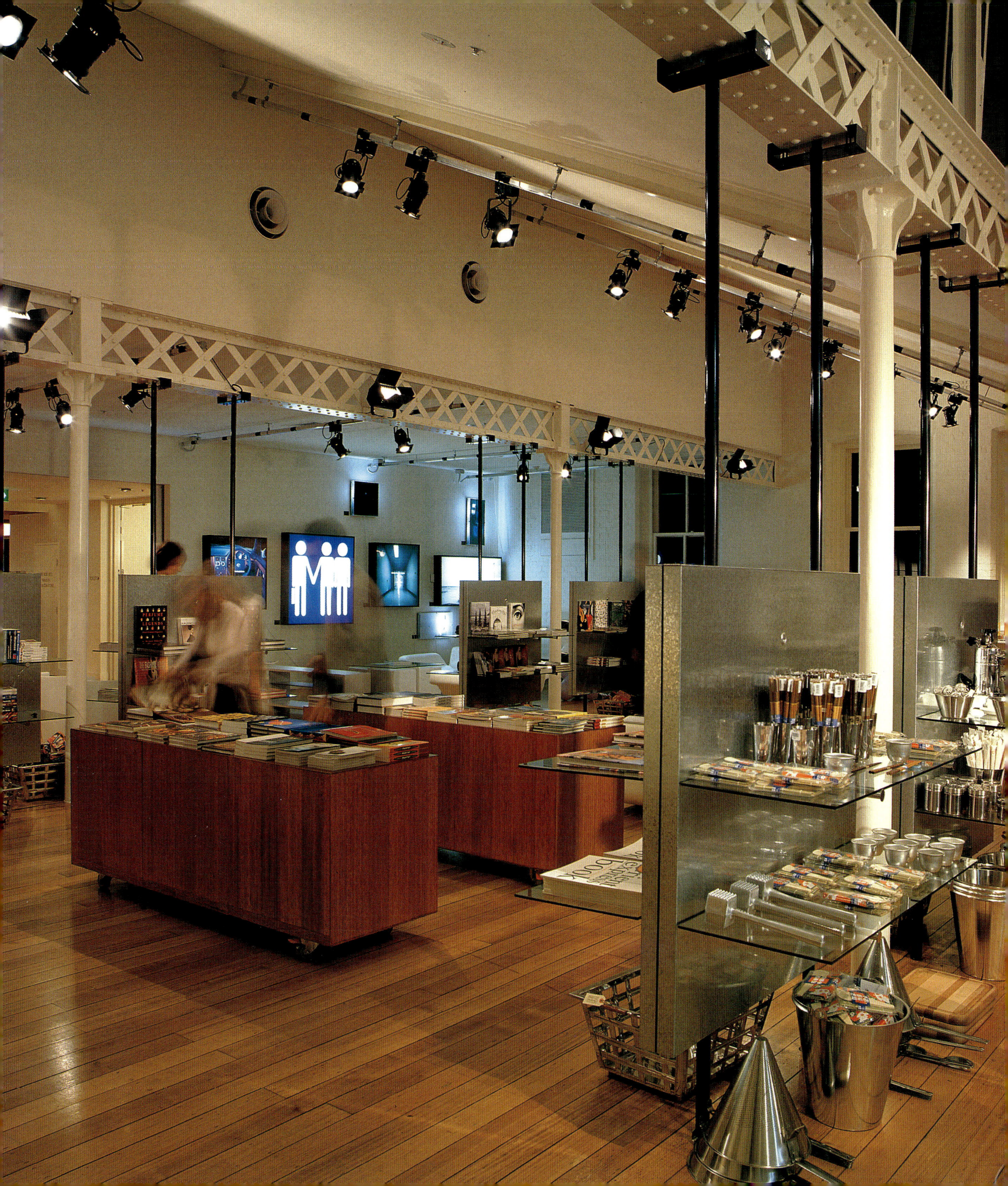

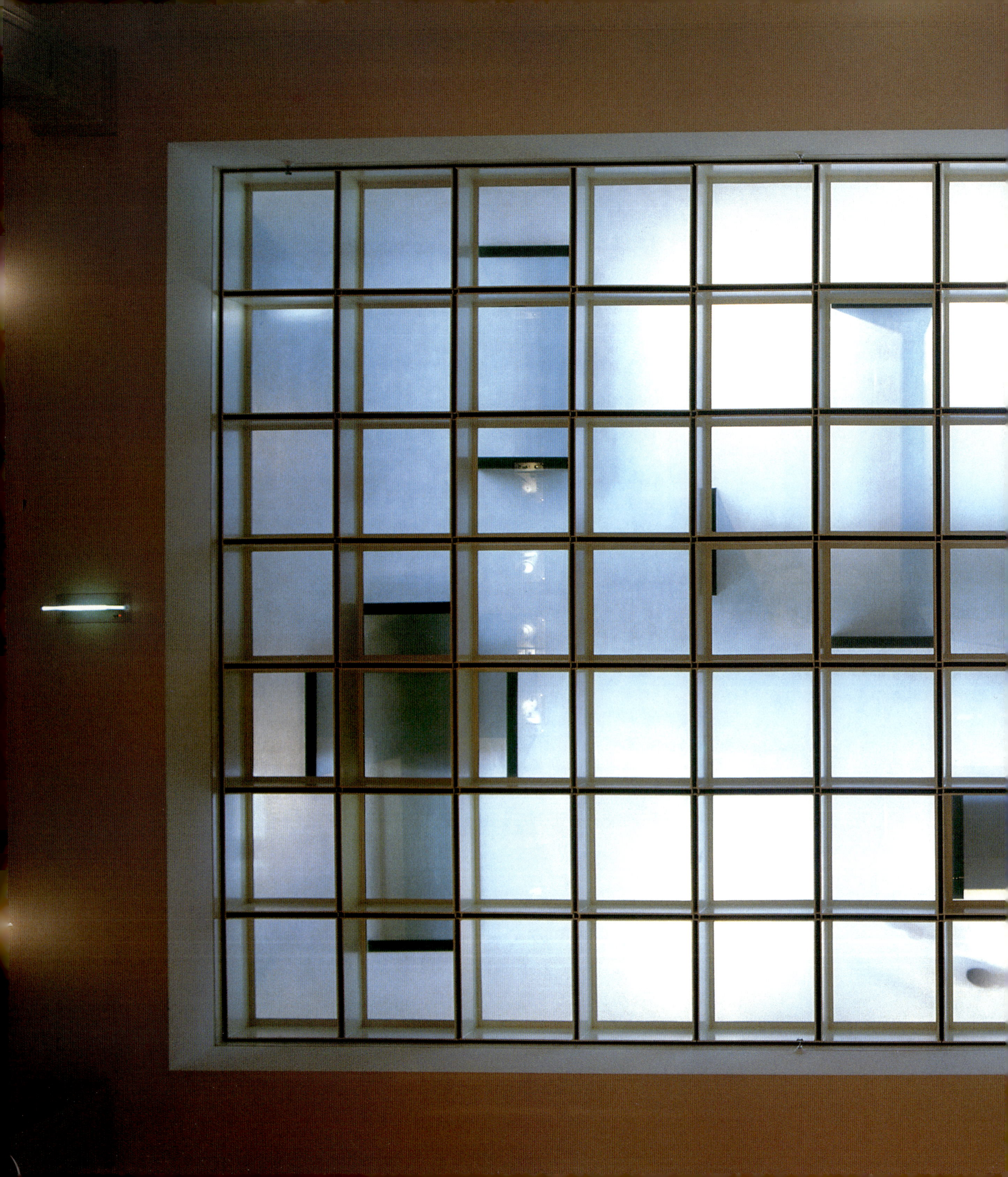

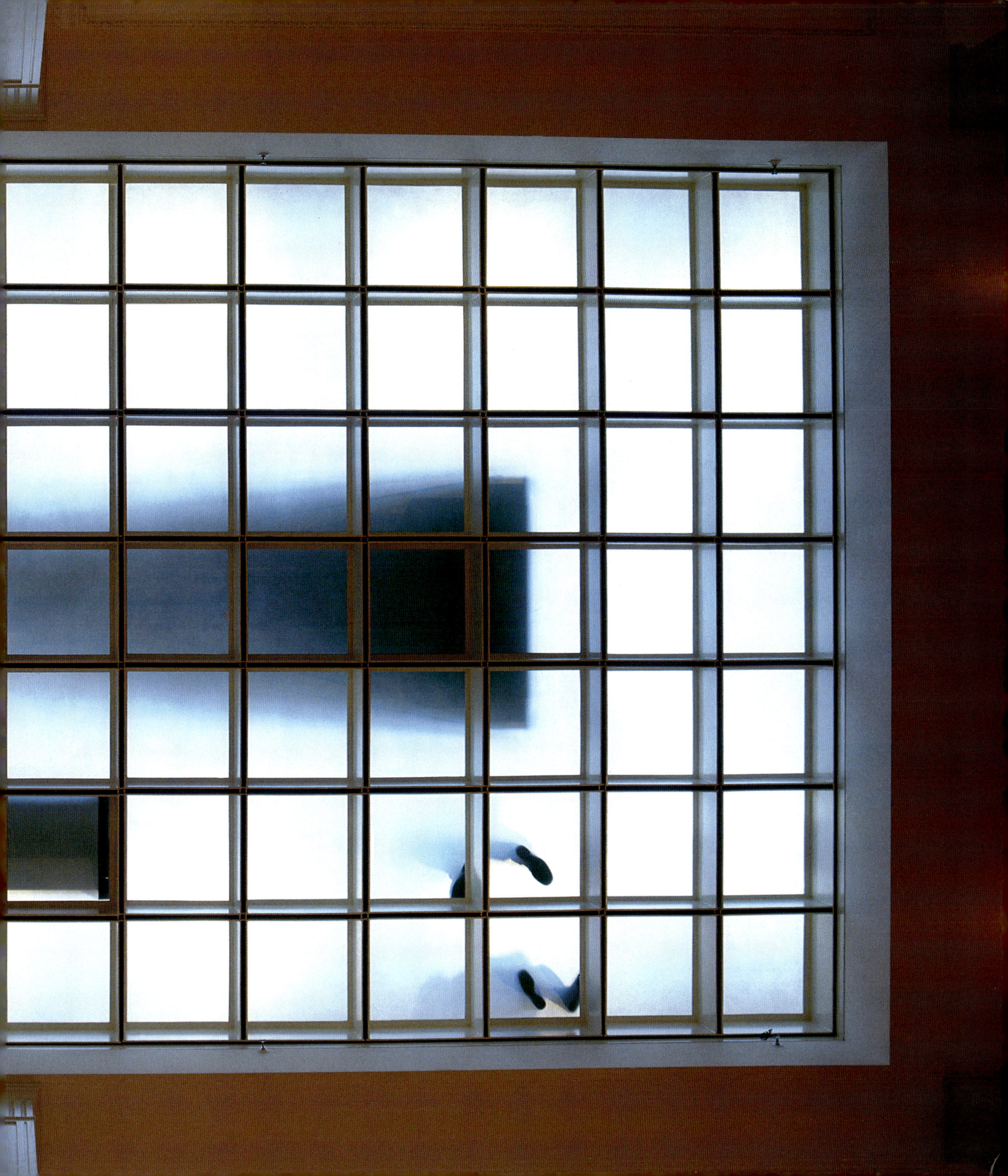

List of Works

Architecture	Tina Engelen Ian Moore	11 12 13 15 17	Davis House – Sydney, New South Wales, Australia Portrait – Ian Moore and Tina Engelen Ruzzene/Leon House – Sydney, New South Wales, Australia Price/O'Reilly House – Sydney, New South Wales, Australia Ruzzene/Leon House – Sydney, New South Wales, Australia Photography – Ross Honeysett
	David Balestra-Pimpini Serge Biguzas	19 20 21 22 25	Hairy Canary Bar – Melbourne, Victoria, Australia Portrait – David Balestra–Pimpini (left) and Serge Biguzas Residence – Surrey Hills, Victoria, Australia Residence – Surrey Hills, Victoria, Australia Townhouse – Albert Park, Victoria, Australia
	Sean Godsell	27 28 29 30 33	Carter Tucker House – Model Portrait – Sean Godsell Godsell House – Kew, Victoria, Australia Gandolfo House – Camberwell, Victoria, Australia Godsell House – Kew, Victoria, Australia
	Shelley Penn	35 36 37 38 39 39	Haddad Apartment – South Yarra, Victoria, Australia Portrait – Shelley Penn Fitzroy Terrace House – Fitzroy, Victoria, Australia Fitzroy Terrace House – Fitzroy, Victoria, Australia Fitzroy Terrace House – Fitzroy, Victoria, Australia Fitzroy Terrace House – Fitzroy, Victoria, Australia Photography Pages 35, 37 – Shelley Penn Photography Page 36 – Kate Gollings Photography Pages 38, 39 – Trevor Mein
	Steven Whiting	41 42 43 44 46 47	Anchor Place Apartment – Prahran, Victoria, Australia Portrait – Steven Whiting Residence – Albert Park, Victoria, Australia Witchery – Store Fit-out Residence – Albert Park, Victoria, Australia Residence – Albert Park, Victoria, Australia
	Kerstin Thompson	49 50 51 53 55	Residence – South Melbourne, Victoria, Australia Portrait – Kerstin Thompson Residence – South Melbourne, Victoria, Australia Residence – South Melbourne, Victoria, Australia Web Street House – Fitzroy, Victoria, Australia
	Christopher Connell	57 58 59 60 63	Snake Pit – St Kilda, Victoria, Australia Portrait – Christopher Connell Queens – South Yarra, Victoria, Australia FIG – South Yarra, Victoria, Australia FIG – South Yarra, Victoria, Australia
	Iain Halliday	65 67 68 69 71	Brave – Paddington, New South Wales, Australia Arkitex Office – Rushcutters Bay, New South Wales, Australia Box – Melbourne, Victoria, Australia Phillip Xavier – Mosman, New South Wales, Australia Arkitex Showroom – Rushcutters Bay, New South Wales, Australia
Graphic Design	Steven Cornwell Jane Sinclair	75 76 77 78 81 82 83	Corporate Brochure – Edwards Dunlop Paper Portrait – Steven Cornwell and Jane Sinclair Corporate Brochure – Ericsson Australia Environmental Graphics – Sir William Angliss Centre Visual Identity – e.g.etal Corporate Identity – Design 481 Environmental Graphics – Crown, Radio Room

	David Band	85	Visual Identity – Melbourne Wine Room
	Fiona Mahon	86	Portrait – David Band and Fiona Mahon
		87	Visual Identity – Melbourne Wine Room
		88	Visual Identity – Pomme
		90	Visual Identity – Café a Taglio
		91	Visual Identity – Café a Taglio
	Visnja Brdar	93	Book Design – *Old Food by Jill Dupleix*
		94	Portrait – Visnja Brdar
		95	Book Design – *Mark Newson, Furniture, Objects, Interiors*
		96	Identity and Packaging – Ariel Booksellers
		98	Poster/Invitation – Royal Australian Institute of Architects
	Andrew Hoyne	101	Book Design – Essential Energy
		102	Portrait – Andrew Hoyne
		103	Corporate Brochures – ANZ Bank
		105	Book Design – Various
		106	Corporate Collateral – Various
	Atia Cader	109	Packaging – G Star
	Andrew Majzner	110	Portrait – Atia Cader (left), Philippa Penndelberry and Andrew Majzner
	Philippa Penndelberry	111	Book Design – The Pratt Foundation
		113	Environmental Graphics – Urban Provisions
		114	Corporate Brochure – Mercedes-Benz
	David Ansett	117	Identity – Hemisphere
	Dean Butler	118	Portrait – Dean Butler (top) and David Ansett
		119	Identity – Paul West Photography
		121	Collateral – St Martins
		122	Book Design – Hailstorm
	Hanna Cutts	125	Wine Label – Grand Orbit
		126	Portrait – Hanna Cutts
		127	Event Collateral – Brisbane Writers Festival
		129	Event Collateral – Livid 98
	Andrew Ashton	131	Event Collateral – Australian Graphic Design Association
	Rick Nelmes	132	Portrait – Graeme Smith (left), Rick Nelmes (centre) and Andrew Ashton
	Graeme Smith	133	Poster – Tomasetti Paper House
		134	Proposal Document – Andrew 'Boy' Charlton Pool
		137	Stamp – Regional Australian Arts Councils
	Ashley Durrans	139	Annual Report – Craft Australia
	Dean Hastie	140	Portrait – Dean Hastie (left) and Ashley Durrans
		141	Corporate Brochure – Integra Information Systems
		142	Exhibition Graphics – Canberra Museum and Gallery
		145	Brochure – Australian Graphic Design Association
Industrial Design	Simon Christopher	149	Lucky Star – Small Pendant Lights
	Celina Clarke	150	Portrait – Simon Christopher and Celina Clarke
		151	Madam Ruby – Table Lamps
		153	Bean Chairs
		154	Amazing Larry – Folding Table
	Marc Pascal	157	Mia – Plate
		158	Portrait – Marc Pascal
		159	Worvo Junior – Pendant Lights
		161	Vaase – Six Stem Flower Vase
	Hugo Davidson	163	Homevox – PABX Telephone System
		164	Portrait – Hugo Davidson
		165	NEC – GSM Mobile Phone
		167	Touchpoint Computer – Detail
		168	LineChippers – Home Banking Terminal

List of Works

	Malte Wagenfeld	171	Thing One – Waste Paper Bins
		172	Portrait – Malte Wagenfeld
		173	Thing One – Waste Paper Bins
		174	Arabesque – Chair and Bench
		176	Es Es – Document Tray
	Mark Armstrong	179	Philips – Remote Controls
		180	Portrait – Mark Armstrong
		181	Sydney 2000 – Olympic Torch
		183	Ryobi – Electric Drill
		184	Dishlex – Dishwasher Detail
	Peter Cooper	187	SpeakerProp – Hybrid Speaker Stand
	Stephen Neil	188	Portrait – Peter Cooper (top) and Stephen Neil
		189	EFTcorp – Smart Card Reader
		190	Quantum – Seating System for Camatic
		193	Quantum – Seating System for Camatic
Interior Design	Nik Karalis	197	Residence – Collingwood, Victoria, Australia
		198	Portrait – Nik Karalis
		199	Just Jeans Office – Richmond, Victoria, Australia
		201	Just Jeans Office – Richmond, Victoria, Australia
		202	Cornwall Stodart – Melbourne, Victoria, Australia
		204	Cornwall Stodart – Melbourne, Victoria, Australia
	Andrew Parr	207	MG Garage – Surry Hills, New South Wales, Australia
		208	Portrait – Andrew Parr
		209	Heat Nightclub – Melbourne, Victoria, Australia
		211	Red Tulip Apartments – Prahran, Victoria, Australia
		212	MG Garage – Surry Hills, New South Wales, Australia
	Jackie Johnston	215	Crown Towers – Melbourne, Victoria, Australia
		216	Portrait – Jackie Johnston
		217	Crown Towers – Melbourne, Victoria, Australia
		218	Crown Towers – Melbourne, Victoria, Australia
	Paul Hecker	221	The Prince Hotel – St Kilda, Victoria, Australia
		222	Portrait – Paul Hecker
		223	The Prince Hotel – St Kilda, Victoria, Australia
		224	The Prince Hotel – St Kilda, Victoria, Australia
		227	Hecker Residence – Melbourne, Victoria, Australia
		228	Hecker Residence – Melbourne, Victoria, Australia
	Kerry Phelan	229	Fidels – Crown Complex, Melbourne, Victoria, Australia
		230	Portrait – Kerry Phelan
		231	Fidels – Crown Complex, Melbourne, Victoria, Australia
		232	Fidels – Crown Complex, Melbourne, Victoria, Australia
		234	Crown Food Court – Crown Complex, Melbourne, Victoria, Australia
		235	Crown Food Court – Crown Complex, Melbourne, Victoria, Australia
	Jeffery Copolov	237	Crown Towers – Melbourne, Victoria, Australia
		238	Portrait – Jeffery Copolov
		239	Clayton Utz – Sydney, New South Wales, Australia
		240	Clayton Utz – Sydney, New South Wales, Australia
	Hamish Guthrie	243	Georges – Melbourne, Victoria, Australia
	Kate Hart	244	Portrait – (left to right) Hamish Guthrie, Kate Hart, Olivia Jackson, Jane Mackay, Geraldine Maher (Rowan Lodge absent)
	Olivia Jackson		
	Rowan Lodge	245	Cornwell Studio – Melbourne, Victoria, Australia
	Jane Mackay	247	Georges – Melbourne, Victoria, Australia
	Geraldine Maher	248	Georges – Melbourne, Victoria, Australia